Britain and America 1850–1939:
A study of economic change

The Authors

Philip S. Bagwell is Professor Emeritus in History at the Polytechnic of Central London. He is a leading authority on transport and labour history, and on these subjects he has been consultant to the BBC for schools history TV broadcasts. His previous books include *The Railwaymen: A History of the NUR* (Allen and Unwin, 1963; Volume 2, 1982).

G.E. Mingay is Emeritus Professor of Agrarian History at the University of Kent at Canterbury, and is currently President of the British Agricultural History Society. His previous books include *English Landed Society in the Eighteenth Century* (1963), *The Victorian Countryside* (editor, 1981) and *The Transformation of Britain 1830–1939* (1986), all published by Routledge & Kegan Paul.

Britain and America 1850-1939
a study of economic change

Philip S. Bagwell
Professor Emeritus in History
The Polytechnic of Central London

G. E. Mingay
Emeritus Professor of Agrarian History
University of Kent

Routledge & Kegan Paul
London

First published in 1970
Reprinted in 1971 and 1987 by
Routledge & Kegan Paul Ltd
11 New Fetter Lane, London EC4P 4EE

Printed in Great Britain
by Billings and Sons Ltd,
Worcester

ISBN 0-7102-1296 8 (C)
ISBN 0-7102-1297 6 (P)

Contents

Figures

Tables

Maps

Preface

While textbooks that deal with Britain and America separately abound, there is, so far as we are aware, no book that compares the two countries' development over even so limited a period as we have selected, the ninety years between 1850 and 1939. The attempt that we make in this volume is therefore something of an elementary pioneer effort in comparative economic history.

We have deliberately pitched our chapters at an introductory level in the hope that they will be the more useful to students and general readers coming fresh to the subject, and we believe that our approach may offer deeper insights and a wider horizon than may be obtained from the study of a single country in isolation. Also, we have thought it more important to sketch an outline of the main framework of the two economies and compare and contrast the factors that made for change (or the lack of it), than to attempt a comprehensive and detailed descriptive survey. In this respect, therefore, this book will be more a supplement to existing national accounts than a substitute for them. At the same time, we have touched on some issues of current interest to historians, and we hope to have provided sufficient material to enable readers to gain an understanding of the differing economic and social characteristics of the two countries, and to find our treatment a little deeper than might be suggested by a bare comparative analysis.

In a book of this kind we have necessarily to lean heavily upon those who have blazed trails before us. Our indebtedness is clear from the references we have given, and at the end of each chapter our suggestions for further reading indicate which works we have thought to be most generally useful for those readers wishing further detail, particularly students of about first-year university level. We have adopted standard abbreviations where necessary, and have omitted the place of publication where this is London.

Philip S. Bagwell
G. E. Mingay

1 Introduction: the British and American economies in the nineteenth century

1 The statistics

The quickest and most effective way of illustrating the essential differences between Britain and the U.S.A. in the middle nineteenth century and after is to place the following figures side by side:

TABLE 1

Population of Britain and U.S.A. 1850-1951

Britain		U.S.A.	
millions		millions	
1851	20·9	1850	23·3
1861	23·2	1860	31·5
1871	26·2	1870	39·9
1881	29·8	1880	50·3
1891	33·1	1890	63·1
1901	37·1	1900	76·1
1911	40·9	1910	92·4
1921	42·8	1920	106·5
1931	44·8	1930	123·2
		1940	132·1
1951	48·9	1950	151·7

Source: *Abstract of British Historical Statistics; Historical Statistics of U.S.*

Already in the middle nineteenth century the population of the United States was larger than that of Great Britain, and because of the high level of immigration, especially in the late nineteenth and early twentieth centuries, and the fairly high rate of natural increase, the American population was over twice as large as the

British population by 1900, and three times as large in the middle of the twentieth century.

In the size of labour force, the U.S.A. did not exceed Britain until about 1880, but by 1900-1 America could command a labour force some 75 per cent larger than that of Britain—29·1m. as compared with 16·7m.; by the 1930s American labour resources were well over twice as great—48·8m. as compared with 21·1m. In the middle nineteenth century, however, the American labour force was two millions smaller than the 9·7m. of Britain, and moreover a much greater proportion of it was engaged in agriculture (together with forestry and fishing).

TABLE 2

Proportion of labour force engaged in agriculture 1850-1–1950-1 (with forestry and fishing)

	1850-1	1900-1	1930-1	1950-1
	%	%	%	%
Britain	22	9	6	5
U.S.A.	64	38	22	12

Source: *Abstract of British Historical Statistics; Historical Statistics of U.S.* and *Output, Employment and Productivity in the United States*, N.B.E.R., 1966, pp. 119-20.

Since these figures also indicate roughly the proportion of National Income produced by agriculture in the two countries, it is clear that the American dependence on the products of the land was very much greater than in Britain although, as the figures show, the importance of agriculture in the American economy has declined very steeply over the last hundred years. By 1850 Britain was already a heavily industrialized country and the proportion of the labour force engaged in manufacturing industry and mining did not rise very much over the following century (although of course the industrial labour force increased greatly in absolute terms). In the U.S.A. only about a fifth of the labour force was engaged in manufacturing, mining, and building in 1850, but by 1900 the proportion had risen to about 27 per cent, around which figure it remained.

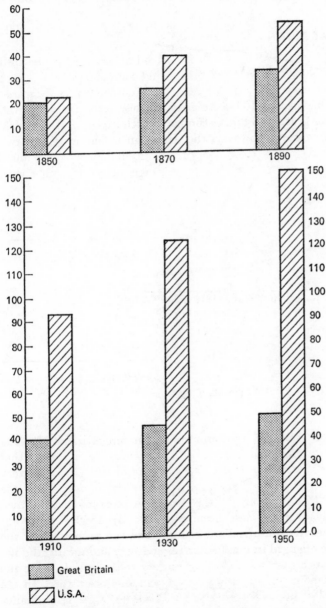

Figure 1. Population of Great Britain and the U.S.A. 1850-1950,
(IN MILLIONS)

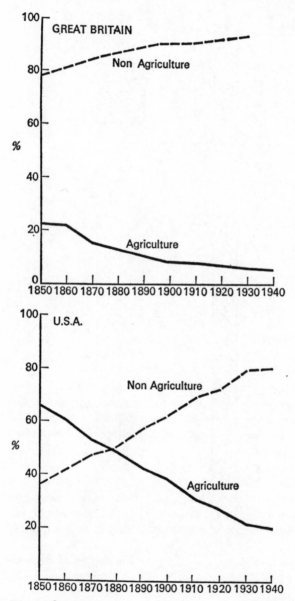

Figure 2. Distribution of farm and non-farm workers: Great Britain and U.S.A. 1850-1940

TABLE 3

Proportion of labour force engaged in manufacturing industry, mining, and building 1850-1–1930-1

	1850-1	1900-1	1930-1
	%	%	%
Britain	43	46	45
U.S.A.	20	27	26

Source: *Abstract of British Historical Statistics; Historical Statistics of U.S.* and *Output, Employment and Productivity in the United States*, N.B.E.R., 1966, pp. 119-20.

The relatively low proportion of the labour force engaged in American industry at the end of the nineteenth century reflected two important differences: the greater (but diminishing) role of agriculture in the American economy, and the already higher output per head of the American worker. It was only about 1890 that the absolute numbers employed in American industry passed those in British industry, but in the output of certain key products such as coal and steel, the United States had forged well ahead by 1900.

With industrialization came urbanization. In Britain, as early as 1841 only 39 per cent of the population was living in rural areas, and by 1911 this figure had fallen to 19 per cent. In the United States, in 1850 only some 3½m. people (15 per cent of the population) lived in places having over 2,500 inhabitants, and only 2m. people (9 per cent) in places having over 25,000 inhabitants. As late as 1910 the rural population of the United States still outnumbered those living in urban areas, and it was only after that date that the urban population came to form the majority. But the tendency for large industrial centres to be created had been marked since the middle of the century, and by 1910 nearly 15½m. people (17 per cent of the total) lived in towns with a population of over a quarter of a million.

Lastly, one important difference concerns the degree of dependence on foreign trade. In 1907 when the role of foreign trade in the British economy had been growing for half a century, about a quarter of the output of goods went for export (over two-fifths of manufactured goods), and imports (including imported raw materials) equalled a third of the total domestic consumption of goods. Corresponding American figures are not available, but only about 5 per cent of American output of manufactures was exported, and only 3 per cent of the total supply of manufactures was imported. However, while the United States' share in a rapidly expanding world trade was a growing one, that of Britain was declining—from over a fifth in the middle nineteenth century to under 15 per cent at the time of the First World War, an ominous indication of the problems to come.

2 The process of growth: Britain

TABLE 4

U.K. National Income 1855-1950

Net National Income (*current prices*)		*National Income per head* (*1913-14 prices*)
	£m	£s
1855	627	19·8
1860	684	21·0
1870	923	26·8
1880	1,079	29·7
1890	1,405	41·2
1900	1,768	45·7
1910	2,078	48.2
1920	5,787	47·7
1930	4,076	49·9
1939	5,182	61·0
1950	10,710	61·33

Source: P. Deane and W. A. Cole, *British Economic Growth 1688-1959* (Cambridge, 1962, pp. 329-331)

In terms of National Income per head at constant (1913–14) prices the above figures show an average rate of growth of 2·0 per cent per annum in the second half of the nineteenth century, with a fall to lower rates thereafter. R. C. O. Matthews's estimates for the growth of real gross domestic product confirm the rate of 2·0 per cent for the second half of the nineteenth century, show a fall to only 1·1 per cent in 1899–1913, and a recovery to 2·3 per cent between 1924 and 1937.[1] There was evidently some retardation in the rate of growth of the British economy in the later nineteenth century, but it is difficult to say just when this began, and how great was its extent. The subject is a complex one, and we consider it in greater detail in Section 3 of Chapter 6. At this point we may confine ourselves to some discussion of the general process of British economic development in the later nineteenth century. Although the rate of growth slowed down, there is no doubt that the overall economic advance was still a remarkable and varied one. What factors lay behind Britain's progress?

First of all, we may say that progress stemmed from a high level of investment. Between 1855 and 1865 the increase in the national capital—about £1,200m.—was equivalent to about one-sixth of the national income; again, between 1865 and 1875 some £2,400m. was added to the capital of the United Kingdom, of which nearly a quarter was invested abroad, one-sixth was invested in houses and other buildings, and one-tenth in railways at home. Probably 'a higher proportion of the national income was being saved and invested in 1872–4 than at any subsequent time'. The mid-Victorian period 'was not a good time in the sense that it brought to most people a reasonable degree of security and comfort. It was not free from sharp interruptions to trade, production, and employment. But if the accumulation of wealth and its application to further accumulation is taken as the criterion of economic success then this was a very successful age. . . .'[2]

Secondly, there had occurred already before 1850 significant technological advances in textiles, and to a lesser extent in coal, iron, and transport. These advances, confined as they were to a limited range of industries, were still of the first importance in reducing costs and making it possible for the country

to concentrate on meeting more efficiently a fairly narrow range of universal human needs. The mid-Victorian world was one in which most people, even in Britain, had little to spend except on the basic necessities of food, clothing and shelter, and a country seeking to expand its economic activity could do so to any great extent only if it could provide these things, or the equipment for producing and distributing them, more cheaply and more abundantly; and that is what the British economy mainly relied on for much of the nineteenth century. The number of manufacturing activities in which the methods and efficiency of production were utterly transformed by mechanical innovation before the middle of the century was small, but it included one group—the textiles—and within that group one industry in particular—cotton—for whose products the demand at home and abroad was enormous and ever-increasing. The transfer of more capital and labour to this group of activities, in which Britain excelled all other countries, was one of the key features of the development of the economy. To maintain and augment the supply of other basic necessities whose production was not aided by such sweeping technological changes—food, garments and houses are the obvious examples—required the retention of a high proportion of the rest of the available labour for this purpose. This need, however, was modified in two ways. Though they were less impressive than those in the textile industries, there were in other basic activities, notably agriculture, changes in organization and technique, made effective by additional investment, that made possible some savings in the use of labour, relative to the amount of the output. And, in addition, the growth of exports permitted some increase in the supply of elementary needs from imports instead of home production. Thus a minor but increasing proportion of the food consumed in Britain was raised abroad and much of the material used in building the rapidly increasing number of houses was imported.[3]

As the century wore on, the range of technological advance widened very considerably. The railways were rapidly improved and brought to a high level of efficiency, to be followed by the slower development of steam turbines which eventually revolutionized shipping, and the coming of internal combustion engines and electrical power. The development of high precision standards in engineering multiplied the efficiency and scope of machine tools, while advances in scientific knowledge played a major part in the appearance of cheap and high-grade steel, synthetic dyes, and drugs. The spread of machinery meant not only the rapid decay of the hand trades but cheap supplies of commodities basic to the standard of living, such as boots and shoes and clothing for the working classes.

The third factor was the growth of the labour force. This was increased by 7m. people, or 72 per cent, in the second half of the nineteenth century, and there was some redistribution of labour which favoured higher productivity (e.g. a decline in the numbers employed in farming, and an increase in those employed in industry, trade, and transport). At the same time improvements in education and training raised standards among manual, clerical, and professional workers and began to widen the scope for women's employment, although the loss of workers through emigration (a net loss of over a million from England alone in the second half of the century) must have made inroads into the supply of skilled manpower. The fall in the death rate which occurred in the last quarter of the nineteenth century meant that the social investment in education and training was yielding a higher return in terms of a lengthening of the average working life, although this also meant that more resources had to be devoted to improvements in public health, such as water supplies, sanitation, and hospitals, and in housing.

Lastly a fourth factor and essential element in the situation was the growth of markets both at home and overseas. The growth of the home market was no mean factor in the demand for goods and services with some 12 per cent extra people added to the population in every ten years during the second half of the nineteenth century, or 16m. people during the whole fifty years; but more important for the growth of the nineteenth-century staples was the development of overseas markets with the expansion of agriculture and industrial activities in other countries. Indeed, in the years after 1850 the growth of British trade, increasingly freed from tariffs and monopolies, was proceeding at a greater rate than was the growth of industry. The overseas demand was not only for textiles and hardware—the traditional British exports—but also increasingly for British coal and machinery, railway equipment and vessels, and for Britain's important re-exports of raw cotton and wool, coffee, tea, oils, oil-seed, and hides—a trade which grew from something over £20m. a year in the later 1850s to over twice that figure by the 1870s, and to over £60m. a year by the end of the century.

The growth of trade meant too a great increase in Britain's invisible earnings. There were widening opportunities for profitable investment abroad, particularly in the Americas and the Empire; the enormous growth in world shipping involved an increasing demand for the products of British shipyards, the world's principal suppliers of vessels; and increased world trade brought about a greater demand, too, for British financial services, short-term credits, exchange facilities, and insurance. Furthermore, the expansion of the world economy meant that Britain's demand for imports, mainly raw materials and food, could be easily and cheaply satisfied. Except for interruptions due to war (as in the Lancashire cotton famine during the American Civil War), the growth of industry was not held up for lack of raw materials, while the increasing imports of flour, feeding stuffs, meat, and dairy produce encouraged or obliged British farmers to concentrate on the products in which they were relatively more efficient producers and to increase output by means of drainage, artificial fertilizers, and machinery, while releasing labour for other employment.

The revolution in transport was a vital part of the economic expansion. British leadership in railway construction, and more especially in the improvements to sailing ships and building of steamships, was the foundation for an important element of the export trade; lower transport costs both at home and abroad widened markets and enabled Britain to import more cheaply; British shipping was a major source of invisible earnings, enabling British consumers to buy more from abroad than they sold, and at the same time to invest heavily in the transport facilities, public utilities, and land and other productive assets in the developing countries, without encountering balance of payments difficulties and while still maintaining a free-trade policy—these were the most important consequences of the improved sailing vessel, steamship, and the steam locomotive (not forgetting also the supplementary role of investment in docks, wharfs, warehouses, navigational aids, and the telegraph). Perhaps, as has been claimed, transport was the key to nineteenth-century development: certainly the conquest of space and time heralded a new age dominated by a more closely linked and inter-dependent world economy which hardly existed in the same sense before the middle nineteenth century.

3 The process of growth: America

TABLE 5

U.S.A. gross national product 1869-73–1950		
	Gross national product *(at current prices)* billion $	*G.N.P. per head* *(at 1929 prices)* $
1869-73	6·7	223
1877-81	9·2	327
1889-93	13·5	424
1897-1901	17·3	496
1907-11	31·6	608
1920	88·9	688
1929	104·4	857
1939	91·1	847
1950	284·6	1,233

Source: *Historical Statistics of U.S.*

Recent estimates of American economic growth go further back than the above national income figures, and suggest that a significant upward trend began about 1839 when a long-term rate of growth developed of close to $1\frac{5}{8}$ per cent per annum per capita. American historians seem now to be in general agreement that the decades of the 1840s and 1850s saw important institutional and technological changes and the beginnings of a new and higher rate of economic progress. They do not agree, however, on the precise causes of the new trend. On the one hand the importance of cotton exports is stressed, together with the growth of inter-regional trade between the North and the South resulting in a high degree of regional specialization and greater agricultural efficiency; emphasis is given also to the growth of urban markets in the north-east, and the rapid growth in the 1840s of a large flow of produce from the west following the development of canal and rail communications; other writers stress the stimulating effects on investment, markets, business organization, and the demand for labour of the rapid spread of rail-roads in the 1850s, together with the adoption of the steamship and the telegraph.[4]

What is quite clear is that the Civil War did not mark the beginnings of industrialization or rapid growth—these were already in train; but the war did bring important changes in banking and tariff policies, western expansion, and a greater degree of mechanization of agriculture and industry. In fact, the war (which may itself have slowed down temporarily the rate of growth) is best seen as a convenient dividing line between the industrializing, but still agriculture-dominated economy of the first sixty years of the nineteenth century, and the increasingly industry-dominated economy of the post-1860 era. Gallman's figures of commodity output show an average rate of growth per decade of 57 per cent between 1839 and 1859, and a rise in annual *per capita* output from $64 to $85 between these two dates. These high *per capita* output figures no doubt reflect the favourable proportion of natural resources to labour, and the rapid growth of both home and overseas markets. Significantly, Gallman's figures show, too, a marked switch of output from agriculture to industry: in 1839 agriculture produced 72 per cent of total commodity output and manufacturing industry only 17 per cent; twenty years later the figures were 56 per cent and 32 per cent respectively.[5] The increased proportion of total output produced by manufacturing industry was undoubtedly an important factor in raising average *per capita* output, and the growth of industry was encouraged by the heavy immigration of the years 1846-55, a period of famine in Ireland and of hard times in Europe generally, but one of boom and prosperity in America. Of no little importance in the long term was the great inflow of capital funds from Europe (principally Britain) seeking investment in American securities. In the seventy years before the Civil War it is estimated that over $500m. (net) of foreign capital came into the country, making possible transport improvements, the expansion of cotton production, and the financing of an import surplus of consumer and capital goods.

In the years after the Civil War foreign capital in the U.S.A. continued to increase in absolute figures but fell greatly as a proportion of the total capital supply. Partly through their rapid growth and expansion into new areas and new products, American business concerns relied less heavily on the ploughing back of a large proportion of each year's profits, as remained largely the case in Britain, and by the later nineteenth century borrowed heavily from the banks and from the investing public by the issuing of bonds. Savings banks spread rapidly before the Civil War and supplied funds to the commercial banks, and to a lesser extent to transport undertakings and industry. More important was the proliferation of commercial banks which lent heavily to transport undertakings, public utilities, industrialists, and farmers. The policies of these banks were often unsound and inflationary, and rash over-optimism led to numerous failures. Nevertheless, it might be argued that economic development would have been less rapid if the banks had sought greater security by adopting a more cautious policy in their lending.

According to Douglas North, the mainspring of economic growth in the 1820s and 1830s was to be found in the expansion of the export trade. The exports of cotton, timber, and foodstuffs provided the link with the rapidly industrializing economy of Britain, and earnings from shipping, too, were not an unimportant element in the total earnings from foreign trade. Before the war cotton dominated exports, rising from $17·5m. in 1815 to $191·8m. in 1860. In 1836-40 cotton formed 63 per cent by value of all American exports, and while falling somewhat from this peak still provided over 50 per cent of total exports down to the Civil War.

The domination of the cotton trade gave rise to the marked inter-regional pattern of American economic development. The increase in incomes in the South derived from the expansion of cotton production (and to a lesser extent from the production of sugar, rice, and tobacco), and the increase in acreage and resources devoted to cotton growing involved a heavier dependence on foodstuffs from the developing agricultural areas of the old North-west: these were the wheat, corn, and meat-producing regions south and west of the Great Lakes, connected with the South by the steamboats and flatboats plying on the Mississippi and Ohio rivers. In addition, both the South and the West depended on the North-east for manufactured goods, luxuries, and financial and commercial services.[6] In an over-simplified way the economy may therefore be seen as consisting of three inter-connected and inter-dependent regions: (1) the North-east, providing capital, manufactured goods, and commercial services; (2) the West, producing primary foodstuffs and raw materials for both the North-east and the South; and (3) the South, whose export staples, and demand for food and manufactures, formed the basis of the system.

The importance of cotton in the economy, although still considerable, declined in the 1840s and 1850s. Expansion was no longer so dependent on the Southern market, and the growth of population in the North-east provided a market 'large enough to support a substantial industrial base. It was, in addition, an ever-growing market for western foodstuffs as canals and railroads bound East and West together . . . the American economy had escaped from the limitations of being tied to a single agricultural export staple. Its future as a manufacturing nation was assured, and the pace of its westward movement was stimulated by the demand for foodstuffs in the East and in Europe. . . . By 1860, New York's population exceeded one million, Philadelphia's nearly 600,000. The growth rate of the major cities in the North-east substantially exceeded the national population increase of 85 per cent between 1840 and 1860.'[7]

By the Civil War, American manufacturing industry had already developed so far as to be competitive with Europe in the production of rough cotton and woollen cloths, boots, shoes and leather, iron and machinery; and the growth of these industries had affected employment in the clothing and machine tool industries. Manufactured goods were of course dominant in American imports, but these consisted mainly of better-quality manufactures, luxury goods,

and producers' goods that the U.S.A. was not yet equipped to produce. The growth and efficiency of American industry before the
war depended on two main factors: the growth of the market, which
made possible specialization and increasing returns to scale, and the
introduction of standardization and large-scale methods of production, both by adopting existing European techniques and by
developing American-invented devices for high productivity. Thus
an increase in industrial productivity was able to compensate for
dearer capital and dearer labour, while the investment in education
and training of labour (widely commented on by European observers)
was an important contribution to this result.[8]

After the war, although the export trade increased greatly in
absolute terms, its relative importance to the American economy
declined.[9] The home market became increasingly important as population rose under the influence of a high (although declining) natural
rate of growth, heavy waves of immigration, industrialization, and
western expansion. Between 1860 and 1914 the market trebled as
population grew from 31m. to 91m., while demand was also affected
by the marked rise in living standards. Transport improvements,
and before the 1850s this meant very largely improvements in water
transport, were the key to the exploitation of the expanding home
market. In seventeen years after 1836 the value of goods shipped to
the western states via the Erie Canal rose nearly ten-fold, and the
development of the western market intensified industrial investment in the East. It also influenced the growth of new large western
cities such as Cincinnati and Chicago, which became the great centres
of production and distribution of industrial goods as well as centres
for the marketing and processing of agricultural produce. Thus in
1835 a French visitor to Cincinnati was already able to make these
remarks:

The Cincinnatians make a variety of household furniture and utensils,
agricultural and mechanical implements and machines, wooden clocks, and
a thousand objects of daily use and consumption, soap, candles. paper,
leather, etc., for which there is an indefinite demand throughout the
flourishing and rapidly growing States of the West and also in the new
States of the Southwest, which are wholly devoted to agriculture and in
which, on account of the existence of slavery, manufactures cannot be
carried on. Most of these articles are of ordinary quality; the furniture, for
instance, is rarely such as would be approved by Parisian taste, but it is
cheap and neat, just what is wanted in a new country where, with the

exception of a part of the South, there is general ease but little wealth and where plenty and comfort are more generally known than the little luxuries of a more refined society. The prosperity of Cincinnati, therefore, rests upon the sure basis of the prosperity of the West, upon supplying articles to fill the basic needs of the bulk of the community; a much more solid foundation than the caprice of fashion upon which the branches of industry most in favour with us depend. The intellectual also receives a share of attention. In the first place, there is a large type-foundry in Cincinnati, which supplies the demand of the whole West and that army of newspapers printed in it.[10]

The railroads supplemented and partially replaced the canals, lakes, rivers, and coastal shipping, and eventually linked the whole vast country by lines connecting the settled areas of the far West, California, Oregon, and Washington, the South-west, and Texas, with the rest of the economy. In general, though, as the population grew, it became increasingly concentrated in large urban centres, especially in the North-east and Lakes states, and here rather than in the West and South were the markets that influenced the general course of the economy. The areas stretching 'from Chicago in the West and from Washington to Boston in the East . . . still contains 68 per cent of United States manufacturing and has 43 per cent of the United States population.'[11] To some considerable extent the industrialized North-east and Middle West formed a self-contained economy, relying only marginally on the markets and production of the agricultural West and South, and also playing an increasing role in the country's growing foreign trade through the export of manufactures and demand for raw materials and luxuries.

The rapid growth of American industry was encouraged by the expansion of markets at home and abroad, by the availability of rich supplies of fuel and raw materials, by the flow of domestic and overseas capital (and especially in the late nineteenth century the growth of investment banking), and not least by the energy, initiative, and ingenuity of the American people themselves, supplemented by the skills and technical knowledge of immigrants. In the later nineteenth century when the westward movement began to lose some of its impetus and prospects of high profits from exploitation of virgin resources of minerals and timber, and from the appreciation of land values, began to look less promising, it seemed that much of the drive and speculative enterprise that had gone into land was transferred to industry and commerce. This was the age of the great industrial 'robber Barons' like Carnegie and Rockefeller, and the great investment Bankers, like Morgan, who built up vast industrial and financial empires, and whose power and influence rivalled, if it did not exceed, that of the President himself.

An important factor in American growth, it is already clear, was the early development of a highly productive machine technology. It was this that largely made possible the high levels of productivity that offset American disadvantages in competition with Europe of scarcer and dearer capital and labour. In 1850 American industry as a whole was generally behind that of Britain, then the world's industrial leader, but significantly, it was already remarkably ahead in the adoption of mechanization, standardization, and mass production in certain fields. Particularly important was the manufacturing of goods by use of interchangeable parts, especially small arms, woodworking, screws, nuts and bolts, nails, locks, clocks and watches, agricultural machinery, footwear, and sewing machines. Before the middle of the nineteenth century mechanization in industry and agriculture was designed to economize in *unskilled* rather than skilled labour, partly because the work performed by the unskilled was more easily adapted to machinery, and partly because liberal land policies, westward expansion, and the demand for unskilled men in transport and construction kept such labour scarce in manufacturing areas. Above all, the high levels of income in agriculture arising from abundance and cheapness of land and the gains from rising land value, and the ease of obtaining land for farming, provided the alternative occupation which kept real wages high in industry. The scarcity and dearness of labour made for rapid improvement and replacement of machinery in both industry and agriculture, and in farming as in manufacturing it was the rising level of demand in the market and the perennial shortage of labour that called forth factory-made cast-iron (later steel) ploughs with interchangeable parts, reapers, mowers, harrows, and threshers some years before mid-century. Again, there was little hostility from the workers towards improvements in productivity—scarcity kept their livelihood and incomes secure.[12]

After the middle of the nineteenth century the costs of taking up farming rose: the cheap or free land was farther away, and eventually only the less fertile, semi-arid or less easily cultivated land was available, so that larger acreages were needed; farming became more mechanized and the capital costs of establishing a farm and providing the equipment became substantial. Agriculture became much less an attractive or feasible alternative to industry and other urban occupations, and moreover, there were periods of falling prices for the agricultural staples. The heavy immigration of the late nineteenth century provided a much more plentiful supply of unskilled labour. Other factors, however, encouraged the continuation of the trend towards a capital-intensive industrial structure with a high degree of mechanization, standardization, and high output per worker. One such factor was the growth of a machine tool industry in the 1850s and 1860s to standardize and cheapen factory machines themselves; another was greater competition between industrial producers as more manufacturers entered the field; and not least there was the rapidly growing home market, more homogeneous in its distribution of income and in its demands for cheap mass-produced goods than the more conservative, class-divided, and locally differentiated consumers of Britain and Europe in general.

The American's attitude to economic development was influenced no doubt by the abundance of natural resources, the relatively free and equal character of American society, and the belief that his country was a land of unrivalled opportunity for all those with energy and initiative. Tocqueville, in his visit of 1831-2, called attention to the universal sense of enterprise and concern with business:

The sole interest, which absorbs the attention of every mind, is *trade*. It's the *national passion*. . . . The American people is, I said, a *merchant* people. That is to say that it is devoured by the thirst for riches, which brings in its train many hardly honourable passions, such as cupidity, fraud, and bad faith. Thus they appear to have but one single thought here, but one single purpose, that of getting rich.[13]

Another considerable influence on the American outlook was education. The early settlers seem to have begun a school almost as soon as they built their first cabins, and in the first half of the nineteenth century there were already technical colleges, mechanics' institutes, and in the northern states, laws requiring the compulsory part-time education of young workers. Education was less well developed in the South where the population was more scattered and there was less concern with the acquisition of industrial skills. The industrial supremacy of the North reflected the differences in educational provision, although it owed a good deal also to immigration of craftsmen from Europe.

Finally a recent American historian has stressed the role of government in the economic growth before the Civil War.[14] The prominent interventions of the post-Civil War Federal Governments are well known, in the fields of transport (land grants for railroad construction and regulation of railroads), settlement of the West (Homestead Acts and other measures concerning the exploitation of the public domain), trade (protective tariffs from the Civil War onwards). and industry (regulation of trusts). But before the war, when the Federal Government's role was a relatively minor one, the promotional activities of the state and municipal governments were in some instances of great importance. A number of semi-public corporations were formed to finance inland navigations, turnpikes, and toll bridges, a well as public utilities, banks, and insurance, while many cities were heavily involved in the finance of road improvements and railroads. However, it has been pointed out that many of the public investments in transport improvements were unsuccessful, and apart from the development of education, the over-all contribution of government to economic growth was probably a modest one.[14a] Transport developments and financial sources were vital conditions for the growth of the economy, but the real growing points—agriculture, trade and industry—depended on private enterprise, on the initiative, enterprise, self-reliance, and rugged individualism of that folk-hero, the American entrepreneur.

4 The Atlantic economy

In recent years the view has been advanced that the links connecting western Europe, and particularly Britain, with America were so strong, the ties of mutual self-interest so binding and pervasive, as to constitute an identifiable entity known as the 'Atlantic Economy'. The basis of this Atlantic Economy was the inter-relationships between an under-developed primary producer on the one side of the Atlantic and a more advanced and rapidly-developing industrial producer on the other. Mutual commercial interests formed the basis of the economy: an eastward-flowing trade in raw materials and foodstuffs and a westward-flowing trade in manufactures and capital goods. But there existed also an Atlantic Economy in another

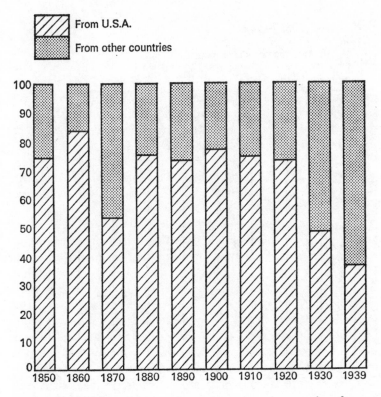

Figure 3. British raw cotton imports: proportion coming from U.S.A. 1850-1939

sense: that of a common pool of resources drawn upon by two geographically and politically separate, but economically inter-linked, centres of production: Britain drew on the American resources of land in the form of agricultural products, while America drew on British supplies of labour, capital, and know-how. The British (and European) demand for American raw materials and foodstuffs was a factor in westward expansion and agricultural specialization in the New World, while British and European labour and capital crossed the Atlantic in search of better opportunities and higher returns.

The Atlantic Economy was in its heyday in the years between 1820 and 1860. This was the period when the growth of the cotton

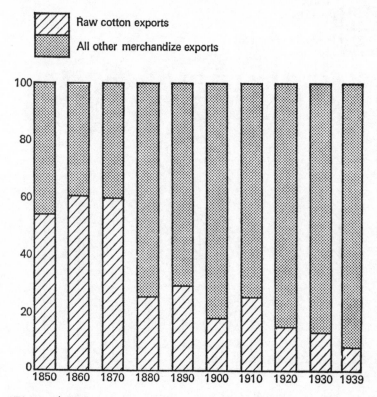

Figure 4. U.S.A.: cotton exports as a percentage by value of total exports 1850-1939

industry and of the British population meant a rising demand for American products, and when Britain was well placed to provide the largely agricultural American economy with the cheap manufactured goods, machinery, capital, and labour that it needed and could not yet produce for itself in sufficient quantities. The three legs of the Atlantic Economy were in fact trade, capital, and labour. Between 1820 and 1860 the American export trade in raw cotton—then the basis of its foreign trade—was closely bound up with the development of Lancashire, while both Lancashire and Yorkshire, together with British iron, hardware, and clothing manufacturers, looked to America for a major part of their markets. More precisely,

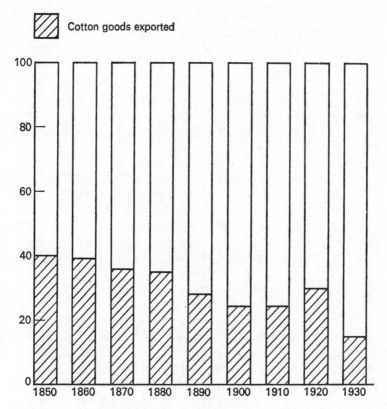

Figure 5. Great Britain: value of cotton goods exports as a percentage of total exports 1850-1930

nearly half of all American exports by value went to Britain (including in addition to cotton, timber, wheat, tobacco, cheese, and meat), and a quarter of all British exports went to America; 40 per cent of all American imports came from Britain (for wool and cotton textiles the figure was 90 per cent); and Lancashire relied on the American south for 80 per cent of its cotton.[15]

British capital was important both for the financing of American public borrowings and for direct investment in railroads and land. About half of the bonds of the 'planters' banks of the southern states were held in England, together with nearly a quarter (in 1828) of the Federal Government's debt. By 1860, 20 per cent of the total

American funded debts were held abroad, much of it still in Britain at a time when the attention of British investors had turned more towards railroad bonds. As important in its sphere as this capital was the availability of British commercial credit to American merchant houses. A great amount of America's inland trade, to say nothing of the Atlantic trade itself, depended on British credit for its functioning, and when the mutual confidence on which this credit depended was shaken, as in the crisis of 1836-7, the Atlantic commerce was brought almost to a standstill.[16]

In the first half of the nineteenth century economic progress in America relied considerably on British immigrants. British farmers (including a sizeable contingent of Scots) were prominent in occupying the newly-opened lands of Illinois and other prairie states from the 1830s onwards, while farm labourers, too, flocked to the emigrant ships, lured by the prospect of higher wages, cheap land, or the opportunity of eventually establishing themselves in business. American industry before 1850 depended heavily on European techniques and on a nucleus of skilled workers from Europe, particularly Britain. The early American cotton industry drew on the labour and knowledge of Lancashire, the American steel and tin-plate industries on South Wales, and American pottery on Staffordshire. In 1860 nearly 600,000 persons in the United States (mainly in the northern seaboard states) were born in England, Scotland, or Wales, representing 14 per cent of the total foreign-born population of the country. British enterprise and skill were invaluable supplements to British capital and credit.

By 1860 all this was changing. The American export trade in grain was about to rival and surpass that in cotton, and the American cotton industry was now producing three times as much manufactured cotton as was imported from Britain and was absorbing as much as 40 per cent of the South's cotton crop. American industry in general had been growing rapidly in the 1840s and 1850s, and some American industrial methods were already ahead of European techniques, particularly in the field of standardization and mass production of common household goods. Immigrants now came in numbers from a wide range of western European countries, and supplies of capital, too, were widening, while the domestic capital supply was now becoming much more ample and was channelled to borrowers through the developing banking system and stock market.

The introduction of high protective tariffs during the Civil War therefore marked America's growing economic maturity and self-dependence, and did not so much begin a new phase in the Anglo-American economic relationship as openly recognize that the nature of the relationship had already changed.

To what extent the transatlantic flow of goods, labour, and capital still deeply influenced the two economies in the later nineteenth century is a question on which historians disagree. It is contended on the one hand that fluctuations in American investment and employment were closely connected with changes in the levels of emigration and domestic investment in Britain, but a contrary view is that the outflow of capital and labour from Britain was related much more to her own internal trends in prosperity, employment, urbanization, and finance. These, however, are complex matters that we must leave for further discussion in their proper place. It is enough to say here that certainly the Atlantic economy, as it functioned before 1860, no longer existed in the same sense.

Notes

1 MATTHEWS, R. C. O., 'Some Aspects of Post-War Growth in the British Economy in Relation to Historical Experience', *Manchester Statistical Society* (Nov. 1964), p. 3.

2 ASHWORTH, W., *An Economic History of England 1870-1939* (1960), p. 7.

3 *Ibid.*, p. 8.

4 NORTH, D. C., *The Economic Growth of the United States, 1790-1860* (Englewood Cliffs, N.J., 1961), esp. ch. 7; TAYLOR, G. R., 'The National Economy before and after the Civil War', in D. T. Gilchrist and W. D. Lewis (eds.), *Economic Change in the Civil War Era* (Eleutherian Mills-Hagley Foundation, Greenville, Delaware, 1965), pp. 9-10; CHANDLER, ALFRED D., Jr., 'The Organization of Manufacturing and Transportation', in *Economic Change in the Civil War Era*, pp. 139-41, 148-9.

5 BRUCHEY, S., *The Roots of American Economic Growth, 1607-1861* (1965), pp. 83-5.

6 NORTH, *op. cit.*, pp. 67-9, 75, 102, 194-6.

7 *Ibid.*, p. 206.

8 NORTH, D. C., 'Industrialization in the United States', *Cambridge Economic History of Europe* VI (Pt. II), (ed.M. Postan and H. J. Habakkuk, Cambridge, 1965), pp. 673-705.

9   With 1913 = 100, American exports rose in value from 33·3 in 1879 to 73·2 in 1900, and to 101·1 in 1912; as a percentage of G.N.P. they accounted for between 6 and 8 per cent. American imports rose less rapidly from 27·0 in 1879 to 53·4 in 1900, and 100 in 1912-13; as a percentage of G.N.P. imports fell from about 6 per cent to a little over 4 per cent in the first three decades of the twentieth century.

10   CHEVALIER, MICHAEL, *Society, Manners, and Politics in the United States* (ed. J. W. Ward, Anchor Books, New York, 1961), p. 197.

11   NORTH, *loc. cit.*, p. 702.

12   See HABAKKUK, H. J., *American and British Technology in the Nineteenth Century* (Cambridge, 1962), esp. ch. 4.

13   PIERSON, GEORGE WILSON, *Tocqueville in America* (Anchor Books, New York, 1959), p. 45.

14   BRUCHEY, *op. cit.*, ch. 6.

14a   NORTH, D. C., *Growth and Welfare in the American Past* (Englewood Cliffs, N.J., 1966), pp. 101-4.

15   THISTLETHWAITE, F., *America and the Atlantic Community; Anglo-American Aspects, 1790-1850* (New York, 1959), ch. 1; 'Atlantic Partnership', *Econ. Hist. Rev.*, 2nd ser., VII (1954-5), pp. 1-17.

16   For details see CHAMBERS, J. D., *The Workshop of the World* (1961), pp. 158-9.

Suggestions for further reading

Texts

ASHWORTH, W., *An Economic History of England: 1870-1939* (1960). *The International Economy since 1850*, (2nd ed. 1962).

CHAMBERS, J. D., *The Workshop of the World* (1961).

CHECKLAND, S. G., *The Rise of Industrial Society in England 1815-1885* (1964).

DEANE, PHYLLIS, *The First Industrial Revolution* (Cambridge, 1965).

NORTH, D. C. *Growth and Welfare in the American Past* (Englewood Cliffs, N. J., 1966).

THISTLETHWAITE, F., *The Great Experiment: an introduction to the history of the American People* (Cambridge, 1965).

Specialized works

BRUCHEY, S., *The Roots of American Economic Growth 1607-1861* (1965).

DEANE, P. and COLE, W. A., *British Economic Growth 1688-1959* (Cambridge, 1963).

HABAKKUK, H. J., *British and American Technology in the Nineteenth Century* (Cambridge, 1962).

MITCHELL, B. R. and DEANE, P., *Abstract of British Historical Statistics* (Cambridge, 1962).

NORTH, D. C., 'Industrialization in the United States', *Cambridge Economic History of Europe* VI, Part II (ed. M. Postan and H. J. Habakkuk, Cambridge, 1965). *The Economic Growth of the United States 1790-1860* (Englewood Cliffs, N. J., 1961).

THISTLETHWAITE, F., *The Anglo-American Connection in the Early Nineteenth Century* (Oxford, 1959) reprinted under title *America and the Atlantic Community; Anglo-American Aspects, 1790-1850* (Harper Torchbooks, New York, 1963). 'Atlantic Partnership', *Economic History Review*, 2nd ser. VII (1954-5).

Trends in the American Economy in the 19th Century (Vol. 24, Studies in Income and Wealth, National Bureau of Economic Research, Princeton, 1960).

U.S. Census Bureau, *Historical Statistics of the United States* (Washington, 1960).

1 British railways: their extent and efficiency

Most of those concerned with the management of British railways in the 1850s were justifiably proud of their country's achievements in railway building during the previous quarter century. With 6,084 route miles open by the end of 1850, Britain possessed a closer network of lines in relation to its area than any other country. London was already in rail communication with all the principal provincial cities. It was possible to travel by rail to Scotland by the fairly direct west coast route through Crewe, Lancaster, and Carlisle or, more circuitously, through Leicester, York and Newcastle. On the other hand East Anglian services were patchy, and Wales was scarcely served at all, except for the Taff Vale Railway running up from Cardiff, and the Chester and Holyhead line in the north.

Through communication had been greatly encouraged by the opening of the Railway Clearing House in 1842, and by the 'end on' amalgamation of smaller companies into the Midland Railway in 1844 and the London and North Western in 1846. The Gauge Act of 1846 provided for the ultimate standardization of tracks on the 4 ft 8½ in. gauge, although the Great Western Railway did not complete the conversion of its lines from the broad (7 ft) gauge to the standard gauge until 1892.

Scheduled railway journey times not appreciably slower than those followed in the 1890s were already achieved in the 1850s. Thus an average speed of 43 m.p.h. was achieved on the London-Exeter run despite seven stops.[1] Whereas it had taken 13 hours to cover a journey of 100 miles by coach in 1830, twenty years later it took but a quarter of the time by rail.

2 British railways: capital

But British railways, though speedily built, were also expensively built. Up to 1914 the average cost of their construction per mile of line was £54,152, compared with £13,000 per mile in the United

States.[2] Many contemporaries contended that a large part of this great difference in cost was due to the payment of 'exorbitant sums' for land.[3] The land bought by the London and Birmingham Railway cost £537,596 or 12·7 per cent of its capital outlay—more than double Robert Stephenson's original estimate. It was pointed out that the average cost of land per mile of track in Britain was £4,000, compared with a mere £235 per mile (including the cost of buildings erected) in the United States.[4] There is little doubt that given a more vigilant public, standing less in awe of the doctrines of laissez-faire and demanding stronger compulsory purchase powers for the railways, land for British railways need not have cost more than 4 per cent of total capital outlay instead of, say, 10 per cent. But the effect on total capital cost per mile of line would not have been great and the effect on shareholders' earnings marginal. Instead of paying an average dividend on capital of 3·55 per cent in 1912, the railways might have paid 3·8 per cent.[5] We can therefore agree with a more recent assessment that 'British railways would have gained if land had been cheaper; but this would not have appreciably reduced the difficulties.'[6]

Part of the extra cost of establishing British railways arose from the expense involved in getting a railway bill through Parliament. The Great Western Railway's parliamentary expenses came to £87,197 but these were modest compared with the Great Northern's half a million pounds. J. S. Jeans estimated that up to 1886 the companies had spent £16m. in obtaining parliamentary powers.[7] But this sum, though large in itself, was small in relation to the estimated £200m. of watered stock (i.e. securities whose nominal value has been increased without any corresponding payment in cash) which burdened the railways in 1913, and smaller still in relation to the £1,282m. total capital of the companies at that date.

Of greater significance than any of the above influences in inflating the capital cost of railways in Britain was the solidity of their construction. Since early locomotives were incapable of tackling steep gradients, and because also engineers became increasingly concerned with speed, lengthy tunnels and substantial cuttings and embankments figured more prominently in the U.K. than they did in the U.S.A. Sharp curves in the permanent way were avoided because British rolling stock did not run on bogies as the American stock did. Stations in the British Isles were built elaborately and expensively. Architects such as Philip Hardwicke (1792-1870) could exercise their talents not only in well-known symbols of the railway age like the Doric Portico at Euston but even in designing the portals of tunnels in remote parts of the country. By contrast, a prominent British railway contractor, Sir Morton Peto, travelling in the United States at the conclusion of the Civil War, noted that 'the original construction of the American railroads was very imperfect'.[8] The fact was that after early, crude, construction the American companies normally improved the permanent way by expenditure out of revenue.

Great Britain had also to pay the price for her pioneering. Part of the capital cost of her railway network comprised expenditure on such items as stationary engines, experimental signalling devices, and the replacement of light cast-iron rails by wrought-iron ones.

If capital had not been available in such comparative abundance, the Boards of Directors of British Railway companies would have been obliged to think in terms of more economical construction, as American directors undoubtedly were. However, the payment of a 10 per cent dividend by the Liverpool and Manchester line for several years after its opening in 1830 unloosed the purse strings of the investors, and there was rarely any difficulty in raising funds for railway building for many years afterwards.

The capital market for British railways was both national and local, with the local element more important before 1850 and the national generally dominant thereafter. Most of the capital for the Stockton and Darlington line in 1825 had been obtained from Quakers in the neighbourhood, and Liverpool merchants, together with Londoners, provided the bulk of the funds for the Liverpool and Manchester railway five years later. But the Liverpool merchant Ellis was 'a shareholder to a great amount' in the Canterbury and Whitstable line before 1830.[9] By the late 1840s the growth of the London and provincial stock exchanges had made the market for long-term railway capital 'impersonal, divisible and capable of easy movement'.[10] At mid-century the 'Liverpool party' was still dominant in the capital of Midland, London and South Western, Great Western, and Eastern Counties railways, but the general public was becoming to an increasing extent railway investment-conscious, with *Herapath's Railway Journal* (which first appeared as early as 1835 as *The Railway Magazine*) offering its expert advice. Even after the main market for railway shares had become a national one, there were examples of important lines built principally with the aid of local capital. Thus the Duke of Buccleugh and the Earl of Burlington, the great land-owners of the district, were the chief backers of the Furness railway at its inception in 1844.

Reckless expansion of competitive lines in the mid-1840s led to a period of meagre financial returns on railway investments in the 1850s when it was more difficult to obtain new funds from the public. By 1863 Richard Moon, Chairman of the London and North Western railway, was complaining 'What is the state of things in England? There is not one of the great companies in this country who can raise sixpence without preference or guaranteed shares. There are no proprietors willing to come forward to make a railway. They are made by contractors, engineers, and speculators who live in the fear of the companies.'[11] *The Economist* estimated that two-thirds of the capital authorized in the sessions 1864-6 was for 'contractors' lines' such as the Metropolitan District, the Cambrian, and the London, Chatham and Dover railways. In these cases the contractors took payment in the form of securities of the railway company for whom they were building, discounting their 'Lloyds Bonds' at one of the great London discount houses when ready cash was needed. The collapse of the greatest of the discount houses, Overend and Gurney, in October 1866, with uncovered liabilities amounting to over £5m., not only bankrupted the contractor, Sir Morton Peto, but also caused railway companies to depend to a greater extent than ever on loans to help them build the remaining 8,000 miles of mainly branch lines before the peak of 20,405 miles was reached in 1926.

Before 1914, in contrast with the situation in the United States, British railways were built without the aid of foreign capital and without material assistance from central or local government. The Hampstead Tube line, in which C. T. Yerkes, a wealthy American, invested £100,000 in 1900, provided a rare exception to the first of these generalizations, and the Hull Corporation's subscription of £100,000 in 1880 to the stock of the Hull and Barnsley railway an even rarer exception to the second.[12]

3 British railways: labour

One reason for the absence of revolution in Britain in 1848 at a time when it was so widespread on the continent was that the peak of railway construction came in the wake of the railway mania of 1845-7. At least 250,000 men—about 4 per cent of the occupied male population—were employed in railway building in 1848, a year in which an additional 1,191 miles of line (an all-time British record) were opened to the public.[13] Had they not been dispersed in contractors' gangs throughout the country, the thousands of Irish-born navvies and unemployed English agricultural labourers would have aggravated the overcrowding in the big cities or been a source of discontent in the villages. Although earnings were high, the conditions of employment, especially with the sub-contractors and 'butty' men, were often deplorable, with overcrowded and insanitary living quarters, a high accident rate and the excessive prices of the truck or 'tommy' shops the principal abuses.

When the pace of construction slackened some members of the contractors' gangs found employment with the railway companies as porters, platelayers, and switchmen. The number of permanently-employed railwaymen rose from 47,000 in 1850 to 650,000 in 1914. Few jobs were so eagerly sought after as those to be found on the railway, despite hours of labour well in excess of most other occupations, since few could offer the same degree of permanency.

The general scarcity of labour in the U.S.A. helps to explain why railway trade unionism became a powerful force earlier in that country than in Britain, where continuity of employment proved a powerful lever to maintain loyalty to the management, especially in such years as 1879 and 1886, when unemployment was heavy outside the railway industry. By maintaining differentials of 100 per cent between the wages of the skilled and the unskilled men, by operating company-sponsored pension schemes, and by many other stratagems, management helped to stave off railway trade unionism in Britain until the foundation of the Amalgamated Society of Railway Servants in 1872. Even then for many years it was touch and go whether the new organization would survive, and it was not until 1911 that the union, with a progressively weaker hold over its locomotive members after the creation of a breakaway union for these grades in 1879, felt strong enough to sponsor a national railway strike in an endeavour to establish collective bargaining with the Companies. In the meantime, in 1907, a Conciliation Scheme for negotiating wages and hours had been agreed by both companies and railway unions. Full collective bargaining was not achieved until the First World War.

4 British railways: economic effects

An American historian has distinguished between transport services which are predominantly 'exploitative' (i.e. carrying more efficiently *existing traffic*), and those which are 'developmental' (or mainly constructed in *anticipation* of new traffic).[14] British railways were for the most part exploitative while American lines were to a greater extent, especially west of the Mississippi, developmental in character. Nevertheless, there were some British railways whose developmental role was uppermost. Thus the Taff Vale railway, opened in 1841, greatly accelerated the growth of coal mining in South Wales and assured the predominance of Cardiff as a coal port. After 1846 the Furness railway played 'a decisive role in opening up . . . a district which was remote and difficult of access' until it became 'one of the important iron districts of the North of England'.[15]

For the most part, however, British railways mainly extended and increased the goods traffic previously carried by canal barge, coastal freighter, and road goods wagon. With the exception of some relatively short coal lines, such as the Stockton and Darlington and the Taff Vale, the increase of goods traffic carried by rail during the second quarter of the nineteenth century was not spectacular. It was possible for Lardner to write in 1850 that 'the transport of merchandise is the branch of railway business . . . which has been hitherto comparatively neglected'. It was quite otherwise with passenger traffic. In the year following the opening of the Newcastle and Carlisle railway in 1839, eleven times as many people travelled by railway as had previously travelled by coach.[16] Within a year of the opening of the Liverpool and Manchester railway in 1830, only one of the thirty stage coaches formerly carrying passengers between the two cities was still operating, and this was supported 'solely by the passengers to intermediate points not lying in the direction of the railway'.[17] In 1848 receipts from passenger traffic still brought in 57·3 per cent of the total revenue of British railways, and it was not until 1852 that freight brought in a greater revenue than did passengers.[18]

The decline in importance of British canals under the impact of railway competition was less severe than has often been suggested. Throughout the nineteenth century the volume of goods carried on inland waterways continued to increase, though at a much slower rate than the increase of rail-borne traffic. The twelve most important canals which in 1838 carried 10,605,957 tons of goods, were carrying 18,837,729 tons (out of a total canal-borne tonnage of 39,350,000) in 1898. However, by the end of the century the canals' share of the combined rail- and waterborne traffic had fallen to just under 10 per cent.[19] The inland waterways' share of goods traffic would undoubtedly have been greater had not about a third of the canal mileage passed into the hands of the railways, mostly during the period 1845-7. The fact that, in this brief span of time, the railways acquired important stretches of canal on such through routes as that from London to Liverpool, and that on the railway-owned canals tolls were higher than on the independently owned canals, restricted the development of cheap long-distance waterborne traffic. In 1900 canal traffic was much more localized than it had been in 1850.

Parliament's attempt to bolster canal competition with the railways at first misfired. Under the Canal Carriers Act of 1845 canal companies were allowed to lease other companies as a means of increasing their joint viability in competition with the railways. The effect of the Act was the opposite to that intended. A railway company which had previously bought out a canal had merely to add the words 'and canal' to its name to enable it to take out a leasehold on any surviving independent canal company and reduce still further existing curbs on the railways' monopoly of inland transport.

The railways had effects on associated industries in raising output and in lowering costs through increased scale of production. According to one authority, at mid-century the building of each route mile of railway in Britain required at least 300 tons of iron. More than a million and a half tons of iron went into the building of the 4,000 miles of track laid down between 1846 and 1850, an amount greater than the total national output of iron in 1844.[20]

No influence was more powerful than that of the railways in raising the mechanical engineering industry from infancy to maturity in the middle years of the nineteenth century. At least a fifth of the industry's output was earmarked for the railways in the later 1850s,[21] and the industry developed new branches such as the manufacture of signalling equipment and automatic brakes. Before long the railway companies themselves were directly engaged in the large-scale production of locomotives and rolling-stock. From small beginnings in 1843, when 423 men were employed, the Great Western railway works at Swindon expanded rapidly to employ 4,000 in 1875, and a maximum of 14,000 in 1905, when it was perhaps the largest establishment, in terms of manpower, in the country.[22]

In Essex there was a rapid increase in the number of brick-making establishments when the Eastern Counties and other railways spread their tentacles through the country. This experience was repeated elsewhere wherever the railway network extended, so that the stimulus to the national economy given by railways' demand for bricks was probably more widespread than that given by the demand for iron. The railways consumed as many as 700m. bricks, or approximately one-third of the national output.

The railways undoubtedly had an impact, too, on the agriculture of the United Kingdom. The railway labourers were prodigious eaters and drinkers. If the man whose daily consumption included seven pounds of meat and nine quarts of gin and ale mixed was at all typical,[23] the arrival of the navvy gangs must have been a godsend to the local fat-stock farmers, even though the welcome afforded by the more timorous of the females of the neighbourhood was a little uncertain.

Lecount, the historian of the London and Birmingham Railway, asserted that the company's payment of £4m. in labourers' wages during the construction of the line, by reducing the volume of rural unemployment, must have eased the burden of the poor rates. Simultaneously the arrival of the railway increased rateable values.

Farms located near the railway immediately appreciated in value. James Smith of Deanston in Scotland, a well-known farmer and publicist, told a Parliamentary Select Committee that a 200-acre farm he knew, located 15 miles from the nearest market, had to pay £142 16s. 3d. a year for transport by road with wagon charges at 6d. a ton mile. At 1d. a ton mile by rail the farm's transport costs had fallen to £40 8s. 9d. A greater quantity of perishable produce hitherto not worth sending to market could now be dispatched at a profit.[24] The consensus of opinion among land agents in the third quarter of the nineteenth century was that the proximity of a railway station increased the letting value of farms by anything from five to twenty per cent. In the second half of the nineteenth century farmers were in a position to meet more closely the needs of the market. Before the railway age heavy stall-fed cattle had lost an average of 56 lb weight while being driven to Smithfield Market. After the advent of the railway it was possible to slaughter cattle locally and send different parts of the carcase to different markets to meet the preferences of customers. Guano and the new artificial fertilizers (publicized by the firm of Gilbert and Lawes from the Rothamstead Experimental Station), reaping machines, and other improved farm implements could now be carried quickly and cheaply to the farms.

In both Britain and the United States in the last quarter of the nineteenth century farmers looked upon the railways with a more critical eye. Helped by the extension of the rail network across the prairies, and the improvements in steam navigation, the area under wheat in the U.S.A. rose from 15m. acres in 1866 to nearly 38m. acres in 1880. British arable farmers found the cultivation of wheat less and less profitable, and they were obliged to diversify the output of their farms by switching to mixed and dairy farming if they were to continue to pay their way. In the 1880s stock farmers were complaining that British railways were carrying American meat from Glasgow to London at 25s. a ton less than they charged for the domestic product, and they found that only by improving quality of breeds of cattle and emphasizing the superiority of British meat could they maintain sales at remunerative prices. Milk sales, however, could be made profitable. From 1872 to 1880 the quantity of milk brought to the Metropolis by the Midland railway alone rose from 940,000 gallons to 5,500,000 gallons a year.[25]

One result of outstanding importance of the coming of the railways was the rapid expansion of the capital market and the increased level of savings. At the height of the railway mania in 1845-7 the London Stock Exchange was 'hard pressed to keep pace with the volume of business' and *The Economist* commented that 'Everybody is in the stocks now. Needy clerks, poor tradesmen's apprentices, discarded serving men and bankrupts—all have entered the ranks of the great monied interest.'[26] The majority of the provincial stock exchanges owed their very existence to railway investment. Those at Manchester and Liverpool were founded during the first railway mania of 1835-6, whilst those at Glasgow, Edinburgh, Birmingham, Bristol, and Leeds were the outcome of the second, and greater, mania of the mid 1840s. Of the 186 securities traded on the Manchester Stock Exchange in 1845, 161 were the issues of the railway companies.[27]

In consequence of the unprecedented boom in stocks and shares, capital investment, which in the early 1830s had been at the level of from 6 to 7 per cent of national income, was raised 'permanently to ten per cent or more by the mid 1850s'.[28] By the time railway building slowed down towards the end of the third quarter of the century, the investment habit was firmly ingrained among much wider sections of the population and the diversion of funds to other forms of new capital ensured the continued rapid expansion of the economy.

5 British railways: public policy

In the second half of the nineteenth century railway questions filled a larger number of pages of the British Parliamentary Papers than did any other aspect of public policy. Paradoxically enough it was principally because of a concern to maintain free competition in transport that so much Parliamentary time had to be taken up in debating railway bills or hearing witnesses summoned before Select Committees and Royal Commissions.

In 1844 the railway interest had been so effectively mobilized to influence Peel and the majority of his cabinet that Gladstone, the President of the Board of Trade, had drastically whittled down those provisions in his Railway Bill which concerned public ownership. Even so, the Act passed that year did give the Government the option, twenty-one years later, to purchase any railway built after 1844. In 1865 a Royal Commission was appointed to examine the case for or against nationalization (and other policies), but despite the advocacy of Sir Rowland Hill, Chadwick, and Walter Bagehot (from the editorial columns of *The Economist*) in favour of a greater measure of government control of the railways, the majority of the Commission was of the opinion: 'that it is inexpedient at present to subvert the policy which has hitherto been adopted of leaving the construction and management of railways to free enterprise of the people under such conditions as Parliament may think fit to impose for the general welfare of the public'.

Parliament followed this advice. In the Regulation of Railways

Act, 1868, it went no further than providing for a standardized
system of railway accounts, a measure long overdue, which enabled
the Government to be more accurately informed on the comparative
efficiency of the various railway companies and the reasonableness or
otherwise of their charges.

Parliamentary inquiries and the legislation which followed them
were closely co-related with the advance of the amalgamation movement. Thus the Select Committee of 1854 presided over by Cardwell,
the President of the Board of Trade, met in the same year in which
the North Eastern railway was formed as a result of the merging of
companies into the most complete regional monopoly so far created.
Although the report of Cardwell's Committee recommended that
Parliament 'should refuse to sanction amalgamation except for working arrangements made for limited periods of time', the Railway
and Canal Traffic Act of 1854 concentrated instead on the kind of
practices which it was believed often paved the way to monopoly. In
language very similar to that which, in 1887, appeared in the U.S.
Interstate Commerce Act, the Act forbade the railway companies 'to
give any undue or unreasonable preference or advantage to or in
favour of any particular person or company or any particular descrip-
tion of traffic'. More positively, the companies were under obligation 'to afford all due and reasonable facilities for forwarding all the
traffic arriving by one of such railways . . . without unreasonable
delay', a clause which proved a great stumbling block to the com-
petitiveness of railways after the First World War, when the railway
monopoly was rapidly undermined by the growth of road goods
haulage which creamed off the most profitable traffic, whilst leaving
the railways with the 'obligation to carry' goods which lorry owners
found it not worth their while to handle.

Leaving aside the Royal Commission of 1865-7, which took place
under the shadow of a major railway amalgamation in Scotland, the
next important occasion on which Parliament was prompted to check
monopolistic tendencies was in 1871-2, when bills were presented for
amalgamations or working arrangements involving 'every important
company in England'.[29] Thus, had the proposal for a merger of the
Lancashire and Yorkshire and the London and North Western railways been sanctioned, the North-west would have had a regional
monopoly every bit as powerful as that already functioning in the
North-east. Whilst the House of Commons effectively vetoed the

project, the Select Committee on Railway Amalgamations, 1872, no doubt influenced by the efficient management of the North Eastern railway, had to admit that past amalgamations 'had not brought with them the evils that were anticipated'. The Railway and Canal Traffic Act, passed the following year, set up a Railway and Canal Commission of three men who became responsible for enforcing the Act of 1854 and for enforcing the obligation of the companies under the 1873 Act to exhibit their books at all stations so that the public should have full information on rates and charges. The Act certainly did nothing to stop the growth of amalgamations.

In 1911 a Departmental Committee of the Board of Trade, surveying developments since 1873, conceded that 'the era of competition between the railway companies' was 'passing away'. There was much evidence of the truth of this statement in the events of the previous twenty years. In 1899 the South Eastern and the London, Chatham and Dover railways, which had operated since 1865 a pooling agreement in respect of their receipts from continental traffic, established a 'working union' by which the two companies' lines were placed under a single management, although the two capital accounts continued to be kept separately. In 1909 the Great Central, Great Northern, and Great Eastern railways were unsuccessful in their attempt to obtain Parliamentary approval for a similar arrangement but, in the meantime, the Midland, London and North Western, and Lancashire and Yorkshire railways had, with less publicity, reached a comprehensive pooling agreement.

Meanwhile, under the Railway and Canal Traffic Act (1888), the Railway (Rates and Charges) Order Confirmation Acts (1891 and 1892), and the Railway and Canal Traffic Act of 1894, the Railway Commissioners (renamed, after 1888, the Railway and Canal Commission) acquired powers to fix maximum rates for each class of goods carried on the railways.

Thus the establishment during the period 1914-23 of a unified system of control through a railway executive committee of ten general managers with a government nominee as chairman, was consistent with the tendencies towards consolidation and unified management which had been accelerating during the previous two decades. It can safely be asserted that, even without a war in 1914-18, the merging of the companies into even larger units would have continued.

Before 1914 the Government had greatly extended the scope of its intervention on behalf of safer railway operation. Initially the principal concern was the safety of passengers rather than railwaymen. This concern lay behind Lord Seymour's Railway Regulation Act of 1840, which required the approval of a Board of Trade inspector before a line was opened to traffic, and the Regulation of Railways Act of 1868 which made compulsory the provision of a communication cord between passenger coaches and the guard's van. Compulsory block signalling and continuous brakes on passenger trains came under the Regulation of Railways Act of 1889. A few years later, under growing pressure from the trade union movement, legislation was extended to give greater protection to railwaymen. The Railway Servants (Hours of Labour) Act of 1893 had the effect of reducing the amount of overtime working and hence indirectly the number of accidents, but the first measure primarily concerned with the safety of the men employed was the Railway (Prevention of Accidents) Act of 1901 which brought in such improvements as the better lighting of goods sidings and the provision of brakes on both sides of goods wagons. Legislation to provide safer working conditions for railwaymen had come long after similar legislation for mines and factories. In this respect the U.S. Congress had acted earlier on behalf of railway employees than did Parliament in Britain.

6 American inland waterways

In the U.S.A. in 1850 water transport was much more extensively used for the carriage of goods and passengers than was the case in Britain. The country was richly endowed with natural waterways whilst the greater average length of canals enabled carriers to enjoy the economies of the long haul. The outstanding example of a successful canal was the 363 miles long Erie canal. Constructed with the aid of a generous land grant from New York state and opened in 1825, it was, at mid century, the principal transport artery between the Atlantic seaboard and the west. The greatest natural waterway was the Mississippi–Missouri river system whose navigation tested to the utmost the skill of the pilots. After a journey from St. Louis to St. Joseph in which encounters with savage-looking snags, reefs, and sandbars were unforgettable memories, Mark Twain, with characteristic hyperbole, observes that the steamboat 'might almost as well have gone to "St. Jo" by land, for she was walking most of the time anyhow—climbing over reefs and clambering over snags patiently and laboriously all day long'. Despite such hindrances to speedy travel, the inland waterways in 1851-2 carried six times as much freight as the railroads. Only by the outbreak of the Civil War in 1861 was the volume of waterborne and rail-borne traffic roughly equal. Thirty years later, in 1890, the railways carried five times as much freight as the waterways. On the other hand in the North-west the commerce of the Great Lakes expanded rapidly. By 1900 the $1\frac{1}{2}$ m. tons of shipping employed in this region was nearly half that employed in the coastwise trade.

Long before the middle of the nineteenth century the United States had an established tradition of government involvement in internal improvement. Although in many matters Americans were intolerant of government interference, transport improvements were regarded as an exception since the state or federal assistance was seen to be a prerequisite to the opening up of the West. In Britain, on the other hand, with more ample private capital resources there was very little support for the investment of government funds in internal improvements.

7 American railroads: extent of network

One reason for the slow eclipse of waterborne traffic was the fact that the 9,021 miles of railroad line opened to traffic in the United States by December 1850 constituted a less adequate transport network than might at first appear to be the case. By 1861 the mileage had been rapidly increased to 31,286, but the country still lacked a satisfactory system of through rail communications. This was mainly for the reason that the railroad companies were chartered by the states and not by the Federal Government and therefore served *state* rather than national ends. Although 53 per cent of the lines were of the standard 4 ft $8\frac{1}{2}$ in. gauge, no less than five other gauges were in use, the most important being the 5 ft (7,267 miles, 21·8 per cent of total), 4 ft 10 in. or New Jersey gauge (3,294 miles, 9·9 per cent), and 5 ft 6 in. (2,896 miles, 8·7 per cent).[30] State legislatures were rarely perturbed by the hindrances to through traffic caused by these gauge differences, since it was no doubt true, as Senator B. Grimes of

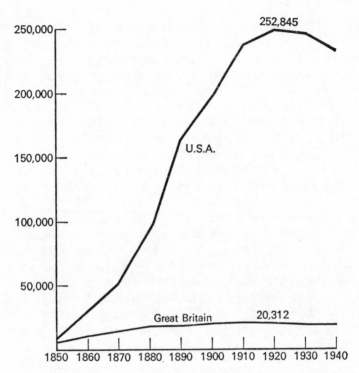

Figure 6. Railways: route mileage, U.S.A. and Great Britain
1850-1940

Ohio said in 1863, that 'Where there is a break in gauge there is a
large amount of business.' Only with the emergency of the Civil War
was there a sufficiently strong reason to remove such obstacles to
through traffic as the absence of a railroad bridge over the Appo-
mattox river at Petersburgh, Virginia.

In the post-Civil War period standardization proceeded apace as
more and more companies adopted the standard gauge already prevalent in the commercially predominant states of New York and
Pennsylvania. On 31 May and 1 June 1886, in an operation which
exceeded in magnitude that carried out on the Great Western railway in England six years later, 13,000 miles of broad-gauge lines in
the Southern States were changed to the standard gauge. Although
in the meantime over 5,000 miles of narrow-gauge lines were built
to tap the mineral deposits of the mountainous west, with uniformity

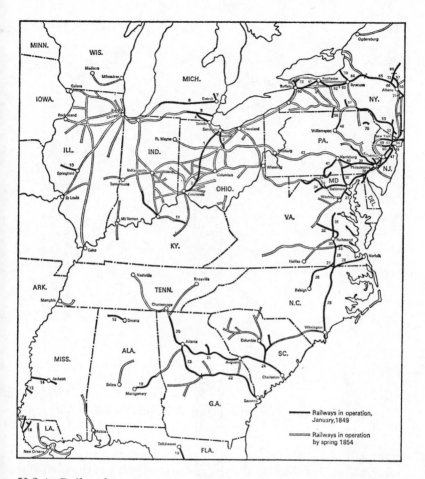

U.S.A. Railroads

of gauge elsewhere railroad building raced ahead until the peak mileage of 254,251 was in service in 1916. If differences of gauge had proved more of an obstacle in the U.S.A. than in England, the costs to the companies of obtaining legislative approval for railroad bills were much lower. Sir Morton Peto observed in 1866 that 'nothing (had) been easier than to obtain from the legislative authority of a state in America . . . a charter to lay down a road.' This did not mean that the social costs of railroad promotion were necessarily any less in the U.S.A. than in Britain. Rather it was the case that in the U.S.A. the public found it necessary to bribe members of the state

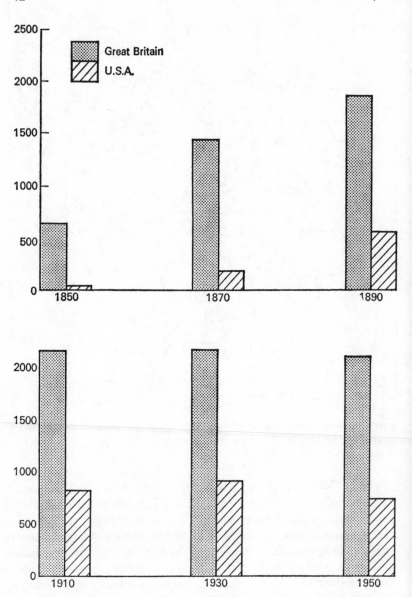

Figure 7. Railways: Great Britain and U.S.A. route miles per 10,000 square miles of land area 1850-1950

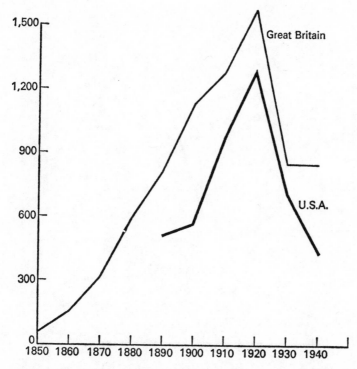

Figure 8. Railways: Great Britain and U.S.A. passenger traffic 1850-1940, (in millions of passengers carried per year)

legislatures and of Congress if the railroad was not to 'pass them by', whereas in England it was the companies that footed the bill.

8 American railroads: capital

Before the Civil War the railroads of the United States were built with capital in part supplied by private investors, in part by state, county, and municipal authorities, and in part by foreign investors. In the 1830s the 'Liverpool party' in English railway finance was matched by the Philadelphia capitalists in American railroad building. In the 1840s New England investors (especially Bostonians) set the pace. When the commercial crisis of 1847 brought a severe check to the fortunes of the New Englanders, New York acquired the dominance which it was to retain for the rest of the century.[31]

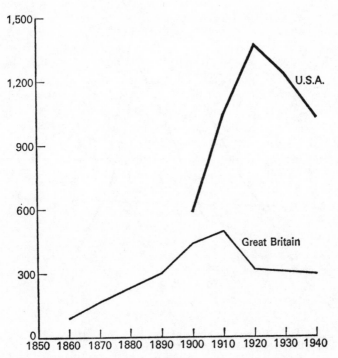

Figure 9. Railways: Great Britain and U.S.A. goods traffic
1850-1940, (in millions of tons carried per year)

By 1861 state and local governments had provided between 25
and 30 per cent of the total funds invested in railroads in the United
States. Infected by a fever of state, county, or even municipal 'mer-
cantilism', representatives of the public had voted no less than
$425m. in cash or credit for internal improvements of all kinds
(roads and canals, as well as railroads). The greater part of this
money was invested by seven Atlantic seaboard states in a bold bid
to breach the Appalachian barrier and capture the increasingly
profitable trade of the Ohio and Mississippi valleys.[32]

The pre-Civil War role of the foreign investor in the direct investment in transport improvements was a comparatively minor one,
although British investment in the Erie canal before its opening in
1825 was of outstanding importance. Indirectly, however, the British
investor contributed substantially to the internal improvements of

this era by his willingness to buy state government bonds. The high tide of state bond issues came in the years 1836-8. Widespread banking failures, in 1839, followed by a protracted depression until 1844, during which eight state governments and one territory suspended interest payments to bondholders, frightened off British investors from much new investment in the United States. This was especially marked during the railway mania (1845-7), when domestic railway investment appeared to be far more attractive. In the 1850s, however, with the fading of the memory of commercial setback in America, and more meagre returns accruing from railway investment at home, British investors showed a renewed interest in American securities.

The Illinois Central railway which in 1850 received through the state legislatures of Illinois, Alabama, and Mississippi, a generous land grant from the federal public domain, was the prototype of those railroads which, in the third quarter of the nineteenth century, received substantial assistance from the federal government. After *The Times* had dubbed the new venture as 'eminently sound investment', and James Caird, the foremost British agriculturist of his day had travelled extensively through the domain of the new railroad and had declared the soil of Illinois was 'abounding in every element of fertility',[33] British investors contributed handsomely to a loan for the building of the line. By 1864 they had the bulk of the 12m. of the company's bonds held overseas and three-quarters of the total stock.[34] Thereafter, until the imperative demands of war compelled their sale in the U.S.A. early in 1915, American railroad securities constituted the most important single element in the typical British investor's portfolio. In 1899 British investors probably held between a fifth and a quarter of the capital of American railroads. By 1914 the aggregate value of American railroad securities held in Britain was £620m., a figure which was approximately 16 per cent of British overseas investments and 15 per cent of the capitalization of American railroads.[35]

In the later history of American railroad finance, the experience of Great Britain was repeated in that the proportion of loan capital to equity stock increased. Whereas in 1850 over half the $800m. invested in American railroads was in equities, in 1916 the loan capital amounted to $9,900m., whilst the stock was only $6,400m.[36] As was the case in England, the most important reason for this change in capital structure was the intervention of the construction company, which received payment for the building of the railroad in the form of mortgage bonds as a first charge on the revenues of the railroad. Whilst the most notorious example of such a concern was the Credit Mobilier, which hastened the completion of the Union Pacific in 1869, similar concerns built all the trans-continental lines and were even to be found in the more settled regions of the east.

After the severe financial panic of 1893 had caused about a quarter of the American railroad mileage to pass into the hands of the receivers, the greater part of the capital of the railroads was consolidated under the control of such great banking houses as J. P. Morgan and Company, Kuhn Loeb and Company (financing Edward H. Harriman), and others, who together concentrated two-thirds of the railroad mileage under the management of no more than seven business concerns.[37]

9 The Federal Government's role in railroad promotion

After the outbreak of the Civil War the Federal Government played a major part in encouraging the extension of the railroad network. If it is a matter of debate whether the railroads were primarily exploitative or primarily developmental in the states east of the Mississippi before the Civil War, there can be less argument on the nature of railroad expansion in the West after 1862. Without Federal Government assistance construction in this region would have been delayed by at least a decade.

A scheme for a transcontinental railroad had been advanced by Asa Whitney in 1845, and the Federal Government financed a survey of possible routes in 1853; but all projects had foundered on the rock of sectional interests. Only when Southern opposition was removed by secession was it possible for Congress to pass the first Pacific Railroad Act on 1 July 1862. Two companies—the Central Pacific which had already been founded, and the Union Pacific set up under the Act—were to complete rail communication across the continent, the C.P. by building eastwards from Sacramento and U.P. westwards from the Missouri. Construction was aided by a grant of land from the federal domain comprising ten alternate sections for each mile of line and a government loan varying from $16,000 per mile on the plains to $48,000 in the mountains. In so far as construction lagged because insufficient capital was forthcoming from the investing public until the (second) Pacific Railroad Act in 1864 had doubled the land grant and given the government a second instead of a first mortgage on the railway, the Union Pacific can be considered a 'premature enterprise'. But the line was busy from the date of its opening and paid an average dividend of 5·1 per cent in the first decade of its operation. Thus, from one viewpoint, the line was premature only in the sense that investors were mistaken as to its likely profitability.

Under the policy of free land grants, continued until 1871, the Federal Government handed over 131,350,534 acres of the public domain to the railways. If the 48,883,372 acres given by the states be added, the total exceeded by 13 per cent the area of present-day France.[38]

10 American railroads: labour

The Irish were as renowned as railroad builders in the United States as they were in Britain. In the 1850s they were employed in large numbers in such states as New York and Pennsylvania. A decade later, on the Union Pacific, they were to be found in the gangs which established the record for track laying in 24 hours—10·6 miles. Such prodigies were achieved only by well-disciplined organization. The food was 'substantial though not elegant', and often comprised buffalo meat, beans, and bacon. The men were fed on specially fitted box cars, tin plates being nailed to the tables to save time with the 'swabbing out' in the few seconds interval between the feeding of one gang and that of the next. Rates of pay were superior to those in England but the work was even more strenuous. On the Central Pacific, Northern Pacific, Southern Pacific, and Atchison, Topeka and Santa Fe lines, tens of thousands of sturdy and industrious Chinese were employed at wages ranging from $26 to $35 a month. Mexicans augmented the labour force in the South-west.[39]

Railroad labour was effectively organized at an earlier date in the U.S.A. than it was in Britain. No doubt the extreme scarcity of skilled labour contributed to the successful launching of the Brotherhood of the Footboard (renamed, a year later, the Brotherhood of Locomotive Engineers) at Marshall, Michigan in April 1863. This organization, like those of the Conductors (1868), Firemen (1873),

Switchmen (1877), and Brakemen (1883), at first concentrated on the provision of friendly society benefits for the membership. But with the onset of economic depression there were some fiercely fought strikes to resist wage reductions, notably on the Baltimore and Ohio railroad in July 1877 and at Pullman, Illinois in 1894. Collective bargaining was achieved on some important lines earlier than was the case in Britain. Thus hard bargaining between the Railway Brotherhood and management on the Burlington Railroad resulted in a collective contract being signed in April 1886. In both Britain and the U.S.A. influential groups of railwaymen became acutely aware of the shortcomings of craft unionism and pioneered the establishment of industrial unions. Eugene Deb's American Railway Union (1893) pre-dated its British counterpart, the National Union of Railwaymen, by twenty years: but whereas the American union had insufficient time to consolidate before becoming involved in the Pullman strike in 1894 when it was smashed by the combined use of the injunction and blacklisting, the N.U.R. was founded just before the industrial truce of the First World War, and was soon strongly entrenched.

The greater strength of unionism on the American railroads led to earlier experiments in industrial conciliation there than in Great Britain. As early as 1889 Congress provided for voluntary railroad mediation, while nine years later the Erdman Act strengthened the arbitration machinery. However, in both countries it was the circumstances of the First World War which did most to establish a permanent system of conciliation.

11 American railroads: economic effects

A distinguished economist, Professor W. W. Rostow, has written that the influence of the railroad was 'decisive' in the 'take off' of the American economy in the years 1843-60. It is a view which is widely supported in textbooks of American economic history.

The reasons that have been advanced for this view are that the railroad was an essential pre-requisite for the growth of intra-regional exchange and hence an extended division of labour; that railroad construction was a 'pace setter' creating a decisively enhanced demand for productive materials, particularly coal, iron and steel, timber, and engineering products; and that the expenditure of money on the labour and materials of railroad building set in motion the 'multiplier effect' which re-invigorated the whole economy.[40]

The above interpretations have recently been subject to critical scrutiny. It has been shown that the rate of structural transformation in the economy in 1843-60 'was not uniquely different from the rates that prevailed in the years that followed' or even preceded it.[41] There is no evidence that the rate of capital formation was radically increased. Further, at no stage in the growth of the American economy did railroad investment constitute so large a proportion of either total investment or of gross national product as was the case with the British economy at the time of the railway manias. In the U.S.A. railroad investment never exceeded the 16 per cent of gross capital formation achieved in the decade 1852-61. It could be argued that the sale of Liberty Bonds after 1917 did more to popularize the investment habit amongst wide sections of the American public than did the sale of railroad bonds. Indeed, it is difficult to find an example of an American stock market which owes its foundation primarily to the need for a market for railroad securities. The exchanges at Philadelphia and New York were founded before the railroad age, while those at Chicago and San Francisco were not established until 1882, after these cities had passed their main phase of railroad development. However, the fact that the headquarters of the majority of the American railroads were in or near Wall Street helped to secure the pre-eminence of the New York exchange: as early as 1835 the bulk of the dealings were in railroad securities.[42]

Earlier claims that the proportion of American pig-iron production going to the manufacture of rails rose from 11 per cent in 1850-5 to 31 per cent in 1866-70 and that 'total railway demand for iron must have been close to 50 per cent of total output in 1871 and 1881', were based on the erroneous assumption that all rails purchased in the U.S.A. were made directly from domestic supplies of pig iron. Until the Civil War (and even later) 40 per cent of the rails bought were imported from England. Of the remainder, domestically produced, 35 per cent were rolled from old rails and 15 per cent were made from imported pig iron. It is indeed arguable that 'nails rather than rails triggered the 1845-9 leap in production' since in 1849, the weight of nails produced was probably twice that of rails.[43] The most that can be said is that railroad demand of all kinds took a quarter of the output of the iron industry in the period 1855-60, and that the proportion may well have been greater in the peak construction years of 1871 and 1881. How far railroad demand produced economies of sale and lowered costs is open to doubt.

The impact of the railroads on the coal mining industry was certainly less in the U.S.A. than it was in England. From the first, British locomotives were fired with coal whereas, before the Civil War, most American locomotives, except in some eastern states, were wood burners. Indirectly, coal used in the manufacture of rails, rolling stock, etc., took 6 per cent of the total output in 1840-60. After the Civil War, with a rapid switch to coal-burning locomotives and a quickening of the pace of construction, the railroads claimed a larger share of the industry's output. The proportion of coal output consumed in locomotives alone rose from 13 per cent in 1880 to 25 per cent in 1921.[44]

Peto's criticism that American railway stations were 'mere wooden erections of a temporary character' and that bridges were also generally built of wood, reminds us that the demand for bricks and stone for railway building in the U.S.A. was nothing like as great as it was in Britain. Most of the timber used for sleepers was locally produced, and this substantial demand had, in consequence, little impact on the growth of timber mills in America. While it is true that the increase in speed and the growing congestion of lines posed new problems which were eventually solved by such specialized engineering firms as Baldwins and the Westinghouse concern, at the time of the Civil War the railroads did not take more than 4 per cent by value of the products of manufacturing industry of the U.S.A.[45]

It may also be questioned whether the new form of transport was responsible for such a decisive break-through in intra-regional exchange, particularly of agricultural produce, as has sometimes been suggested. Those who wrote the eighth Census Report in 1860[46] claimed that the reduction in transport charges which was a consequence of railroad building in such states of the old North-west as Ohio, Michigan, and Illinois, had for the first time secured the farmer 'very nearly the prices of the Atlantic markets'. By giving the producer the benefit of the best market and higher prices the railroads had increased the agricultural production of the interior states 'beyond anything heretofore known in the world'. Largely because of the railroad, the price of good farmland in Illinois had risen from

$1·25 to $20 an acre in the decade since the Illinois Central Railway was chartered in 1850.

But the initial reduction in costs provided by water transport as compared with wagon haulage, was greater than the fall in railroad rates in the second half of the century. Indeed, it is not always appreciated that railroad rates remained *above* those charged for river and canal transport. The fall in water transport costs was dramatic indeed: by 1830, following the introduction of steamboats on the Mississippi, Missouri, and Ohio rivers, the river freight rate had fallen to a mere thirtieth of the wagon rate. Canal rates fell sharply after 1830, and by 1850 were only a twentieth of wagon rates. In 1850 railroad rates were as much as four times higher than canal rates, and although the differential was subsequently reduced, railroad freight charges remained substantially higher than the cost of water transport.[47]

The effect of this great reduction in water transport costs before 1850 was decisive for the opening of the substantial trade between the east and the west. 'It was by means of canals that Americans . . . were for the first time able to make effective use of the great interior and to establish a national market on which industrial development could be based.'[48] During the period 1820-50, the population of Ohio, Indiana, Illinois, and Michigan rose from 8 per cent to 18·1 per cent of the national total. It was the opening of the Erie Canal which was largely responsible for this rapid growth. Only when the canals could no longer adequately cope with the growing traffic in produce from the old North-west did the rapid building of railroads take place. At least for this region 'it was the demand factors which stimulated the building of railways rather than the reverse.'[49]

West of the Mississippi where there were few canals and where the natural waterways provided less adequate alternative means of transport, the railroad was to a greater extent playing the part of innovator. This can be seen in the transport situation of states newly admitted to the union. The twelve states accepted into the union in the period 1830-65 had put 400 miles of railroad at the time of their admission; the twelve admitted between 1865 and 1914 had 23,000 miles. In most cases these western states had a nucleus of railroads at least a decade before they had sufficient population for them to qualify for admission to the union. Clearly in the West, the railroads performed the role fulfilled further east by the canals. It would be difficult to imagine the rapid rise of the cattle industry in Wyoming and Montana to its peak of activity in 1886 without the existence of speedy rail communication with the union stockyards in Chicago.

The western railroads were great colonizing agents. Since they were often generously endowed with land it was in their interest to sell it to potential railroad users as quickly as possible. The consequent publicity campaigns were not characterized by an excessive modesty. The Northern Pacific (in a pamphlet) claimed that 'the only illness which remotely touched the residents of Montana was the pangs of over-eating, resulting from the excessive indulgence of the hearty appetite attendant on the invigorating atmosphere',[50] whilst the London agent of the Galveston, Harrisburg and San Antonio railroad assured his audiences that the atmospheric conditions on *his* line produced 'flexibility of joints, lightness of limbs and a buoyancy of spirit'.[51] With the existence of such a paradise in western latitudes it is not surprising that the Northern Pacific had, by 1883, sold nearly three million acres of land and had directly settled 16,000 heads of families. (The families settled on land initially purchased by speculators were far more numerous.) Over a longer period of time (1854-1914) the Illinois, Central Railway directly settled between 30,000 and 35,000 families.[52]

12 American railroads: State and Federal Government regulation

Partly because farmers' expectations of the benefits of railroads had been unduly raised, their resentment was all the greater, when, after the first enthusiasm of settlement, they confronted the problem of selling their produce in distant markets. By the late 1860s and early 1870s farmers organized in the Granges were demanding legislation to curb the railroads' monopoly of grain elevators and to put an end to their practice of granting rebates and of discriminating in freight charges in favour of the long haul.

Between 1871 and 1873 the legislature of Illinois established a Board of Warehouse and Railroad Commissioners which determined passenger fares and enforced freight charges that were strictly proportional to distance. The example of Illinois was quickly followed by Minnesota, Iowa, and Wisconsin, and the laws were, by implica-

tion, upheld by the U.S. Supreme Court in the case Munn *v.*
Illinois in March, 1877. Nevertheless, increasing doubt was expressed
of the adequacy of control at state level. In 1870 three railroads,
each having terminals at Chicago and Omaha, reached an informal
agreement to share traffic and restrict competition between these
two cities. This 'Iowa Pool' was beyond the control of a single state
legislature since, in its sphere of operation, it transcended state
frontiers. The South Western Railway Rate Association (1876,
covering the Chicago–St. Louis region) and other pooling agreements
followed.

The first preoccupation of the U.S. Congress when it began to
consider a policy for railroads was similar to that of the English
House of Commons throughout the nineteenth century—how to
maintain competition. Central Government control was given less
attention than was the case in Britain, but the Windom Committee
in 1874, convinced that 'cheap transportation is to be saved through
competition', recommended Government ownership or control of
'one or more railroads' to link the Mississippi Valley to the Atlantic
seaboard in order to act as a yardstick for the efficiency of lines
privately owned.[53] It was not a policy which found favour with a
majority of Congressmen, and no legislation along these lines
resulted.

Paradoxically, to the extent that state legislation succeeded in
controlling *local* rates so did the case for national regulation increase,
since railroads sometimes raised *through* rates as compensation for
being obliged to lower *local* ones. The question assumed a much
greater urgency, however, when the Supreme Court in the case
Wabash, St. Louis and Pacific Railway *v.* Illinois in 1886, invalidated part of the Granger legislation and ruled that: 'A regulation of
commerce . . . must be of that national character, and the regulation can only appropriately exist by general rules and principles
which demand that it should be done by the Congress of the United
States under the Commerce clause of the constitution.'[54] By this
time many railroad managers were in favour of federal regulation
of railroads in the hope that the government might forbid rate
cutting and enforce pooling agreements. The City Chambers of
Commerce were also urging greater federal control.

The Interstate Commerce Act of 1887 embodied many of the
recommendations of the (Senate) Cullom Committee of 1885. It

ruled that all interstate rates were to be 'reasonable and just', but it did not define justice or reason! Under section four of the Act discrimination in favour of the long haul was forbidden: 'It shall be unlawful for any common carrier . . . to charge or receive any greater compensation . . . of passengers or of like kind of property, under substantially similar circumstances and conditions, for a shorter than a longer distance over the same line in the same direction, the shorter being included within the longer distance.' The pooling of traffic and the granting of rebates and drawbacks were prohibited and, as a protection for the public, rate schedules were to be published in every depot or station. Enforcement was to be through a five-man Interstate Commerce Commission which could issue 'cease and desist' orders but whose final sanction was the Federal courts.

The achievements of the Commission in the first decade of its life were unimpressive. Those who filed suits against the railroad companies under the Act had ample experience of the law's delays. In cases where the companies appealed against the decision of the lower courts the average time taken before the Supreme Court rendered its verdict was four years, and there were even instances where the delay extended to nine years. Even then the judgement—from the point of view of the complainant—was often not worth waiting for! Of the sixteen appeals to the Supreme Court on rate questions between 1887 and 1905 all but one were decided in favour of the railroads,[55] and in the Maximum Freight Rates case in 1897 it was ruled that, whilst the Commission was empowered to determine the reasonableness of rates which had applied in the past, the Act had not given it 'the legislative function of prescribing rates which (shall) control the future'.

In the early years of the twentieth century, however, Congress returned to the attack. Rising freight rates provoked the inevitable crop of protests from traders, and the success of the consolidation movement of the companies after 1898 led to renewed accusations of monopoly. The new legislation took the form of a tightening up of the provisions of the Interstate Commerce Act. By the Expedition Act of 1903, where the Government was the complainant, the case was to be given precedence in the courts to expedite judgement. In the same year the Elkins Act made the receiver of a rebate as well as the railway company granting it, guilty of an offence. To increase the influence of the Commission, the Hepburn Act in 1906 increased its membership from five to seven and gave it authority over other common carriers besides the railroads. Finally the Mann-Elkins Act in 1910 gave the Commission power to suspend proposed rate increases and obliged the companies to show good reason why such added charges were necessary.

Nevertheless, despite some success in closing the vast loopholes of the original Act, we can agree with Professor Kirkland that 'the railroad reform movement failed, however, to solve the dilemma as to whether competition or railroad operation under Government control was the better way to end the abuses against which it protested.'[56]

The United States entry into the First World War made possible a temporary resolution of the dilemma when President Wilson, in December 1917, placed all the railroads as well as the coastwise and inland water transport under the Secretary of the Treasury as Director General.

13 Conclusion

By the middle of the nineteenth century industrialization and capital accumulation had proceeded much further in Britain than in America. Thus ample capital was available from private sources for the construction of canals and railways. In America, where private capital was less abundant, but the public domain was vast, the government played a more positive role in the promotion of internal improvements. Before the Civil War state governments made the greater contribution, principally in the form of loans and subscriptions to capital stock. In the third quarter of the nineteenth century to encourage more rapid settlement of the west, the Federal Government gave the railroads generous grants of land from the public domain. Because of more favourable geographical conditions, inland waterways made a relatively larger contribution to overall transport services in America than in Britain.

In the thirty years before the outbreak of the First World War on both sides of the Atlantic there was an increase in Government intervention to check rate discrimination and rebates and to promote greater safety for both travellers and railwaymen. But the American Government took a much more hostile attitude to pooling agreements than did Parliament in Britain, with the result that railroad managers and investment bankers sponsored consolidation as a method of evading the drawbacks of competition. In Britain on the other hand pooling agreements kept alive a proportionately larger number of companies and tended to delay the standardization of equipment.

Notes

1 LEWIN, H. G., *The Railway Mania and its Aftermath* (1968 ed.), p. 424.

2 SAVAGE, C. I., *An Economic History of Transport* (1959), p. 44.

3 JEANS, J. S., *Railway Problems* (1887), p. 430.

4 *Ibid.*, pp. 34, 431.

5 POLLINS, H., 'A Note on Railway Constructional Costs, 1825-1850', *Economica* n.s. 19 (1962), p. 395.

6 SIMMONS, J., *The Railways of Britain* (1965), p. 15.

7 Jeans, *op. cit.* p. 40.

8 PETO, M., *The Resources and Prospects of America* (London and New York, 1866), p. 268.

9 FELLOWS, R. B., *History of the Canterbury and Whitstable Railway* (Canterbury, 1930), p. 28.

10 POSTAN, M., 'Recent Trends in the Accumulation of Capital', *Econ. Hist. Rev.* VI (1935), p. 1.

11 Cited by POLLINS, H., 'Railway Contractors and the Finance of Railway Development in Britain', *Jour. Transport History* III (1955), p. 44.

12 LEE, C., *Fifty Years of the Hampstead Tube* (1957), p. 12; PARKES, C. D., *The Hull and Barnsley Railway* (1948), p. 2.

13 LARDNER, D., *Railway Economy* (1850), p. 55.

14 GOODRICH, CARTER, *Government Promotion of American Canals and Railroads, 1800-1890* (New York, 1959), p. 15.

15 POLLARD, S. and MARSHALL. J. D., 'The Furness Railway and the Growth of Barrow', *Jour, Transport History* I, 2 (1953), p. 109.

16 *Select Committee on Railways*, B.P.P. 1839, Q. 3818.

17. JEANS, *op. cit.*, p. 6.

18 LARDNER, *op. cit.*, p. 277.

19 *Report of R.C. on Canals*, B.P.P. 1906 XXXII. Appendix 1.

20 ROBBINS, M., *The Railway Age* (Penguin ed. 1962), p. 30.

21 MITCHELL, B. R., 'The Coming of the Railway and U.K. Economic Growth', *Jour. Ec. Hist.* XXIV (1964), p. 315.

22 EVERSLEY, D. E. C., 'Engineering and Railway Works', *V.C.H. Wilts.* IV (1959), pp. 208-18.

23 Cited by CHADWICK, E., in a paper read before the Statistical Society of Manchester *On the Demoralisation and Injuries occasioned by the want of proper Regulations of Labourers engaged in the construction and working of Railways* (Manchester 1846), p. 39.

24 *Select Committee on Railway Acts Enactments,* B.P.P. 1846 XIV, Minutes of Evidence Q. 3152-61.

25 *Royal Commission on Agriculture,* B.P.P. 1882 XIV, Minutes of Evidence Q. 8096 *et seq.*

26 *The Economist,* 28th June 1845.

27 MORGAN, E. V. and THOMAS, W. A., *The Stock Exchange: its History and Functions* (1962), pp. 108, 141.

28 MITCHELL, *loc. cit.*, p. 331.

29 CLEVELAND STEVENS, E., *English Railways: their development and their relation to the State* (1915), p. 238.

30 TAYLOR, G. R. and NEU, I. D., *The American Railroad Network, 1861-1890* (Camb., Mass., 1956), p. 14.

31 CHANDLER, A. D., JR., *Patterns of American Railroad Finance, 1830-1850,* Mass. Inst. Tech. Publ. No. 15 (1955), *passim.*

32 GOODRICH, CARTER, *op. cit.*, p. 268.

33 CAIRD, JAMES, *Prairie Farming in America with notes by the way on Canada and the United States* (1859), p. 58.

34 GATES, PAUL W., *The Illinois Central Railway and its Colonisation Work* (Harvard, 1934), p. 68.

35 JENKS, L. W., 'Britain and American Railway Development' *Jour. Ec. Hist.* XI (1951), p. 375.

36 STOVER, JOHN F., *American Railroads* (Chicago, 1961), pp. 30, 176.

37 FAULKNER, H. U., *The Decline of Laissez-Faire* (New York, 1951), pp. 191-8.

38 STOVER, *op. cit.*, pp. 88-9.

39 WINTHER, O. O., *The Transportation Frontier: the Trans-Mississippi West, 1865-90* (New York, 1964), pp. 108-13.

40 JENKS, L. H., 'Railroads as an Economic force in American development', in *Essays in Economic History* III (ed. E. M. Carus-Wilson, 1962), p. 222.

41 FOGEL, R. W., *Railroads and American Economic Growth* (Baltimore, 1964); COONTNER, P. H., 'The Role of Railroads in U.S. Economic

Growth', *Jour. Ec. Hist.* XXIII (1964), p. 477. For a concise summary see D. C. North, *Growth and Welfare in the American West* (Englewood Cliffs, N.J., 1966), pp. 110-21.

42   DICE, C. A. and EITEMAN, W. J., *The Stock Market* (New York, 1952), p. 90.

43   FOGEL, *op. cit.*, pp. 135, 193.

44   *Ibid.*, pp. 135-6.

45   *Ibid.*, p. 146.

46   *Influence of the Railroads upon Agriculture*, Census of 1860: Agriculture (Wash. D.C., 1863), pp. clxv-clxix.

47   NORTH, D. C., *Growth and Welfare in the American Past* (Englewood Cliffs, N.J., 1966), pp. 110-12.

48   SEGAL, H. H., 'Canals and Economic Development', in Carter Goodrich (ed.) *Canals and American Economic Development* (New York and London, 1961), p. 249.

49   COONTNER, *loc. cit.*, p. 505.

50   HEDGES, J. B., 'The Colonisation Work of the Northern Pacific Railroad', *Mississippi Valley Historical Review*, Dec. 1926.

51   WINTHER, O. O., 'Promoting the American West in England', *Jour. Ec. Hist.*, XVI, 4 (1956), p. 508.

52   GATES, *op. cit.*, pp. 256 *et seq.*

53   Report of the Select Committee on Transportation Routes to the Seaboard, *Senate Report No. 307, Part I* 43rd Congress 1st Session, pp. 140-1, 156-61.

54   Cited in KIRKLAND, E., *Industry Comes of Age* (New York, 1961), pp. 125-6.

55   FAULKNER, *op. cit.*, p. 188.

56   KIRKLAND, *op. cit.*, p. 135.

Suggestions for further reading

Texts

ASHWORTH, W., *An Economic History of England 1870-1939* (1960), ch. 5.

FAULKNER, H. U., *American Economic History* (New York, 1964), ch. 14, 23.

JONES, G. P. and POOL, A. G., *A Hundred Years of Economic Development* (1940), ch. 2.

NORTH, D. C., *Growth and Welfare in the American Past* (Englewood Cliffs, N.J., 1966), ch. 9.

ROBERTSON, R. M., *History of the American Economy* (New York, 2nd edn., 1964), ch. 6, 12.

Specialized works

COONTNER, P. H., 'The Role of the Railroads in U.S. Economic Growth', *Jour. Ec. Hist.* XXIII (1964).

FOGEL, R. W., *Railroads and American Economic Growth* (Baltimore, 1964).

MITCHELL, B. R., 'The Coming of the Railways and U.K. Economic Growth', *Jour. Ec. Hist.* XXIV, 3 (1964).

ROBBINS, R. M., *The Railway Age* (Penguin Books, 1965).

SAVAGE, C. I., *An Economic History of Transport* (1961).

CLEVELAND-STEVENS, E., *English Railways: their development and their relation to the state* (1915).

STOVER, J. F., *American Railroads* (Chicago, 1961).

TAYLOR, G. R., *The Transportation Revolution, 1815-1860* (New York, 1951).

3

Agriculture

1 The agricultural labour force

In the middle of the nineteenth century American agriculture employed some 64 per cent of the labour force and accounted for a slightly smaller proportion of the national income. In Britain, the comparable figure in both cases was about 20 per cent, only about a third of the American figure. In both countries agriculture declined sharply in relative importance during the next eighty years. In 1900-1 British agriculture employed less than a tenth of the labour force, by 1930-1 only a little more than a twentieth. In America the proportion in agriculture was under two-fifths by 1900, and under a quarter by 1930.

TABLE 6

Labour engaged in agriculture 1850-1–1930-1

| | *Proportion of labour force engaged in agriculture* | | *Total numbers employed in agriculture* | |
	Britain %	U.S.A. %	Britain '000	U.S.A. '000
1850-1	22	64	2,017	4,550
1900-1	9	38	1,425	11,749
1930-1	6	22	1,353	10,633

Source: *Abstract of British Historical Statistics, Historical Statistics of U.S.* and *Output, Employment and Productivity in the United States*, N.B.E.R., 1966, pp. 119-20.

It is worth noting that the British agricultural labour force reached its peak in absolute numbers about 1850 and then declined sharply to the end of the century, recovered slightly between 1901 and 1921, and then declined again at a slower rate to the present. In America the agricultural labour force was at its absolute peak about 1910 (11·77m.), and then declined slowly until the 1930s, when a more rapid rate of decline in numbers set in during the depression. In both countries the fairly prosperous period of farming between 1900 and 1920 saw near-stability in the labour force; the onset of depression conditions in the 1920s, together with widespread technical advances involving electrification of farms, use of tractors, new and more prolific strains of seeds, and other developments which substantially increased output per man, began a new phase of declining manpower which has not yet come to an end.

2 Differences in agrarian structure

The essential difference in the agrarian structure of the two countries was that between a farming system in England dominated by large proprietors (who did not usually farm commercially), and a system in America dominated by owner-occupiers. In England the so-called 'tripartite system' prevailed. In the nineteenth century most of the land—about 85 per cent of it—was owned by large and middling owners (the great landowners and the gentry) who let it out to tenants, except for a small proportion which landowners retained as parks and gardens round their residences, and as woods, and home farms kept mainly to supply produce for the house. In return for rent, the landlords provided the land itself together with fixed capital, such as the farmhouses, farm buildings, farm roads, walls, and fences. The tenant-farmers, the second element in the system, provided the working capital, such as teams, livestock, implements, carts, and barn machinery, and also of course they supplied the management of the farm and stood to gain or lose according to their degree of skill and enterprise. In 1881 there were 233,943 farmers and graziers in England and Wales, a figure which remained nearly constant to the end of the century. They occupied a cultivated acreage of some 27m. acres. The holdings figures of 1885 show that only 29 per cent of the acreage was in holdings of over 300 acres, i.e. large farms, and 42 per cent was in holdings of medium size farms 101-300 acres, while 14½ per cent was in holdings of 51-100 acres. The figures are not easily interpreted in detail, but clearly the country was primarily one of medium and small farms.[1]

The labourers made up the third element of the tripartite system. In 1881 there were 890,175 agricultural workers of all kinds on farms in England and Wales. Of these, nearly 20,000 were farm bailiffs or foremen, and a substantial proportion of the rest were skilled men in charge of teams and livestock, expert ploughmen, thatchers, hedgers and ditchers, and other specialists. Many of these men still lived in with the farmers, had their keep free, and were hired and paid by the year. The rest were day-labourers, paid at daily or piece-rates, with little formal security, although many worked for years on the same farm. The day labourers' average weekly wage varied with the availability of alternative employment. In the north, where there were large areas with industrial employment within easy reach, it averaged 16*s.* 9*d.* in 1882, but only between 11*s.* and 16*s.* 6*d.* over the rest of the country. (Allowances in kind, such as free or low-rented cottages and gardens, fuel, food and drink, and piece-work and overtime earnings, are not included in these figures.) Agricultural wages were slowly rising—improving faster, in fact, in real terms than in money terms—and the main factors in the rise were the decline in the numbers of workers and the increase in labour productivity with greater use of machinery on farms.

The English tripartite system had defects. Many great estates were too heavily encumbered with debts (largely inherited) for the landowners to be able to spare capital for expensive improvements, such as drainage and new buildings, so that farming was less efficient than it might have been. Although the position varied from one area to another, the majority of tenants had no lease and therefore no legal security of occupation, and this, together with inadequate arrangements for compensation for improvements, discouraged them from investing in improvements on their own account. Parts of some states were subjected to the needs of sport, and crops were subject to depredations from the game preserved for hunting or shooting. Nevertheless, it is easy to exaggerate the extent of these defects. Despite the stagnation on the estates of heavily-encumbered proprietors, landlords as a whole poured some £24m. into drainage and other permanent improvements on some 4-5m. acres of land in the thirty years 1846-76. The return on this investment was only about three per cent or less; in economic terms it did not pay, and 'in effect the landlords were subsidizing the farmers by an uneconomic use of capital—an expensive aberration that sprang partly from the strength of the tradition of the landlord's function and partly from a miscalculation as to the long-term returns of high farming.'² The absence of leases was not such a serious drawback as might be supposed: farmers in fact enjoyed great security of tenure even on annual agreements and good tenants were seldom, if ever, turned out, while the uncertainty of future price movements was such that many tenants preferred not to be tied down by a lease. Lastly, the management of large estates was marked by increasing professionalism and efficiency, and the agents of the large owners were often key figures in the technical advances of the day. Perhaps the clearest evidence of the success of the tri-partite system was the technical leadership in intensive farming that English agriculture assumed in the nineteenth century.

The great advantage of the English landlord-tenant system was its flexibility. There was a division of responsibility in the provision of capital, and the tenant-farmer could devote all his resources to providing working capital for the farm. (Indeed, English landlords refused to let farms to men of insufficient capital.) Land was thus cultivated efficiently, and when times were bad the tenant could look to the landlord for relief through some reduction of his normal outgoings, the landlord coming to the tenant's assistance with rent abatements and frequently with help in such matters as rates and repairs. In America, of course, most of the farmers were owner-occupiers—men who owned or were in the process of buying their farms. In addition to buying their land they had to find the working capital for farming it, and through their local taxes bore much of the burden of providing roads, railroads, schools, and other amenities, which in England were provided by private enterprise or through taxes which fell on a wider community. Not all American farmers, however, were the owners of their farms: in many areas the propor-tion of tenants was surprisingly high. In Iowa, Kansas, and Missouri, for example, a quarter of the farmers in 1890 were tenants. And in the South, where share-cropping was an important system of pro-duction, the proportion of tenants ranged upwards to nearly a half. Over the whole country the proportion of tenants rose from 25 per cent in 1880 to 42 per cent in 1935. It is unrealistic to suppose that the granting away of the public domain at low prices and the gen-erous terms of the Homestead Acts created a farmer-democracy in the United States. In fact, through the provisions of the various land acts, through the railroad land grants, through speculation in negotiable federal scrip, manipulation of loopholes in the legislation, political influence, and downright fraud, vast areas of land, and much of it the best land too, came into the hands of monopolists, both companies and individuals. 'Before 1870 William Scully, an Irish-American, accumulated some 250,000 acres in Illinois, Missouri, Kansas and Nebraska. . . . William S. Chapman bought for cash at the land office 650,000 acres in California and Nevada. Then he added "swamp" lands in California till his total was above 1,000,000 acres. . . . In 1886 there were 29 foreign syndicates and individuals who held 20,747,000 American acres. Eleven timber firms in later years got hold of over 12,000,000 acres.' California was the scene of vast engrossment: 'Henry George declared that a strong man on a good horse could not gallop across one of the larger holdings in a day. By 1870, the greater landlords, particularly the Southern Pacific railroad, ran the state government to suit themselves.'[3]

As a class, American farmers were debtors rather than creditors. They borrowed to buy land—even after the Homestead Act the better land could be acquired only by purchase—they borrowed to buy the seed, tools, wagons, livestock, and machinery for their farms and to tide them over a bad season. Machinery assumed an early importance in sections of American agriculture because of the invention of valuable processing machinery such as the cotton gin, the natural suitability of the level prairie soils and the high mobility of labour and existence of local labour shortages. But although prices of machines tended to drop in the later nineteenth century while their design and efficiency improved, the cost of equipping northern farms was still considerable: in 1851 a reaper cost $125, a drill $125, and a threshing maching $175. As the years went by new and improved machines appeared, such as the twine binder, which in 1880 cost between $175 and $325. Between 1850 and 1900 the average value of machinery and implements on farms in Iowa rose from $79 to $254 per farm. Indeed, the increasing outlay on machinery was a factor in adding to the numbers of tenants, especially in the north-central states where the bulk of machinery was used.[4]

As a consequence of these factors American farmers as a whole were considerably in debt, and in 1890 the average amount owed on mortgage was as much as $1,224. Rates of interest were relatively high in western rural areas, and farmers found it more difficult to get credit as the more cautious national banks replaced the small local banks after 1865. The post-Civil War deflation and the long-term fall in prices of farm produce between the Civil War and the end of the century made debts more onerous and more difficult to repay, and these grievances were factors that contributed to the farmers' movements of the period.

American farming was more capitalistic than is often supposed, and even before 1860 a capital of $1,000 was necessary for success. In 1850 the total investment in an average farm business was $1,454 in Iowa, and $1,667 in Illinois. By 1900 the figures had risen to $9,497 and $8,492 respectively, most of the increase representing the greatly higher value of land and buildings.[5] It followed that the way to independent farm ownership was open principally to persons of some capital, and to the sons of farmers who would inherit their father's farm or who could marry a farmer's daughter with similar expectations. Although they might have hopes of one day setting up on their own, many rural workers were therefore in the position of permanent agricultural labourers, and their numbers grew roughly in line with the growth of the farming population as a whole. The proportion of agricultural labourers to the total agricultural population remained fairly stable between 1860 when the figure was 49 per cent, and 1900 when it was 43 per cent. While immigration in the later nineteenth century was directed mainly towards the large urban centres, the heavy immigration of the 1890s was reflected in substantial numbers of immigrant farm labourers (13·1 per cent of all farm labourers in 1890), with Germans, Scandinavians, Irish, British, and Canadians the most numerous. The generally low and static levels of farm wages reflect the growth in numbers of farm labourers and throw some doubt on whether labour shortages in agriculture were more than local occurrences, although it is true that the labour supply tended to be uncertain, men seldom staying long in one place. Wages showed great geographical variations according to remoteness, mobility of the labour force, and the availability of alternative employment. Thus in the South, where an immobile negro labour force kept wages down, they could be as low as $2–6 a month, or $9 without board; while in a remote western state like Nevada they might be as high as $75 without board. It is clear, therefore, that while the owner-occupied family farm was the typical unit of American agriculture, neither farm tenants nor permanent labourers were by any means unimportant elements in the industry.

3 The expansion of American agriculture

In 1860, after a decade of heavy land speculation and expansion of
settlement, the frontier reached well beyond the Mississippi into
Minnesota and Iowa in the north, and had taken in Missouri,
Arkansas, and much of Texas in the south; while through the gold
rush of 1849 settlers had jumped the great plains (the 'Great
American Desert', as this vast area was known) and the Rockies,

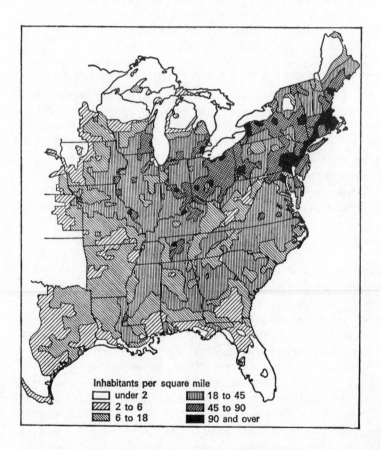

U.S.A. Density of population: 1860. (Reproduced by permission of
The Carnegie Institution of Washington from *Atlas of Historical
Geography of the United States*)

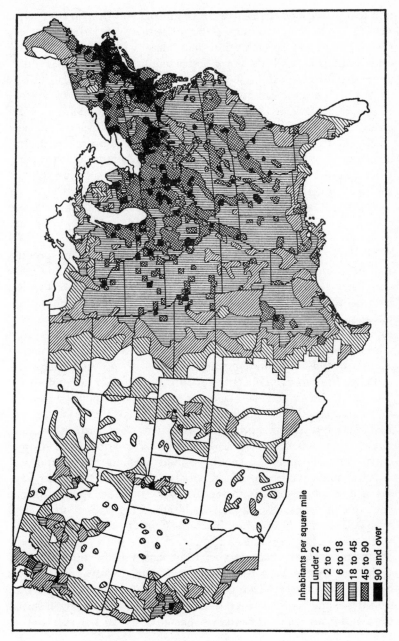

U.S.A. Density of population: 1900. (Reproduced by permission of The Carnegie Institution of Washington from *Atlas of Historical Geography of the United States*)

and had established themselves in California and Oregon (see maps, pp. 66, 67). Within this huge, and for the most part sparsely settled, area agricultural specialization had already developed. Leaving aside California, with its as yet restricted outlets for farm produce, American farming can be seen as falling into three broad regions.

In the South the great staple export crop was of course cotton, although it is interesting to notice that corn, grown for human and animal consumption locally, occupied over three times the acreage of cotton; in 1849 18m. acres was in corn as compared with 5m. acres under cotton. The production of cotton had expanded rapidly before the Civil War from an output of 73,000 bales in 1800 to reach 1·35m. bales in 1840, and 3·84m. bales in 1860. Originally established on the coastal areas of Georgia and South Carolina, the cotton region had spread westwards as land became exhausted and richer areas were opened up in the lower Mississippi valley. By 1860 Mississippi, Alabama, and Louisiana each exceeded the production of Georgia, while Texas, Arkansas, and South Carolina were also large producers. Cotton was suited to plantation production because the work of planting, chopping (thinning), cultivating, picking, ginning, baling, and haulage called for labour all the year round and made the keeping of slaves an economic proposition. And while the gin had speeded up the process of separating the cotton fibre from the seeds and had made it possible to expand acreage, the principal limitation on output remained the number of hands available for picking when each labourer could cope with only about six to nine acres. Large plantations prevailed in the black belt of Alabama, but the majority of producers were farmer-planters, having each less than 200 acres and under twenty slaves. Lower down the scale came the small 'yeoman' farmers whose land provided a subsistence in corn and pork, as well as a little other livestock, and cotton or tobacco for the market. These farmers might keep one or two slaves for household and farm work, but in 1860 over half of the 800,000 families in the South owned no slaves at all.

In terms of acreage tobacco was now a minor crop in the south, occupying only 400,000 acres in 1850, but it had a high value in yield per acre. Like cotton it was spreading westwards from its original locations in Virginia, Maryland, and North Carolina into Tennessee and Kentucky. Again like cotton it was a crop well suited to slave labour, since it required constant care all the year round.

However, it rapidly depleted the fertility of the soil and could only
be grown continuously for three or four years, so that fairly large
acreages were required to allow for soil exhaustion and to combine its
cultivation with wheat, corn, and other crops. Of the other crops in
the south, sugar and rice were confined to limited areas, the first
near the Mississippi in southern Louisiana, and the other chiefly
on the lower reaches of rivers in Georgia and South Carolina. Both
were grown on large plantations with hundreds of slaves and were
essentially capital-intensive crops, partly because of the need for
costly processing machinery, but also because of the heavy outlay in
making and maintaining embankments, drainage ditches, and
access roads, as well as the intensive and unhealthy work of cultivation itself. In Kentucky hemp was important for making baling
cloth for cotton, rope, and clothing for negroes.

In the north an early trade in grain and meat with the south
developed via the flatboats and steamboats of the Mississippi and
Ohio rivers. The centre of grain cultivation was shifting westwards
to the newly-opened states of the 'old North-West'. In 1839 Ohio,
Pennsylvania, New York, and Virginia had produced about 62 per
cent of the total wheat output, but by 1859 their production, still
about the same in absolute figures, contributed only 30 per cent of
the total. The more westerly prairie states of Illinois, Indiana, and
Wisconsin, formerly only small producers, now produced a third
of the total. The prairie soils, after initial difficulties of dealing with
the tough matted sod, and of overcoming the shortage of timber for
making houses and fences, proved ideal both for wheat and for corn,
Yields could be obtained of up to thirty bushels of wheat per acre,
and 100-120 bushels of corn, while the level and unobstructed sur-
face lent itself to the use of horse-drawn machinery. Wheat production and corn were combined, with wheat providing the cash crop
and corn the food for the farmer and the means of fattening his hogs
and cattle, and of making whisky.

With the spread westwards of grain production and fattening,
and the opening of communications to the Great Lakes area by
water and rail (Erie Canal 1825, Erie railroad from Buffalo to New
York 1852, Chicago connected to New York by rail 1855), agriculture in the north-eastern states became severely affected by western
competition. This region suffered from certain natural disadvantages:
the New England states possessed only thin soils and a harsh climate,

land had been exhausted by over-cropping, while insect pests and crop diseases affected production over much of the region. Fortunately, compensation was found in the growth of large centres of population such as New York, Boston, and Philadelphia, and the consequent growth of demand for produce that the west could not supply. This meant that local farmers could profitably specialize in dairying—New York became the leading dairying state—in 'truck farming' or market gardening, in fruit, hay (consumed by urban as well as rural livestock), fat cattle, wool for the New England factories, and in supplying firewood, charcoal, and building materials such as sand, timber, and stone.

The development of transport facilities encouraged western expansion, not only by opening up eastern and overseas markets to western farmers, but also by making it easier and cheaper for farmers to move west and obtain supplies of seed and farm equipment. Focal points of transport and communications such as Cincinnati, Buffalo, and Chicago developed into great marketing, distributing, and processing cities and important centres of industrial production. The growth of the market and development of communications were fundamental to western expansion, and indeed the big surges of land settlement in the late 1860s and 1880s were influenced by upward swings in agricultural prices.

The expansion of American agriculture occurred not only in a spatial sense, but also in terms of yields per acre and per man-hour, and the latter development was encouraged by the growth of agencies for the improvement of scientific knowledge. These included agricultural societies, fairs, and periodicals, the establishment of the Department of Agriculture in the Federal government (1862)—itself an important agent in introducing new crops, fighting pests and diseases, and establishing better standards of farming— and the agricultural colleges and experimental stations. The year 1862 was a crucial one for it saw not only the establishment of the Department of Agriculture but also the acceptance by Congress (in the absence of southern opposition) of the Homestead Act and the Morrill Land Grant College Act. The latter act allowed states to establish agricultural colleges with an endowment of 30,000 acres of public land for each representative and senator in Congress. By 1898 sixty-four colleges and universities had been established through this act, and by that date the agricultural colleges of the

Middle West were providing valuable comprehensive courses in the practical and scientific aspects of farming, as well as carrying on research and providing advice to practising farmers.[6] The Hatch Act of 1887 was also of importance for establishing experimental stations for agricultural research, while the Smith-Lever Act of 1914, which developed extension work among the farmers by means of county agents, resulted in a raising of farming standards and has been described as 'a vital factor in the transformation of American agriculture.[7]

One of the key factors in agricultural expansion was the adoption of liberal land policies for the transfer of the public domain into private hands. Between 1860 and 1900 the number of farms in the United States rose from 2m. to 5·7m., and the total land in farms increased from 407m. acres to 829m. acres. In this enormous growth the Homestead Act of 1862 was itself only a minor factor, merely one of a long series of acts, and affecting itself only a small proportion of the new land that was settled after the Civil War.

The Homestead Act allowed any adult of American citizenship to claim free (except for a small commission fee) 160 acres of public land after having cultivated or resided on the claim for five years. Important as it may have been for its contribution to the ideal of creating a democracy of family farmers, it must be doubted how far the act itself was a magnet which attracted European immigrants to the west.[8] It must be noted, too, that only 80m. acres of the 432m. acres of land added to the farm acreage between 1860 and 1900 represented holdings under the Homestead Act, while by comparison as much as 125m. acres were granted to the railroads in the years after 1862. There were, of course, many homesteaders who genuinely attempted to create a permanent farm and failed; but other 'homesteaders' were really petty speculators who were, in effect, obliged to take up farming while waiting for further settlement in the area to raise the value of their holdings; and there were yet others who were 'merely the hired pawns of land monopolists who took over the land as soon as the final patents were received. . . .' Possibly only an eighth, or even only a tenth, of the additional farm land of 1860-1900 consisted of free homesteads.[9] The Homestead Act was thus only one factor in expansion, more important as a token of the policy of rapid western settlement than for its practical results.

There were many reasons for the limited value of the Act. Down to 1891 cash sales of the public land continued and even increased, and, indeed, more land was sold to farm-makers than was homesteaded. The would-be homesteader found that much of the best land in the West was already in the hands of railroad companies, large landowners, and speculators. Syndicates bought the best land in blocks of 100,000 acres or more, and land, timber, and mining companies employed squatters to file homestead claims on land they subsequently turned over to the companies. Claims were even staked on behalf of non-existent individuals, and there was graft and corruption also on the part of the land office officials. Homestead land was often 20 miles or more from the nearest railroad track, and for this reason farmers were obliged to buy from the railroad company or other holders of land nearer the track. But most important perhaps, was the fact that the bulk of the land available for homesteading was west of 100th meridian, was subject to periodic droughts, and had an average rainfall of only 10-18 in. On such land 160 acres was of little use; it was too large an area to irrigate, and too small to be used for grazing.

Subsequent legislation attempted to remedy some of the defects of the 1862 Act and also recognized the need for conservation of the country's natural resources. But the Desert Lands Act of 1877 (which offered 640 acres of arid land to anyone who would irrigate within three years), the Timber Cutting Act of 1878 (offering free lumber as an incentive to purchasers of public lands), and the 1878 Timber and Stone Act (offering, at $2·50 per acre, land unsuited to agriculture but valuable for timber and minerals) benefited the large grazing interests, the millowners, lumber companies, mining corporations, and speculators, rather than the farmers. From 1891, with the repeal of the Timber Cutting Act and the ending of sales from the public domain, the era of conservation really dawned. Subsequent acts led to the encouragement of irrigation, set aside large areas as national forests, and reserved minerals on remaining public lands to the government. The official declaration that the frontier had disappeared had little real meaning since vast areas of arid and semi-arid lands remained unsettled, and Acts of 1904, 1909, and 1916 enlarged the Homestead grants to 320 acres in some states, and to 640 acres in areas suited to stock-raising. More land was, in fact, homesteaded after 1900 than in the four preceding decades. Of the homestead claimants before 1890, as many as two-thirds failed; only about 400,000 families obtained free land and succeeded in keeping it; some seven million others bought farms or became tenants and labourers. Indeed, in view of the two long periods of agricultural depression—between the Civil War and 1896 and in the inter-war period—it might well be argued that in the long run the policy of rapid western settlement was a mistake, or at least was overdone.

4 Markets, prices, and the course of agricultural development

In Britain, also, the middle decades of the nineteenth century were ones of increasing expansion and specialization. A good deal of the specialized production arose, as in America, from the growth of urban markets and improvements in transport. The growth of the urban population, associated with a substantial rise in real incomes, meant not only an increase in the total demand for agricultural produce but also a relatively greater demand for meat, dairy produce, vegetables, and fruit at the expense, principally, of wheat. The shift in emphasis was made the more necessary by the Repeal of the Corn Laws in 1846. Grain imports had been growing since the later eighteenth century, and the effect of the protection offered by the Corn Laws was mainly to keep out foreign grain supplies when the home harvest was good. After Repeal imports increased steadily and formed a larger proportion of the total grain supplies. The result up to the middle 1870s was that grain prices remained at a roughly stable level, while the prices of other agricultural commodities rose by between 20 and 50 per cent. In these circumstances, there was a tendency for the arable acreage—probably at its peak about the middle of the century—to shrink slightly, while the area under permanent and rotational grass increased. Rail transport, providing speedy communications with the large centres of population, offered greater advantages to the dairy farmer and fat-stock specialist than to the corn producer, and these branches of farming expanded. At the same time, arable farming was not stagnant but was showing evidence of improved techniques, flexible rotations, and subtle shifts of output to meet market conditions. In particular, the larger arable farmers concentrated more on producing roots and green crops for the fattening of bullocks, and in some years of low prices even wheat might be used as cattle food. The end products of the complex system of mixed arable farms thus shifted somewhat towards meat and drink-corn (barley), and away from bread-corn (wheat).

The era was dominated by 'high farming', i.e. a system of intensive farming using large amounts of capital on good-sized farms to achieve through drainage, artificial manures, machinery, advanced design of farm buildings, better strains of seed, and improved breeds of cattle and sheep, the highest output per acre. Some landlords and tenants spent large sums on drainage of heavy soils, new buildings, steam-driven barn machinery, steam cultivation, and even light railways for horse or man-drawn haulage on the farm. Progressive farming was fostered also by the encouragement given by scientific discoveries: by experiments and discussions stimulated by Liebig, the great German chemist, Sir John Lawes and the work of the Rothamsted Agricultural Research Station, the Royal Agricultural College at Cirencester, and the shows and publications of the Royal Agricultural Society and local societies. How far an improvement in standards was general is difficult to say, but farming certainly became a more complex and more capital-intensive industry, and it may be that the gap between the standards of the small and large farmer was, if anything, widened. Even in 1880, in contrast to the highly-mechanized methods of high farming, some farmers still got their harvest in with the sickle, much land still remained to be drained, and buildings were still often ancient and inadequate.

In its day, high farming was technically very efficient, but its survival as a viable farming system depended on the continuation of a profitable level of prices. In the middle 1870s prices turned downwards and English agriculture reeled from the successive blows of extraordinarily bad seasons and outbreaks of animal disease, unprofitably low prices for wheat, and increasing competition and lower prices in the meat and dairy produce markets. There had, of course, been some bad years in the middle decades of the century: a short depression followed the Repeal of the Corn Laws until 1853, while bad weather and animal disease marked the years 1860, 1864, 1865-6, and 1868, but the general buoyancy of prices had kept the atmosphere prosperous. In the twenty years after 1875 wheat prices were halved, and home-produced butter, cheese, and meat fell by a little over 10 per cent. Free trade in agricultural produce, ushered in by the Repeal of 1846, was now really effective for the first time. Now a bad harvest was not compensated by a rise in prices, because the market was governed not by the home harvest but by imports. In 1879, the worst harvest of the century, wheat sold for 43*s.* 10*d.*, while in the five worst years of the 1860s it had been about 60*s.* Developments in American farming, and in transport costs in America, Russia, and elsewhere, brought about a general downward price trend. In America the railroads were opening up the western prairies and the great plains, barbed wire and artesian wells made possible grain farming on the high plains, and machinery made it possible to cultivate and harvest large acreages with a small labour force. Railroads and cheap water transport brought the grain to the eastern seaboard, and steamships and sailing vessels competed to bring it across the Atlantic. The cost of carrying a quarter of wheat from Chicago to Liverpool averaged 11*s.* in 1868-79, 4*s.* 3*d.* by 1892, and only 2*s.* 10½*d.* in 1902. In 1894 wheat reached its lowest point of 22*s.* 10*d.* a quarter and then recovered to a little over 30*s.* in 1907–13. Imports of wheat and flour rose from a little over 40m. cwt. in the early 1870s to an average of nearly 70m. cwt. in the later 1890s, and to over 100m. cwt. by 1910-13.

The consequences were obvious. Despite heavier unemployment in industry, the market trends were still generally favourable for large branches of English farming, with 10m. people added to the population during the depression period, and real wages continuing to rise down to the 1890s. Farmers shifted away from wheat and away from the mixed farming system altogether, turning more towards the production in which they met little or no competition and for which the markets were expanding—fattening on permanent pasture, dairying, market gardening, fruit, vegetables, poultry, and other specialities. Competition increased also in meat and dairy produce, however. The first shipment of frozen Australian meat arrived in London in 1880, five years after the first trial shipment of 'chilled' meat from New York, and butter, cheese, and bacon came in from Denmark, Holland, and France. However, imports of meat and dairy produce, although growing, were still only a small proportion of the total supply and their prices fell only by about 20 per cent. Consumers preferred the home-produced alternatives, the prices of which fell only by a little over 10 per cent. The acreage under wheat fell from 3·4m. acres in 1871 to 1·7m. acres in 1901, and in the same years the area under permanent grass rose from 11·4m. acres to 15·4m. acres.

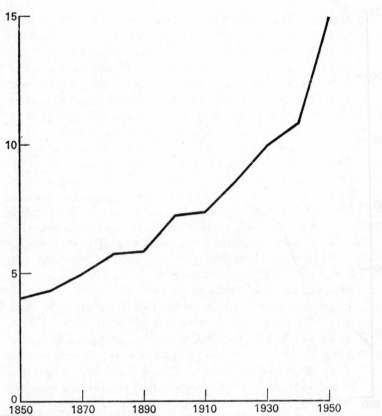

Figure 10. U.S.A.: agriculture. Persons supplied by one farm worker 1850-1950

While all farmers suffered to some extent from the bad weather and animal disease of 1879-82, the depression of the 1880s and 1890s was not a general one. Arable farming was concentrated in the south and east of the country, and here rents and profits fell heavily; indeed on some properties in counties such as Essex net rents fell to zero, which meant that, after paying taxes and meeting essential repairs and other outgoings, the landlord received nothing from his land. In the more pastoral west and north, however, there was a general and quiet prosperity: even here, however, the arable districts shrank and farmers moved more towards concentration on fattening and dairying; they suffered from the excessively wet

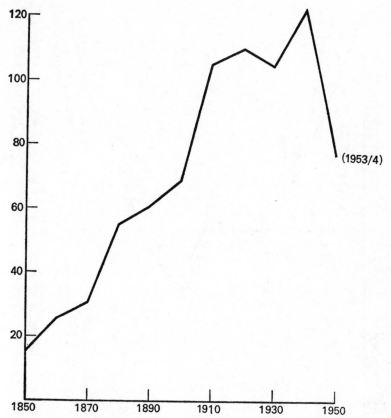

Figure 11. Great Britain: wheat imports, in thousands of hundred-weights, 1850-1950

seasons in the early years of the depression and experienced heavy losses of beasts, but on the whole rents and profits fell only slightly, and in real terms not at all. The farmers in the north and west were fortunate in producing commodities the prices of which fell relatively little, and for which outlets were expanding. Moreover, the fall in feed prices was of direct benefit to the pasture farmers in reducing one of their major costs of production, while the adjustments they were obliged to make to meet market trends were relatively less great and less difficult.

The adjustment facing arable farmers in the south and east, on the other hand, was a formidable one, and involved in the extreme

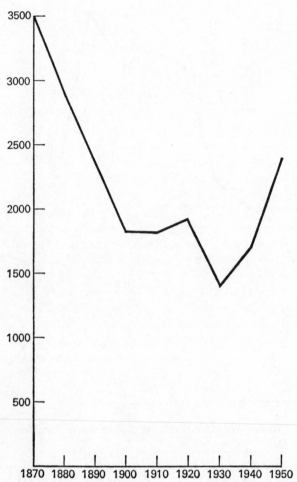

Figure 12. Great Britain: acreage of land under wheat 1870-1950, (in thousands of acres)

cases the conversion of entire arable farms to pasture. Some historians have criticized the tardiness with which the transformation was undertaken, but it may be objected that in fact the eventual extent of the shift from wheat, as illustrated by the figures above, is remarkable evidence of the degree of flexibility in English farming. The permanence of the lower levels of grain prices was, of course, by no means certain, and the early years of poor seasons and

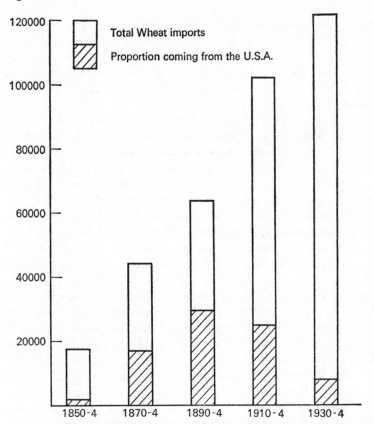

Figure 13. Great Britain: wheat imports, in thousands of hundred-weights, 1850-4–1930-4

heavy losses both misled as to the need for making permanent changes and, by diminishing their capital resources, reduced the farmers' and landlords' ability to undertake the necessary changes. Capital was crucial because the change to pasture required not only expenditure on buildings, seed, and stock, but also time for the sward to establish itself, and for the better returns from dairying and fattening to appear. No doubt it also required flexibility of mind, and it is significant that the shift towards grass followed in many areas upon the influx of Scottish and west-country farmers, new men with the necessary capital and enterprise, and with experience of the new lines of production. With the readjustment came a moderate measure of renewed prosperity, for in the early years of the new century prices moved hesitantly upwards again, and with lower costs, a smaller labour force, and a pattern of output more closely in line with the market, farmers began to find a new confidence in their ability to navigate the uncharted seas of international competition.

The Civil War in the United States affected agriculture in three main ways. First, the absence of Southern opposition from Congress made it possible to pass the Homestead and Morrill Land Grant Acts and so ushered in the era of rapid western expansion discussed above. Second, Northern agriculture was influenced by wartime demands for wool (used for uniforms and blankets), and by labour shortages caused by the large flow of agricultural labour into the Union armies. Sheep numbers increased in such states as Ohio and Iowa, while labour shortages accelerated the adoption of farm machinery, especially in wheat production. The output of farm machinery and implements expanded by 110 per cent between 1849 and 1859, and by 1866 farmers had three times the number of machines they had available in 1860. With horse-drawn ploughs, drills, corn planters, and reapers, every stage in grain production could be carried on by horse-drawn machines. Thus occurred what Rasmussen has called the 'first revolution' in American agriculture— the transition from man power to animal power.[10] The third major change occurred in Southern agriculture where loss and destruction of livestock, dwellings, equipment, and stocks of cotton, together with the worthlessness of Confederate notes and bonds, produced a drastic fall in liquidity and land values, and led to numerous sales. The plantation system proved unworkable with wage-labour, and share-cropping and division into small tenancies provided the solution to obtaining a constant supply of submissive labour at the lowest cost. By the end of the nineteenth century, three-quarters of all cotton workers were either tenants or sharecroppers, and white sharecroppers had come to outnumber the black:

	White	Black	Total
Cash tenants	150,000	233,000	383,000
Sharecroppers	402,000	229,000	631,000

The sharecroppers received a third of the produce if they provided labour only, or two-thirds if they also provided the beasts, seed, and implements. They were in a very weak position, having no legal claim to a renewal of their holding, and even uncertain of keeping their hut through the winter. Both cash tenants and sharecroppers relied on the country storekeepers and local banks for credit for the purchase of food, seed, fertilizer, and other necessities, and since the storekeepers handled the marketing side, it was the crop itself that provided the security on which sharecroppers' borrowings were based. Interest charges were very high, ranging from 40 to 110 per cent, a feature of the system that took account of the high risk of crop failures and the possibility that the borrower might abscond. Another serious drawback of this crop-lien credit system was that it encouraged the persistence of monoculture, since the northern merchants and bankers, who were the ultimate source of the credit, insisted on its being secured only on cash crops. This led to over-production, low prices, and soil exhaustion. Further, the storekeepers' dislike of the croppers having their own vegetable gardens and pigs meant that the unfortunate cultivators had to exist on a monotonous and inadequate diet, which robbed them of energy and left them subject to the scourge of malnutrition and diseases such as pellagra.

Between the Civil War and the end of the century, the general characteristics of American agriculture may be summed up in the one word *expansion*. There was expansion in land area with the settlement of the western prairies and the great plains, so that the improved acreage rose more than two-fold, and the number of farmers three-fold. The area under wheat rose from 15·4m. acres in 1866 to 44m. acres in 1898, and net output rose from 148m. bushels in 1860 to 522m. bushels in 1900. The cotton acreage increased in 1866-98 from 6·3m. acres to 24·9m. acres, and output of cotton lint rose from 1,890m. lb in 1860 to 4,702m. lb in 1900. The corn crop was some 839m. bushels in 1860, and reached over 2,000m. bushels in the 1890s. Although yields per acre rose, the major advance in productivity came from the better utilization of labour with technological developments and improved farm organization.

The great expansion in output was encouraged by the rapid growth of the home market from 31·5m. people in 1860 to 76·1m.

in 1900, and by the rapid growth of large urban centres served by a network of rail and water communications. The value of livestock and livestock products nearly doubled between 1860 and 1900, and dairy products (whose output was closely related to the growth of urban markets) more than trebled. Export markets were also of great importance, and between 1860 and 1900 agricultural produce accounted for about three-quarters of all exports. For some agricultural products export markets were crucial: over three-quarters of the cotton produced was exported, and between two-fifths and four-fifths of the tobacco, while in 1880 some three-eighths of the wheat crop was exported. Nevertheless, the dependence of certain crops on foreign markets should not obscure the over-riding importance for agriculture as a whole of the home market: between 1869 and 1900 82 per cent of farm products by value was sold on the home market, and, as export markets declined in the twentieth century with growing international competition in farm produce, the importance of the home market became even more marked.

The response of farmers to growing markets and plentiful land was indeed *too* ready, for the period between the middle 1860s and the later 1890s was marked by generally falling prices. The average farm price of a bushel of wheat fell from over $1.50 to a mere 50 cents in these years, while cotton fell from 18 cents per lb in 1871 to 6-7 cents. Cattle prices fluctuated considerably but were particularly low in 1875-81 and again in 1890-7. In terms of money income this tendency for prices to fall meant difficulties and poverty for many farmers. The average cotton producer's family could earn only about $300 a year even when cotton was at 10 cents, and the settlers on the great plains must have wondered whether wheat at 80 cents was worth all the enduring of extreme heat and cold, and the hazards of droughts, crop failures, grasshopper plagues, and dust storms. But since the general price level was also falling (and perhaps falling faster than farm prices), the farmers came out not too badly in terms of real consumption, although it remains true that low farm prices formed the environment in which foreclosure and failure were commonplace, and agrarian unrest was a marked feature of the country.

This unrest took a variety of forms, and because of regional variations in the nature and organization of agricultural production, it tended to express local rather than national grievances. Not that there lacked general problems that affected the great majority of farmers: many farmers felt that their position and status, their role in the nation, was being diminished by the rise of big commercial, financial, and industrial enterprise over which they had little or no control. They felt themselves exploited (as indeed they often were) by big landowners who monopolized the best land; by middlemen and processors of farm products, the grain elevator companies, for example, who stood between them and consumers, and seemed to make more out of marketing the produce than the farmers did in growing it; by bankers and storekeepers who advanced credit on restrictive terms at high rates of interest, and who secured a stranglehold on them through the power to foreclose on mortgages; and by railroads which kept back large areas of fertile land from the market, charged excessive rates, and provided a poor transport service; lastly by the government, dominated increasingly by the interests supporting high tariffs and deflationary monetary policies, measures which increased the real burden of farm debt. Consequently, in addition to complaints against railroads and tariffs, a constant theme of the farmers was the concern with the 'greenback' and free coinage of silver issue, a concern with securing more currency, cheaper credit, and higher prices as antidotes to the deflationary trends which threatened their survival.

It must be observed, however, that recent evidence suggests that some of the farmers' principal complaints had little foundation. Certain years, such as the 1870s, do appear to have been bad ones, but conditions varied greatly from area to area. Farm prices certainly fell between the middle 1860s and the middle 1890s, but so did prices in general, and perhaps more than farm prices, as we have noted. Railroad rates also fell steeply, providing the farmers with cheaper transport, while the growing efficiency of processing and marketing organizations helped to give the farmer an eventually larger share in the final return for the product. While it is true that a high proportion of farms were mortgaged where agrarian unrest was concentrated (as in Kansas), in 1890 less than one farm in three was mortgaged on average, and then only up to about a third of the value of the farm for an average period of a very few years. Rates of interest at between 7 and $8\frac{1}{2}$ per cent in the North Central region were higher than in the East, but lower than the 10 per cent common in the 1850s. Nevertheless, the complaints about poor

railroad services, difficulties in obtaining short-term credit to tide
over bad seasons, and the exercise of monopolistic power by the
elevator companies, were often justified. As D. C. North has pointed
out, prices fluctuated far beyond the farmers' control or understanding. Grain prices, in particular, were subject to world-wide
climatic vagaries as the international grain trade spread to all five
continents, while prices in the domestic market were affected too by
the widely varying areas over which crops were grown and the
sudden surges of supply as new areas were opened up. But most of all
the farmer felt the deterioration in his personal position:

Throughout all of our earlier history, his had been the dominant voice in
politics and in an essentially rural society. Now, he was being dispossessed
by the growing industrial might of America and its rapid urbanization. The
farmer keenly felt his deteriorating status. His reading matter was full of
warnings and complaints against the evils and moral decay of the city and
its malign influence over the countryside. His disenchantment was an
inevitable component of the vast and complex economic-sociological phenomenon that was taking place, involving both the commercialization of
agriculture on a vast scale in a worldwide market and the farmers' becoming
increasingly a minority group in American society.[11]

The various short-lived farmers' movements were broadly combinations of farmers' clubs and individuals directed towards the
securing of particular reforms. The Granger movement started in
1867 and was strong in the middle west and north-western states,
where it was successful in getting laws to regulate railroad rates and
in establishing co-operative enterprises for the sale of merchandise
and implements, and for the storage and processing of farm products.
As the Grange declined in the late 1870s, the Farmers Alliances
developed. State alliances of farmers were consolidated into regional
organizations, the Southern Alliance and the Northwestern Alliance. The principal aims again were monetary reform (including
flexibility in issuing greenbacks and free coinage of silver), government regulation of large landowners, and higher taxes on railroads.
By the 1880s the various Alliance movements were coming together
on a broad platform of monetary reform and government ownership
and control of railroads. In the election of 1890 alliance groups
secured a number of successes, and by 1892 the new People's or
Populist party was in being. The Populists allied themselves with the
Democrats in the 1896 campaign, but the demand for free silver

failed to win enough support to gain the day. By this time improving conditions for farmers, with rising prices, began to take much of the steam out of the movement, and it was significant also that in subsequent years many of the reforms demanded by the Populists were passed into law. The prosperous years between 1896 and 1920, however, served not only to quieten the farmers' complaints and send the Populists into oblivion, but also to lay 'the basis for the next era of farm depression'. By the end of the First World War the farmers were again undertaking speculative expansion, and again were only too easily exposed to the destructive effects of a new period of over production and falling prices, credit restriction, and foreclosure.[12]

5 The urban drift

Despite the vast increase in the cultivated area of the United States and the trebling of the number of farmers between 1860 and 1900, there was a marked trend towards the concentration of population in towns. In this period the proportion of population living in towns of 8,000 and more inhabitants doubled to reach a third of the total population: the total farm population rose by 50 per cent; the total town population by 400 per cent. The theory that a 'safety-valve' for urban discontent was offered by the prospect of free or cheap land in the west must be severely discounted. For every city labourer who took up farming, twenty rural workers flocked to the city, and the city workers who did go west usually did not farm but took up urban jobs or entered mines and factories. In fact it might well be argued that the true position was 'that the rise of the city in the nineteenth century was a safety-valve for rural discontent.'[13] However, by the 1890s the attraction of the city was beginning to decline and the urban drift fell off, until in the 1930s there was no net shift of population between town and country. But in more recent years a variety of factors—the large margin between farm and urban incomes, the inferior amenities of schools, roads, and public health in rural areas, and a general sense of rural isolation—has again renewed the townward movement.

In England, a parallel drift to the towns (and overseas) occurred. Between 1851 and 1871 the number of agricultural workers fell by over 250,000 or 22 per cent, a shift large enough to influence wages

and improve labourers' conditions, while encouraging the farmers
to make greater use of machinery. By the 1870s heavy migration
had spread from the south and east to the south-western counties and
to Wales, and in the 1880s northern migration was considerable,
while that from Wales rose to a peak. By the nineties the drift was
on the decline: 'Fewer potential migrants were being born, because
the parents who might have reared them had already migrated.'
The average annual outflow of rural population (which of course
included industrial as well as agricultural workers) was over 75,000
between the 1850s and the 1890s, but there was no general fall in
the numbers still living in the countryside: it was the increase which
was absorbed by migration, leaving behind a changing but numeri-
cally stable rural population.[14] After the 1890s the migration
continued at a much reduced rate, but by 1911 the proportion
of hired workers to each farmer was only a little over three to
one.

In England the principal effects on agriculture of the outflow of
labour were to slowly raise the wages and living conditions of
labourers, and to add the pressure of labour shortages to other
factors encouraging farmers to make greater use of machinery. Both
these effects have continued to be felt since the First World War,
helping to limit (but never closing) the gap between farm and
industrial wages, and creating an agriculture that has become one of
the most highly mechanized in the world. In the late nineteenth
century a great deal of public concern was felt over 'rural depopula-
tion', a concern which sprang from intensified urban unemployment
and over-crowding, the inadequate physical state of townsmen as
revealed by recruiting figures, and other factors, in addition to the
frightening prospect of deserted countryside. Remedial measures
included the introduction of parish councils (1894) and Small-
holdings Acts in 1892 and 1907 designed to give the rural worker a
greater stake and interest in his native village; but, as it proved,
'more than Acts of Parliament were needed to turn a centuries-old
rural proletariat into a race of peasant cultivators.'[15]

6 Conclusion

In addition to the basic differences in land area, scale of production,
types of crops, agrarian organization, and role within the national

economy referred to in this chapter, we should perhaps conclude by drawing attention to some other rather less obvious points of contrast. While the increased output and greater efficiency of English agriculture in the nineteenth century were important in providing foodstuffs, raw materials and (after 1850) labour, for a rapidly industrializing and urbanizing economy, the corresponding role of American agriculture was of far greater significance. American agriculture provided foodstuffs and raw materials for an economy that grew even faster than Britain in terms of population and industrial output; and through agriculture's dominant part in American exports it helped pay for imports of goods and of money capital necessary for American economic development; while thirdly, in its own rapid growth in land area and numbers employed, and in its demand for implements, machinery, transport, processing and storage facilities, it constituted a major force making for the general expansion of the American economy—a fact of the greatest importance. Further, the large outflow of cheap American grain and flour in the later nineteenth century was a key factor in the reshaping of English agriculture, releasing labour from the land for other employments, and helping considerably in the substantial rise in living standards of the English working classes that occurred in the period.

The cultivated acreage in America was of course very much greater than that of England, but it might be noted that to some extent the large margin between the total value of agricultural output of the two countries was reduced by three factors: the relatively greater shift in England towards products whose prices showed less tendency to fall; the much greater concentration in England on intensive methods of production, resulting in much higher returns per acre; and the low or nil returns on much American land due to land wastage—soil exhaustion, erosion, and dust-bowls caused through long years of monoculture (as in eastern areas) and through application of unsuitable farming methods (as in semi-arid regions of the West).

American farming was wasteful of land but efficient in terms of output per head. Land and capital were readily expended in order to get the best return from manpower. Output per man-hour in the production of wheat and oats rose four-fold between about 1840 and the early years of the twentieth century, and this rise was due partly to the westward expansion to more fertile soils, but was mainly the result of mechanization.[16] The mechanization of American agriculture was earlier and more extensive than in England, where labour costs and shortages were only gradually felt in the years after 1850. Moreover, English farming with its predominantly mixed character, its small average size of farms and multiplicity of small fields, its generally hilly terrain and moistness of climate, was less well suited to the application of machinery. Particularly was this so in the adoption of harvesting machinery for grain, in which the most notable early progress was made in America. The two world wars, however, together with rising labour costs and renewed prosperity from the early 1930s, have brought British farming practice much into line with that of America, especially in the transition from animal to machine power, as seen in the adoption on a large scale of the internal combustion engine and electrical power since the early years of this century.

The agrarian unrest in America, with the rapid growth of organizations for expressing farmers' discontents, have no close parallel in England. English farmers grumbled but made little attempt to improve matters through combination. Their complaints concerned mainly the burden of rates on agricultural land in a period of falling prices and profits, the need for regulation of the compensation for improvements, manures, etc. paid to outgoing tenants by the new occupants of farms when land changed hands, and the preferential rates given to importers by the railway companies. It was not until the 1930s, when agricultural protection and regulation were revived by the state, that the Nation Farmers Union became a power in the land. Among the important factors in the American farmers' movements were the rapid decline in the status of American agriculture in both economic and political terms, and also a tradition of looking to government for intervention (as seen in the legislation dealing with the public domain, conservation, and agricultural education), trends which were less marked in England between 1850 and the 1930s. Finally, while both countries experienced an urban drift due to greater attractiveness of urban employment and town life, this was accompanied in America by expansion in both the cultivated area and the number of farms; it is only in fairly recent years that agricultural conditions and the decline in rural population have given rise to the kind of public concern which in England produced the 'back to the land' agitation of the late nineteenth and early twentieth centuries.

Notes

1 It is important to avoid the common fallacy that because land was predominantly owned in large units farms were large in size; the size of an estate (the unit of landownership) had no necessary connection with the size of the farms (units of production) which made up the estate.

2 CHAMBERS, J. D. and MINGAY, G. E., *The Agricultural Revolution 1750-1880* (1966), pp. 163-4.

3 SHANNON, F. A., *The Farmer's Last Frontier* (New York, 1961), pp. 71-2.

4 GATES, PAUL W., *The Farmer's Age* (New York, 1965), pp. 288, 291; SHANNON, *op. cit.*, pp. 140, 146. BOGUE, ALLEN G., *From Prairie to Corn Belt* (Chicago U.P., 1963), p. 286.

5 BOGUE, *op. cit.*

6 For details, see SHANNON, *op. cit.*, pp. 272-7.

7 RASMUSSEN, WAYNE D., 'The Impact of Technological Change in American Agriculture, 1862-1962', *Jour. Ec. Hist.*, XXII (1962), p. 587.

8 DOVRING, FOLKE, 'European Reactions to the Homestead Act', *Jour. Ec. Hist.*, XXII (1962), pp. 461-72.

9 SHANNON, *op. cit.*, p. 51.

10 RASMUSSEN, WAYNE D., 'The Civil War: a Catalyst of Agricultural Revolution', *Agricultural History* 39 (1965), pp. 187-95; and 'Impact of Technological Change', *loc. cit.*, p. 578.

11 NORTH, D. C., *Growth and Welfare in the American Past* (Englewood Cliffs, N.J. 1966), pp. 137-46.

12 For details of the farmers' movements see SHANNON, *op. cit.*, ch. 13-14, and his *American Farmers' Movements* (Princeton, 1957). See also HOFSTADTER, RICHARD, *The Age of Reform* (New York, 1955).

13 SHANNON, *The Farmer's Last Frontier*, p. 359.

14 CAIRNCROSS, A., 'Internal Migration in Victorian England', in Cairncross, *Home and Foreign Investment, 1870-1913* (Cambridge, 1953), pp. 75, 77.

15 See Chambers and Mingay, *op. cit.*, pp. 186-9, 196-7.

16 PARKER, WILLIAM N. and KLEIN, JUDITH L. V., 'Productivity Growth in Grain Production in the United States, 1840-60 and 1900-10', in *Output Employment and Productivity in the United States after 1800* (N.B.E.R., New York, 1966), pp. 533, 543.

Suggestions for further reading

Texts

CHAMBERS, J. D. and MINGAY, G. E., *The Agricultural Revolution 1750-1880* (1966).

EDWARDS, EVERETT E., *American Agriculture–The First 300 Years* (U.S. Dept. of Agriculture Yearbook 1940).

GATES, PAUL W., *The Farmer's Age: Agriculture 1815-60* (New York, 1960).

NORTH, D. C., *Growth and Welfare in the American Past* (Englewood Cliffs, N.J., 1966), ch. 10-11.

WHETHAM, E. H. AND ORWIN, C. S., *History of British Agriculture 1846-1914* (1964).

SHANNON, FRED A., *The Farmer's Last Frontier: Agriculture 1860-1897* (New York, 1961).

Specialized works

FLETCHER, T. W., 'The Great Depression of English Agriculture 1873-1896', *Econ. Hist. Rev.* 2nd ser. XIII (1960–1).

GATES, PAUL W., *Agriculture and the Civil War* (New York, 1965).

JONES, E. L., 'The Changing Basis of English Agricultural Prosperity, *Agricultural History Review* X (1962).

RASMUSSEN, WAYNE D., 'The Civil War: a Catalyst of Agricultural Revolution', *Agricultural History*, 39 (1965). 'The Impact of Technological Change in American Agriculture, 1862-1962', *Jour. Ec. Hist.* XXII (1962).

SHANNON, FRED A., *American Farmers' Movements* (Princeton, 1957). THOMPSON, F. M. L., *English Landed Society in the Nineteenth Century* (1963).

BOGUE, ALLAN G., *From Prairie to Corn Belt: Farming on the Illinois and Iowa Prairies in the Nineteenth Century* (Chicago U.P., 1963).

4

International trade and the movement of factors 1850-1914

1 The growth of trade

A remarkable growth of world trade was a dominating feature of the years between 1850 and 1914. The total value of world international trade (i.e. total exports and total imports, plus transport costs) was perhaps £800m. in 1850, nearly £3,000m. in the late 1870s, and nearly £4,000m. by the end of the century. An enormous expansion in the early years of the twentieth century took the figure to over £8,000m. in 1913. Thus there occurred something like a ten-fold increase over some six decades.

The import and export trades of Britain and America were very important elements in this great expansion of international trade. British exports increased in volume by 57 per cent between 1871-5 and 1896-1900, and by 46 per cent between 1896-1900 and 1911-13. As a proportion of total world trade, however, Britain's share fell from the 20-25 per cent maintained between 1850 and 1875 to 14 per cent in 1911-13. (As a proportion of world exports of manufactures, however, Britain's share fell from 41·4 per cent in 1880 to 29·9 per cent in 1913.) To some extent, Britain's reduced rate of growth of exports after 1875 was compensated by the terms of trade, which turned markedly favourable after 1885 and made possible a more rapid increase in the growth of imports.[1]

American exports increased in volume by 120 per cent between 1879 and 1900, and by 37 per cent between 1900 and 1913. America's share in world trade (by value) rose from about 10 per cent between 1850 and the 1870s to reach some 14-15 per cent in 1900-13. (As a proportion of world exports of manufactures, the American share rose from 2·8 per cent in 1880 to 12·6 per cent in 1913.) Terms of trade tended to be unfavourable, so that the net value of the big advance in exports in the later nineteenth century was somewhat reduced.

American trade increased as follows:

TABLE 7

American commodity trade 1850-1913

	Imports		Exports	
	Value	Volume	Value	Volume
	$m.	1913: 100	$m.	1913: 100
1850	178	—	152	—
1879	460	27·0	735	33·3
1900	930	53·4	1,499	73·2
1913	1,923	100·0	2,615	100·0

Source: *Historical Statistics of the United States*

2 The changing character of trade

There were important shifts during this period in both the composition
and the direction of trade. The position of the great nineteenth-century staples in British exports tended to decline as industrialization
spread to new areas of the world. Manufactured goods fell from
some 90 per cent of total exports in the middle years of the century
to 75 per cent by 1911-13. Textiles, in particular, which had
dominated British exports for so long, fell to less than 40 per cent of
the total. Between the 1850s and 1911-13 the proportion of coal in
total exports more than trebled to reach 9 per cent, while engineering
products (machinery, railway rolling stock, ships' hulls, etc.)
doubled to reach 10 per cent. The proportion of foodstuffs in British
imports increased in the 1870s to reach the same proportion as raw
materials, but in the last quarter of the nineteenth century the most
important change was the rapid growth of imported manufactures,
which rose from a very small proportion to a fifth of total imports
by 1900.

The pattern between 1900 and 1913, therefore, was one of
roughly 40 per cent foodstuffs, 40 per cent raw materials (considerable quantities of which were re-exported, together with some foodstuffs), and 20 per cent manufactures. The growth of manufactured
imports in the later nineteenth century reflected growing inter-

national specialization in industrial production and rising living standards. The latter influence could be seen also in the changing proportions of the different foodstuffs imported, dairy produce and animal products rising more rapidly in absolute quantities imported than sugar, tea, grain, and flour. Changes of emphasis in British industry also led to rapidly increasing imports of certain raw materials such as copper, mineral oils, and rubber, as well as manufactured products such as iron and steel, specialized machinery, chemicals, and paper products.[2]

The changes in the direction of British exports were connected both with the industrialization of important markets such as the United States and Germany, and with the advance of the little-developed regions of the world. The proportion of British exports going to North America, always a fluctuating one, declined: in the 1860s North America took 16 per cent of exports, in 1911-13 only 11·5 per cent. Trade with Africa, Asia, and Australia grew from 33 per cent in the 1860s to nearly 42 per cent in 1911-13; while exports going to South America declined, but not markedly, and in 1911-13 stood at 11·7 per cent. On the import side, Europe and North America increased their share from 57 per cent to 62·7 per cent, while Australian imports rose sharply from under 4 per cent to over 8 per cent. The share of imports coming from Africa, Asia and South America, while of course growing in absolute terms, fell relatively from over 39 per cent to 29 per cent.[3] In general, the shares of Europe and the Empire in British trade did not change very much between the 1860s and 1910-13, and the continuing large share of Europe in British trade (38·1 per cent of imports in the 1860s, 40·5 per cent in 1910-13; 35·5 per cent and 34·7 per cent of exports respectively) provided an important element of stability.[4]

The changes in the composition of American trade were more dramatic and reflected the development of the internal resources of the country and her rise towards economic maturity. In exports the main changes were the substantial and long-term fall in the share of crude materials (especially cotton); the growth in the last quarter of the century, and subsequent decline, of crude and manufactured foodstuffs (principally grains, flour, cheese, and meat); and the long-term rise in the share of finished manufactures and semi-manufactures (machinery, iron and steel products, and petroleum).

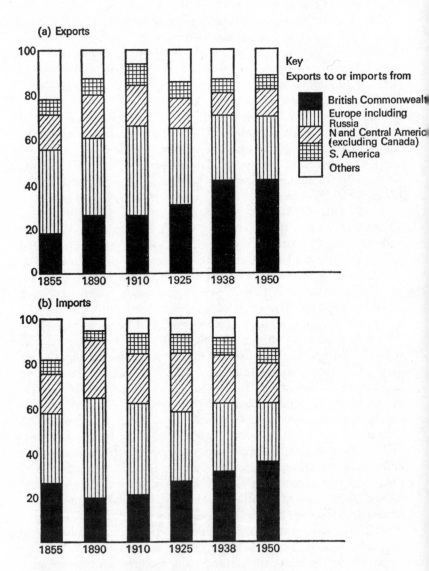

Figure 14. British foreign trade: distribution by area 1855-1950

TABLE 8

Percentage composition of U.S. commodity exports,
1851-60–1906-10

	Crude materials	Crude foodstuffs	Manufactured foodstuffs	Semi-manufactures	Finished manufactures
1851–1860	61·7	6·6	15·4	4·0	12·3
1876–1880	32·2	23·9	24·4	4·6	14·9
1896–1900	26·1	18·9	24·0	9·6	21·4
1906–1910	31·7	8·9	18·1	14·2	27·1

Source: *Historical Statistics of the United States*

The corresponding figures for the change in the composition of imports are as follows:

TABLE 9

Percentage composition of U.S. commodity imports,
1851-60–1906-10

	Crude materials	Crude foodstuffs	Manufactured foodstuffs	Semi-manufactures	Finished manufactures
1851-1860	9·6	11·7	15·4	12.5	50·8
1876-1880	18·6	18·2	21·5	12·4	29·3
1896-1900	29·5	15·1	15·9	13·3	26·2
1906-1910	34·6	11·0	11·8	17·8	24·8

Source: *Historical Statistics of the United States*

The growth of American industry is reflected in the rising proportion of imports consisting of crude materials (rubber, wood pulp, hides, furs, wool, silk, copper, tin, jute, petroleum, nickel, vegetable oils, and steel alloys), and the falling proportion of manufactures. Crude foodstuffs and manufactured foodstuffs fell as a proportion after 1876-80, although they continued to grow in absolute terms. These consisted principally of tropical foodstuffs, coffee, tea, cocoa, tropical fruits, nuts, sugar, and vegetable oils.

The direction of American trade also saw significant changes. In 1860 three-quarters of American exports went to Europe, and over three-fifths of American imports came from that continent; by 1906-10, however, the European share in American exports and imports had fallen to 68 per cent and 51 per cent respectively. In the same period exports to Canada rose from under 7 per cent of the total to over 10 per cent, and those sent to Asia from 2·4 per cent to 5·5 per cent. Exports to other areas did not change very significantly. In imports the decline of the European share was offset mainly by increased shares from Asia and South America.[4a].

Trade between Britain and America expanded considerably over the period, although American exports to Britain rose much more rapidly than did the counter-flow of goods. British exports to America rose only from some £20m. a year in the 1850s to some £37m. in 1900, and to £60m. in 1911-13. Moreover, in the case of a number of Britain's staple exports to America—iron and steel products, textiles, glass, earthenware, and china—her share in total American imports fell sharply, more of the market going to European competitors.[5] American exports to Britain, on the other hand, rose from some £25m. in the later 1850s to £139m. in 1900, and £133m. in 1911-13. A trade gap of about £5m. in the 1850s had risen to one of £73m. a year in 1911-13. Cotton remained a major export to Britain, rising in volume from 682m. lb in 1855 to 1,811m. lb in 1911-13, and in value from £17m. to £50m. Wheat exports were at their peak in both volume and value in 1878-82; by 1911-13 wheat averaged only £9·2m. in value as compared with £19m. in 1878-82. There was a significant long-term rise in the value of other commodities over the period—from a mere £8m. in 1855 to £69m. in 1911-13—although the pre-1914 peak in the total value of American exports to Britain was reached in 1900-1 with £140m.

3 The balance of payments

a **Britain (United Kingdom)**   Commodity trade is of course only one element, if the major one, in the balance of payments. In addition, the 'invisible' items (trade in services), and bullion movements, have to be brought into the reckoning. As British commodity trade developed in the nineteenth century a large gap opened up between earnings from exports and expenditure on imports: we always tended to export less than we imported. Fortunately, the earnings from invisible items not only covered the gap but provided a surplus,

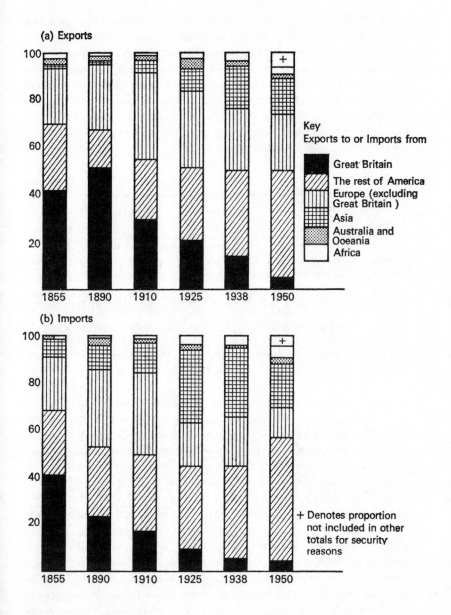

Figure 15. U.S.A. foreign trade: distribution by area 1855-1950

from which in most years a substantial annual outflow of capital was financed. Before 1914 Britain came to be the world's largest exporter of capital—a development we shall look at again in a later section of this chapter—and the large outflow of capital to the under-developed areas of the world played an important part in the growth of world trade which we have already discussed. The healthy state of the balance of payments enabled Britain to export capital, and run a deficit on visible trade, *and* maintain a free trade policy, all at the same time—a remarkable state of affairs.

TABLE 10

Britain's balance of payments 1850-1913 (in £m.)

	1850	1870	1900	1913
Exports	83·4	244·1	354·4	634·8
Imports	103·0	303·3	523·1	768·7
Balance of commodity trade	− 19·6	− 59·2	−168·7	−133·9
Net invisible earnings	+ 31·2	+112·1	+212·7	+367·8
Surplus on current account (excluding capital and bullion movements)	11·6	52·9	44·0	233·9

Source: *Abstract of British Historical Statistics*

The invisible earnings were thus crucial to Britain's role as a great free-trading and capital-exporting nation. And among the invisible items the earnings of British capital invested abroad bulked large. Thus a beneficial circle appeared: as we have seen, the in-visible earnings (in which the earnings of capital abroad were a major element) met the deficit on visible trade and provided the annual surplus from which new capital investment abroad was financed; this made it possible to run a large deficit on visible trade at the same time as maintaining a free trade policy—a situation which helped the overseas borrowers of British capital to service their loans by exporting to Britain's free trade market (although with the expansion of world trade on a multilateral basis, and the growing importance of sterling as a world currency, free access to the British market, while valuable, was not vital). British capital exports helped in the expansion of world trade and in the development of countries that could supply cheaply large quantities of agricultural produce and primary materials, so that Britain's demand for these commodities could be readily satisfied, and for part of the period was satisfied at falling real cost in terms of exports.

TABLE 11

Britain's net invisible earnings 1845-54–1900-08 (in £m.)

Source	1845-54	1865-74	1895-1904	1900-08
Shipping	16·5	46·4	64·1	75·7
Capital invested abroad	10·3	37·0	103·6	121·9
Other (including overseas money earnings of London money market, insurance, etc.)	7·1	33·2	38·6	44·3
Total	33·9	116·6	206·3	241·9

Source: *Abstract of British Historical Statistics*

It is clear from the table above that in addition to the earnings of capital invested abroad the other major contribution—and a rapidly growing one—was that of shipping. Despite a huge expansion of world shipping, Britain's merchant fleet expanded at the same pace, and represented about a third of the total; moreover, until the 1890s the British fleet had the highest proportion of steamships, which gave it a great advantage over the merchant fleets of other countries.[6]

The apparent ease with which Britain financed her trade deficit and export of capital in the period before 1914 masked several underlying or potential weaknesses in her economic position. Her reliance on foreign trade for the employment and standard of living of the population became very great: in 1907 about a quarter of the total output of goods was exported, while retained imports accounted for a third of the total consumption of goods;[7] furthermore, cheap imported food was a major factor in the rise of living standards in the last quarter of the nineteenth century. Unlike other European countries, Britain took advantage of the agricultural productivity of newly opened areas, and to a large extent her superior living standards depended on the maintenance of a free flow of cheap food imports. Further, Britain's ability to pay her way and continue in her role as the world's largest supplier of capital depended, as we

have seen, on her earnings from capital invested abroad, her shipping services, and the earnings of the London money market. All
these constituents of her invisible income depended in turn on the
maintenance of a high level of world investment and trade. Moreover, since about 1870, the growth in size and variety of import
requirements, and the widespread nature of British overseas investments, resulted in a situation where there were fewer and
fewer countries with which Britain had a favourable balance of
payments (taking into account both commodity trade and capital
exports).

Down to 1914, however, Britain's reliance on a high level of
multilateral trade rarely led to serious difficulty because of the
factors favouring rapid growth in world economic activity. These
factors included the growth of population and the industrialization
of formerly agricultural countries, with consequent growth in
demands for food and raw materials, and the opening up of new
productive areas in the Americas, Australasia, Africa, and Asia,
which created a demand for manufactures and for capital goods to
build railways, harbours, and public utilities. At the same time, trade
was moving on to a more multilateral basis: this arose partly through
the gradual adoption by the world's leading currencies of the gold
standard, i.e. a fixed rate of exchange in terms of gold, with a gold
reserve as the basis for the internal currency. With the main trading
currencies freely convertible into gold at fixed rates of exchange it
mattered little if a country had large deficits in some areas, so long
as there were offsetting surpluses elsewhere. Sterling, in fact, became the world's leading currency, and many of the smaller countries came to settle their trade accounts in sterling rather than in
gold, since the stability and convertibility of sterling were never
seriously in doubt. Moreover, sterling was in plentiful supply
because of Britain's large appetite for imports from all over the
world and the domination of London in the business of providing
loans.

The settlement of Britain's own trading accounts relied heavily,
in fact, on the growth of British trade in Asia, especially India.
Receipts from India covered a large and growing proportion of
Britain's trade deficits (rising up to about one-half by 1910), and the
remainder was covered by surpluses with China, Japan, Turkey, and
Australia. Fortunately these countries could meet the cost of British

imports and interest payments on British loans (the latter important only in the case of India and Australia) by exporting food and raw materials to Europe and the Americas, areas with which Britain herself was in deficit.[8]

Thus, so long as the world economy was expanding, and Britain was able to take advantage of the growth of a multilateral system of payments to balance her trading accounts, all was well. But what if this happy state of affairs should be disrupted?—this was the problem that Britain had to face with the outbreak of war in 1914.

b **The United States**

TABLE 12

U.S. balance of payments 1850-1913 (in $m.)

	1850	1870	1876	1900	1913
Imports	195	449	470	858	1,829
Exports	153	413	562	1,395	2,600
Balance of commodity trade	−42	− 36	+ 92	+537	+771
Net invisible earnings	+ 4	− 97	−134	−265	−604
Balance on current account	−38	−133	− 42	+272	+167
Capital movements	+29	+ 97	+ 42	−271	+ 87
(net inflow + net outflow −)					

Source: *Historical Statistics of the United States; Trends in the American Economy in the Nineteenth Century* (Nat. Bureau Econ. Research Princeton 1960), pp. 699–705.

It will be seen from the table above that between 1870 and 1900 a fundamental change occurred in the American balance of payments. This change was the emergence of a large surplus on commodity trade transactions, and if we attempt to pinpoint more exactly when this occurred we can say that a substantial annual surplus on visible trade of about $100m. or more began to appear in 1876 and was the general rule thereafter (except for a spell of small deficits in 1887-9 and in 1893, and only moderate surpluses in 1882, 1884, 1886, and 1890).

Before 1876 a moderate deficit (or in some years a small surplus) on visible trade was the usual state of affairs, and the growing deficit on invisible transactions was offset by the inflow of capital from abroad. Payments of interest and profits on foreign capital invested in America accounted for most of the deficit on invisibles, but travel by Americans abroad was important, and from the 1880s immigrants' remittances also became a major factor.

The importance of the new trend that appeared after 1876 was that gradually a moderate and, in time, very substantial surplus on commodity trade met the large and still growing deficit on invisible transactions, so that dependence on imports of capital from abroad in order to achieve overall balance was reduced. Taking the balance of payments as a whole, overall surpluses in the current account were achieved in 1877-81, and markedly after 1896. Indeed, from 1897 to 1905 American investments abroad exceeded the inflow of capital into the United States by amounts ranging from $23m. in 1897 to $245m. in 1901. (In the remaining years before 1914, American investments abroad were still considerable—averaging $131m.—but except for 1908 were more than offset by heavy inflows of foreign capital.)

Thus the United States balance of payments followed the reverse pattern of that of the United Kingdom. Whereas Britain depended on her invisible earnings to cover her deficit on visible trade and finance her capital exports, America after the middle 1870s could use her customary surplus on visible trade to cover part or all of her unfavourable invisible transactions, and also about the turn of the century begin in a modest way to assume her modern role as the world's greatest supplier of capital. In the last quarter of the nineteenth century, therefore, America moved from the status of an 'immature debtor nation' (a condition in which the annual outflow of interest and dividends on accumulated foreign investment is less than the annual inflow of new capital from abroad) to that of 'mature debtor' (when the annual outflow of interest and dividends is met by an export surplus).

Britain's balance of payments position was so strong, of course, that down to the First World War she was able to sustain a policy of free trade. In 1842 Peel took the bold political step of re-introducing the income tax in order to provide a surplus of revenue which could make possible reductions in customs duties. The crucial stage was reached with the total abolition of the Corn Laws in 1846-9 and the repeal of the Navigation Laws (1849); and in subsequent years Peel's work was continued by Gladstone. By the early 1860s Gladstone had completed a policy of taxing imports for the purpose of revenue only and not for protection, making no distinction between colonial and other imports, and avoiding taxation of common foodstuffs such as sugar, while concentrating revenue duties on former luxuries such as tea, tobacco, and alcohol. Free trade became associated in the minds of the British people with prosperity and plenty, and certainly cheap imported food played a major part in raising living standards before the end of the century, and helped, as we have seen, to keep at a high level a multilateral system of trade, payments, and investment.

By contrast, the drift of American commercial policy was towards the introduction and maintenance of high protection. The decisive change came with the Civil War, which put an end to the trend towards lower tariffs which had developed after 1832. The war created an urgent need for revenue, and in the absence from Congress of southern opposition there was little difficulty in imposing on the country an elaborate system of excise taxes and import duties. In 1864 the average rate of duty was raised to 47 per cent, as compared with a level of about 20 per cent in 1860. What was first regarded as a temporary emergency measure hardened during the years after the war into a policy of permanent high protection. Frustration met the attempts to reverse the policy, as in 1872 and 1882, and in Grover Cleveland's administrations in the middle 1880s and early 1890s. Only in 1913 did the Democrats under Woodrow Wilson secure the first real reduction in tariffs since the Civil War. While the revenue position of the Federal Government hardly justified such a high level of tariffs, and the farmers and the Progressives of the late nineteenth century represented the main anti-tariff forces, the vested interests supporting protection were too powerful to be overcome.[9]

The high tariff could be held to offer four valuable advantages: provision of Federal Government revenue, restriction of imports, protection of the American labour force from the competition of 'cheap European labour', and the fostering of new American industries. All four supposed benefits may be challenged, however. Certainly the tariff produced a large share of total Federal revenues (rather more than half in the 1870s and 1880s, and generally under a half from the middle 1890s). But revenue tended to grow in excess of requirements, and after the expiration in 1871 of the income tax introduced during the Civil War (and with the exception of the 1894 income tax which was declared unconstitutional in 1895), America was without a tax on incomes until 1913. Thus revenue was collected by taxes which fell hardest on the lower incomes, and the gap between rich and poor was inevitably widened.

Import restriction was certainly achieved by the high tariffs, and this may have played a part in the growth of the large surpluses on commodity trade which marked America's shift to the status of a mature debtor nation, as mentioned above. The large outflow of interest and dividends on foreign-owned capital, and the growth of heavy immigrants' remittances in the late nineteenth century, called for the development of an offsetting surplus on commodity trade, but as one writer has said, 'it cannot be proved, however, that the protective tariff was responsible for it'.[10] And, on the other hand, it might well be argued that restriction of imports was a factor in raising living costs and keeping down living standards—certainly the farmers thought so—and may have encouraged retaliatory measures against American exports. Further, the continuation into the post-1914 era of high protective tariffs was inconsistent with America's role as the world's greatest lender, and was a factor in the breakdown of the international economy in the 1930s.

Protection of the American worker from the competition of cheap European labour was hardly a valid argument for the tariff while unrestricted immigration from Europe was permitted and the inflow of cheap labour into America reached the high levels that it did in the closing years of this period. If this was a function of the tariff, it was equivalent to bolting the front door while leaving the back door wide open. In any case, the higher productivity of the American worker meant that even under conditions of free trade he had little to fear from his European counterpart, who worked with so much less in the way of capital equipment, and whose production was less efficiently organized.

Lastly, did the protective tariff foster American industry? Again, no clearcut answer is possible: undoubtedly certain industries owed their beginning, and possibly their continued existence, to tariff protection, but this would not be true of industry in general. The shipbuilding industry is an example of the *adverse* effects of high tariffs. Its production costs were raised by the high cost of imported

iron and steel after the Civil War, and American shipbuilders were
encouraged to cling to the old methods of building wooden sailing
vessels, a policy that proved disastrous.

In conditions of free trade the growth of American industry
would have depended on the level of costs of production and distribution relative to those of Europe, and numerous factors—ample
supplies of raw materials, intensive capital investment, mechanization, and early adoption of assembly-line mass production methods,
together with closer proximity to the market—favoured the
American producer. Protection added to these one more favourable
factor, and tended merely to reduce, or in some cases eliminate,
foreign competition, and perhaps encouraged, as was widely argued,
combinations of producers and higher prices than would otherwise
have ruled.

4 The movement of factors: 1 Capital

Among the influences that encouraged the growth of world trade in
the later nineteenth century were the growth of markets, the
expansion of population, and the spread of industrialization in
Europe, the development of communications (with railways,
developments in shipping, harbour facilities, and the telegraph), and,
the opening up and bringing into production of large new areas of the
world rich in natural resources. The new area that is immediately
relevant here is the interior of the United States. The rapid opening
and settlement of the American west and the Pacific seaboard, and
the rise of new major cities as route centres and bases of industries
for processing agricultural produce, supply of machinery, equipment, and consumers' goods—such as Chicago, Minneapolis, Omaha,
Kansas City, Portland, and Seattle—owed much of course to the
land and railroad policies of the American government, the westward
flow of capital from the expanding industrial centres of the east, and
not least, to the enterprise and hardiness of migrating American
farmers, ranchers, prospectors, and lumbermen.

A significant share of the new capital and labour required in the
rolling back of the American frontier came from western Europe,
and a large proportion of this came from Britain. British capital
invested in the United States is estimated as reaching £200m. by
1871, £525m. by 1899, and £755m. by 1914. At the last date this

represented about a fifth of total British overseas investment, and the largest amount invested in any one country. Large as was the British stake in America in absolute terms, and relative to total British overseas lending, how significant was British capital in the total capital supply of the United States? It is clear from the figures for average gross capital formation in the United States ($1,328m. in 1869-78, $3,311m. in 1894-1903, and $5,684m. in 1904-13) that the inflow of capital from Britain provided only a very small proportion of total capital supply. Nor can it be argued that British capital assumed a role of risk-taking; rather, with some exceptions (e.g. British investment in bonanza farming in the west), most British investors played safe by keeping to government bonds and railroad securities. At best, British capital helped to keep down interest rates, and with the other external capital released American funds for other investments.

From just before the beginning of the present century the United States herself became an important exporter of capital. Until the First World War she remained on balance a debtor country, but by 1914 she already had foreign investments totalling $2,600m. (over $860m. in Canada, $850m. in Mexico, $692m. in Europe, $635m. in South America, and large sums in the Pacific and Far East). The main object of the investments in Central and South America was the exploitation of undeveloped areas principally for oil, raw materials, and foodstuffs, such as Cuban sugar and tobacco, Mexican oil, minerals, and cattle, as well as oil and minerals in Peru, Chile, Venezuela, and Colombia. In the Pacific and Far East American capital concerned itself with Hawaiian sugar and pineapples, in the Philippines with sugar, hemp, coconut oil and other commodities, and in China with railroads. In Canada, however, American capital was attracted only in part by raw materials—lumber and minerals; also attractive was investment in manufacturing industry with the object of jumping over the barrier of the Canadian tariff.

The export of capital from the United States was thus primarily influenced by the needs of the American economy for raw materials and foodstuffs, and was particularly connected with American political interests in Central and South America, and in the Pacific and Far East. 'Dollar imperialism' in the Americas and East—the 'great aberration' in American history—was the American counter-

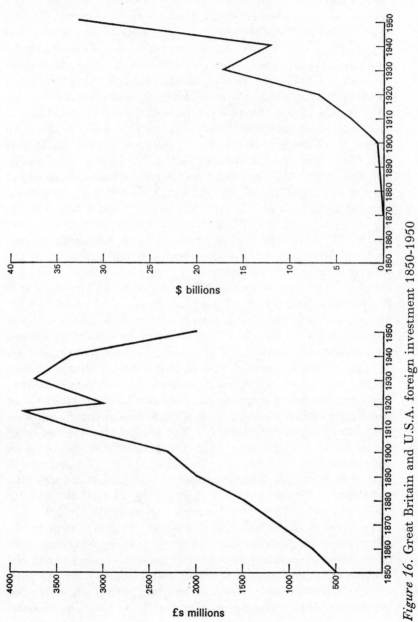

Figure 16. Great Britain and U.S.A. foreign investment 1850-1950

part to the European 'grab for Africa', the new imperialism of the late nineteenth and early twentieth centuries. The export of capital from Britain, on the other hand, was less directly connected with the supply of raw materials and foodstuffs or the development of markets for British goods, although it certainly had effects in these directions. Capital left Britain basically because the return on overseas investments of a kind similar to those popular at home was substantially higher. There were other factors, of course, and it is relevant, as Cairncross has pointed out, that the issuing houses were geared much more to overseas than to home investment; at least half of the additions to capital of British firms came out of undistributed profits, and it was easier for the ordinary investor to hear of good opportunities abroad than at home.[11] Nevertheless, in general British capital followed the rules of the market and flowed where it was most productive and received the highest return.

Thus, in the 1870s U.S. government bonds offered an average yield of $7\frac{1}{2}$ per cent, while Consols produced under 4 per cent; the average yield on British railway stocks was only a little over 4 per cent, while U.S. rails yielded 9·3 per cent, South American rails 8·1 per cent, Indian rails 6·3 per cent, and colonial banks 12·4 per cent. As the yield on overseas government bonds became less attractive so there was a shift by British investors towards overseas industrial securities, especially rails. By 1913, 41 per cent of all British holdings of overseas securities were in railways, as compared with 30 per cent in government and municipal bonds. Just as home rails had exercised such a magnetic attraction to British investors in the middle decades of the century, so foreign rails exercised a similar magnetism in the half-century before 1914. Railways—the great invention of the age—were also the greatest field for overseas investment.[12]

It was inevitable that in developing countries railways and governments should have the largest appetites for capital. In 1913 £617m. of the £755m. British-owned capital in the United States were in railways. In addition to railways and government bonds, other fields for British capital were still closely concerned with communications, power, and primary production: telegraphs and telephones, trams, canals and docks, gasworks and water supplies, electric light and power, land, mines, oil, rubber, tea and coffee plantations, iron and steel, banks, and breweries. Total capital

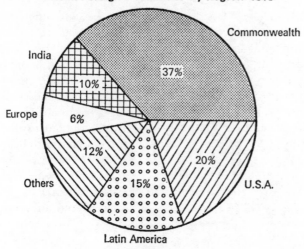

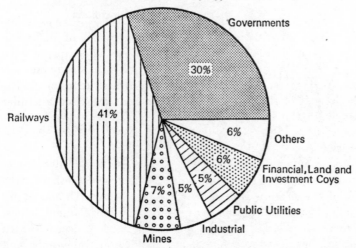

Figure 17. British foreign investment by region and by type 1913

U.S.A: Foreign Investment by Region, 1938

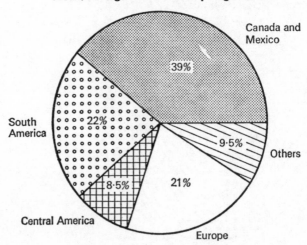

U.S.A. Foreign Investment by Type, 1935

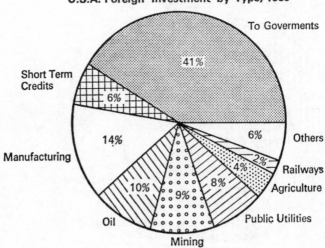

Figure 18. U.S.A. foreign investment by region 1938, and by type 1935

invested abroad rose from some £200m. in 1850 to about £700m. in 1870, £1,500m. in 1885, £2,400m. in 1900, and £4,000m. in 1913.[13]

The returns on this heavy investment of capital overseas were important in a variety of ways. While there was no necessary relation between exports of capital to a particular country and the direction taken by British trade, nevertheless a period of heavy British investment was followed by a growth of exports to the country in question. The direct returns of interest and dividends grew from about £50m. a year in the 1870s to £188m. in 1911-13, amounting to nearly 10 per cent of the national income at the latter date.[14] These earnings of British capital abroad were a major and expanding element in Britain's growing invisible earnings which performed so valuable a function in the balance of payments, as we noted in section 3 of this chapter. The invisible earnings not only enabled Britain to obtain a surplus on current account, from which the annual capital outflow could be financed, but also enabled Britain to maintain a free trade policy and 'increased the consumption of imports even while little more was being earned by exports.' (Between 1871-5 and 1896-1900 the total value of imports rose by 31·7 per cent, and between 1896-1900 and 1911-13 by 54·2 per cent.)[15]

Capital exports to primary producing areas such as the Americas and the British Empire might be expected to improve the terms of trade in Britain's favour, until eventually a state of over-supply of foodstuffs and raw materials, resulting in falling prices, made further development of such areas less promising as a field for investment. As Cairncross points out, the improvement in Britain's terms of trade which began from about 1885 and lasted until the first years of the new century, was at first accompanied, not preceded, by heavy investment in Australia, Argentina, and the United States. In the early 1890s, however, 'the boom in foreign investment was finally brought to an end by a sharp break in the price of foodstuffs and raw materials. . . . About 1903, when the terms of trade had ceased to move in Britain's favour, foreign investment revived. The great burst of investment after 1906 coincided with a period of rising import prices and practically stationary terms of trade.'[16]

While capital exports were important for our invisible earnings and capacity to import, were they harmful for home investment and the development of British industry? There is no evidence that the drain of capital abroad had the effect of raising long-term interest rates unduly (periodical increases in overseas investment were accompanied, however, by rises in short-term rates); but it has been argued that if more capital had sought investment in the home market new British industries might have developed more rapidly, and that a higher level of home investment (e.g. in house-building) would have reduced the level of unemployment.[17]

Given that in the era before 1914 public opinion and policy were not yet ready for large-scale intervention by government in the housing market (and many hospitals and schools derived from private rather than public enterprise), the level of investment in house-building depended mainly on the domestic trends in migration, urbanization, and finance. Only in the 1880s with sustained emigration (associated with heavy capital investment abroad, which, however, does not seem to have affected adversely the availability of funds for building), was the level of British housing development affected through a reduction in the demand for houses. External influences played relatively little part for most of the later nineteenth century in determining investment in house building.[18]

Looking at the economy more generally, it is evident that when overseas lending was heavy, home investment was low, and *vice versa*. On balance, this tended to have the effect of depressing the economy: the rise in exports resulting from an increase in foreign lending was less powerful than the decline in home spending, so that activity tended to be damped down and unemployment was increased. (These circumstances help to explain why Britain was able to lend large sums abroad without straining the balance of payments.)[19] The home boom of the 1890s was influenced, among other factors, by a falling off in foreign investment.[20] However, it has been suggested that in the slowing down of Britain's industrial growth the question of capital supply was probably of minor importance. British firms tended to remain family concerns, conservative and complacent in outlook, and relied on profits to finance what new developments were felt to be necessary. Domestic capital went into British government stock and foreign issues rather than home industry 'because of the paucity of domestic issues in which to invest or because English firms were on too small a scale to attract the issue houses.'[21] How far the weaknesses of British industrial growth in the later nineteenth century were related to developments in British commodity exports (as distinct from exports of capital) we discuss in the following chapter.

5 The movement of factors: 2 Labour

Economic conditions greatly favoured an increase in the migration of labour in the later nineteenth century. Improvements in shipping made it easier, cheaper, and safer to reach distant countries (the steerage fare across the Atlantic fell to only £3 in the 1880s), and railways rapidly transported newly-arrived migrants to developing

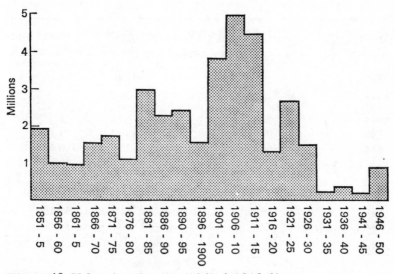

Figure 19. U.S.A. immigration 1851-5–1946-50

industrial centres and newly-opened farmlands. Workers in Britain and the rest of Europe were becoming better educated and more aware of the opportunities provided by the Americas, South Africa, and Australasia. Newspapers were more widely read, and railway and shipping companies made it their business to attract emigrant traffic with alluring (and sometimes misleading) descriptions of the employment, high wages, and rich farmland in the new countries. There were few or no restrictions on the movement of white people, and the letters of friends and relations who had already emigrated brought with them encouragement, advice, and often the fare for the journey.

Passengers sailing from British ports to destinations other than in Europe (only a very rough guide to the numbers of emigrants) fluctuated considerably from under 100,000 in slack years such as 1858-63 to over 200,000 in a number of years before 1900, rising after that date to an average of 460,000 in 1911-13. Irish emigrants made up a large proportion of the total passengers sailing from U.K. ports to the United States until the early years of the new century. The figures are as follows:

TABLE 13

Outward movement from Britain to United States of America 1853-1914

Year	England and Wales	Scotland	Ireland	Great Britain and Ireland
1853	26,512	7,470	156,970	190,952
1854	37,644	4,888	111,095	153,627
1855	25,278	3,797	57,164	86,239
1856	31,194	4,960	58,777	94,931
1857	33,966	5,490	66,060	105,516
1858	14,469	3,389	31,498	49,356
1859	13,065	2,851	41,180	57,096
1860	13,556	2,220	52,103	67,879
1861	8,741	1,210	28,209	38,160
1862	14,180	1,025	33,521	48,726
1863	32,570	3,481	94,477	130,528
1864	29,811	5,986	94,368	130,165
1865	30,816	5,562	82,085	118,463
1866	38,421	6,825	86,594	131,840
1867	38,231	8,249	79,571	126,051
1868	40,365	10,463	57,662	108,490
1869	63,044	17,226	66,467	146,737
1870	68,935	16,640	67,891	153,466
1871	71,926	13,271	65,591	150,788
1872	82,339	12,691	66,752	161,782
1873	78,968	12,226	75,536	166,730
1874	56,388	9,250	48,136	113,774
1875	43,867	5,893	31,433	81,193
1876	34,612	3,510	16,432	54,554

Year	England and Wales	Scotland	Ireland	Great Britain and Ireland
1877	28,074	3,416	13,991	45,481
1878	32,099	3,993	18,602	54,694
1879	52,402	9,346	30,058	91,806
1880	69,081	14,471	83,018	166,570
1881	90,527	18,238	67,339	176,104
1882	94,599	19,004	68,300	181,903
1883	93,392	15,332	82,849	191,573
1884	83,324	12,752	59,204	155,280
1885	73,789	13,241	50,657	137,687
1886	83,066	16,786	52,858	152,710
1887	107,069	25,373	69,084	201,526
1888	103,674	26,006	66,306	195,986
1889	93,307	17,567	57,897	168,771
1890	86,442	13,861	52,110	152,413
1891	87,581	15,376	53,438	156,395
1892	84,667	16,406	48,966	150,039
1893	83,293	16,534	49,122	148,949
1894	54,253	10,151	39,597	104,001
1895	61,211	13,244	52,047	126,502
1896	48,434	10,535	39,952	98,921
1897	43,381	9,121	32,822	85,324
1898	42,244	7,372	30,878	80,494
1899	45,723	8,128	38,631	92,482
1900	49,445	11,504	41,848	102,797
1901	57,246	11,414	35,535	104,195
1902	58,382	12,225	37,891	108,498
1903	68,791	15,318	39,554	123,663
1904	76,546	17,111	52,788	146,445
1905	58,229	19,785	44,356	122,370
1906	76,179	23,221	45,417	144,817
1907	91,593	24,365	54,306	170,264
1908	49,841	14,720	31,518	96,079
1909	50,787	21,486	36,611	108,884
1910	62,127	27,918	41,019	131,064
1911	60,054	23,441	36,613	120,108
1912	37,623	13,974	28,086	79,683
1913	46,435	15,936	32,320	94,691
1914	35,066	10,451	24,138	69,655

Source: *External Migration: A Study of the Available Statistics 1851-1950* by N. H. Carrier and J. R. Jeffery (H.M.S.O. (1953)).

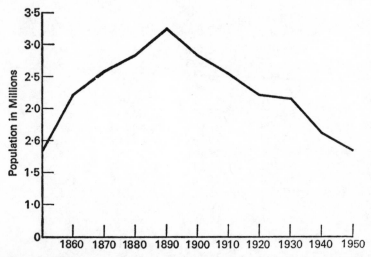

Figure 20. Natives of Great Britain and Ireland resident in U.S.A. 1850-1950

Among those who stated their occupation when leaving for the United States (over two-thirds of the total), labourers and domestic servants dominated down to the early 1890s (many of the former were building labourers, miners, and general labourers); after that period their numbers were matched or exceeded by the skilled workers, always a sizeable element in the total. Merchants and professional people fluctuated at roughly 5-10 per cent of the total, although many of these were not emigrants but merely temporary visitors to America. Farmers and farm labourers constituted a major element from the 1880s, reaching an early peak of 81,000 in the later 1880s, and 51,000 in 1891-5, with a later minor peak of 44,000 in 1906-10.[22]

Most of the farmers and agricultural labourers took up farming in America: the attraction of owning one's own land was a powerful one, although the well-informed realized that hard work, and some capital, were necessary for success. The Homestead Act of 1862 made little difference to the numbers seeking land: the frontier was a very long way from the east coast, and all the good land had already been appropriated and had to be paid for. Between 1870 and 1890 the proportion of British-born immigrants engaged in the United States as farmers fell from 19·2 per cent to 12·9 per cent of the total

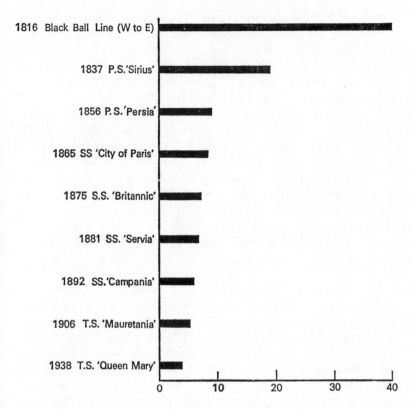

Figure 21. Time taken on the Atlantic crossing (in days) 1816-1938

British-born, while the proportion of British-born who were farm labourers fell from 7·7 per cent to 3·6 per cent. The proportion of manual workers in industry and service occupations remained steady at between 55 and 57 per cent, while some 6-8 per cent of the British-born were businessmen, and a growing proportion were professional men, clerks, and public officials (9·2 per cent in 1870, and 15·3 per cent in 1900).[23] The proportion of immigrants of all nationalities in the total American population remained fairly stable at about 14 per cent in the later nineteenth century.

As the American frontier receded and American farming became more capitalistic, a growing proportion of British immigrants sought the towns and industrial occupations. This trend reflected the growth of American industry, and also the urbanization of Britain, as a growing proportion of immigrants came from towns rather than the country. American wages were high, and the rapid development of American cities offered great numbers of unskilled jobs, not only as factory workers, but also as policemen, carters, porters, street-sweepers, waiters in restaurants, and the like.

A complex and changing relationship existed between the fluctuations in economic activity and the flow of immigrants. Jerome found that the inflow was dominated on the whole by conditions in the United States, and that from 1889 cyclical changes in employment in America had corresponding influences, after a short time-lag, on immigration.[24] More recently, Brinley Thomas has argued that the evidence suggests a structural change in the American economy just after the Civil War, with the effect of changing the direction of lag between immigration and American economic activity. Before the war, immigration preceded railroad building and followed coal output, after the war, both immigration and coal output lagged behind railroad building. This suggests that before the 1870s, when the exploitation of natural resources made transport developments of prime importance, the rate of American expansion was conditioned by the arrival of new labour. 'The railways could not have been built without the gangs of labourers, many of them Irish, recruited in the east and transported to the construction camps.' But after the war 'the American economy evolved into a more mature phase, and railway building ceased to be the dominant force which it had previously been. Changes in the rate of inflow of population were now induced by changes in the general levels of investment'—a conclusion in line with the findings of Jerome and others.[25]

The first major influx of immigrants was in 1844-54, when 2,871,000 Europeans joined a population which in 1844 was only 19·5m: 'it is not surprising that this formidable invasion had a profound effect on the labour market and on the growth of investment. . . .' A second influx began in 1863 when the result of the Civil War was in sight, and lasted to 1873: it preceded fixed capital investment. But the third upswing of 1878-88, and the fourth of 1898-1907, were influenced by the prior upswings of capital investment, especially in railroads. Investment in building in the United States, however, lagged behind the influxes of migrants. The last great influx of 1898-1907 was very largely of agricultural workers from southern and eastern Europe, and this 'new' immigration was practically simultaneous with high capital investment as represented by pig-iron output and railway freight ton-miles.[26]

The Dillingham Immigration Commission of 1911-12 gave statistical support to the public fears aroused by the large inflow from southern and eastern Europe in the years before 1914. In the northern industrial area east of the Mississippi almost 40 per cent of the wage-earners were Italians, Poles, and Slavs, who formed ghettoes in the large cities, were generally poor and subject to unemployment, and seemed more resistant to integration into American life than had been the earlier immigrants from north-western Europe. Their great numbers, and their tractable nature, lowered wages and kept working conditions poor in the industries they entered, and so discouraged continued immigration from the older sources of north-western Europe. Their lack of skill made for the more widespread adoption in industry of processes and machinery which reduced or eliminated the need for skill and experience. The hostility felt by native American workers who found their jobs and living standards threatened by the mass influx was perhaps unfounded since the newcomers took the lowest-paid jobs while native Americans moved a step higher up the ladder. Nevertheless, this hostility was behind the restrictive legislation which began with the Chinese Exclusion Act of 1882 and led to the first Quota Act of 1921, restricting entry on a basis highly favourable to the old north-western European countries.

But, in fact, the Dillingham Commission exaggerated the differences between the old and the new migration. Like the newcomers, a high proportion of the old immigrants were agricultural workers: in 1849-54 80 per cent of the two million immigrants were peasants from Ireland and Germany, and in the later peaks of 1867-73 and 1881-8 two-thirds of the migrants were from Ireland, Scandinavia, and Germany, and were mainly of rural origin. A large proportion of the English, Welsh, and Scots, too, were also agricultural, especially in the earlier years. While many of the peasants from Scandinavia and Germany took up farming, others, the Irish especially, went to work in the cities. It was not true, as the Dillingham Commission argued, that the 'old' immigrants included a high proportion of skilled workers who brought great advantages of training and experience to America.

Among the more important of the general effects of immigration on the American economy were the influences upon the composition, geographical distribution, and growth of the population. The immigrants included a high proportion of males of working age, and the high birth-rate of immigrant families helped to offset somewhat the fall in birth-rate that was occurring among the native population, while perhaps contributing to the conditions which encouraged the native birth-rate to fall. (The immigrants' death-rate was also higher, owing partly to a higher proportion of the foreign-born being in the upper age-groups, and their concentration in cities where the expectation of life was less than in rural communities.) The tendency for the 'new' immigrants to flock to the larger cities greatly reinforced the townward drift already prevalent among native Americans. Between 1890 and 1930 the proportion of foreign-born whites living in cities rose from 62 per cent to 80 per cent, and that of the native whites rose also from 26 per cent to 48 per cent. The fact that the larger cities contained a higher and rising proportion of recent immigrants, while the rural areas were populated predominantly by native Americans, tended to emphasize the rural-urban conflict, and and to add ethnic and religious factors to the small-town American's suspicions of the alien character of the large city.[27]

The organization of workers in unions was both stimulated and frustrated by the 'new' immigration. While the foreign-born supplied prominent union leaders and often made determined rank-and-file members, the advantage of large-scale immigration lay with the employer, for the flood of uprooted was too great for the labour movement to assimilate, and indeed employers imported immigrants specifically as strike-breakers. Many unions consisted of conservative groups of skilled workers, who viewed the newcomers with distrust and sought only to preserve the superior standards of their trade. Immigration tended to lower the wages of the unskilled, especially in mines, railroads, and factories, and made for high rates of urban unemployment; indeed, considerable numbers of immigrants continued to arrive even in depression years. Between 1900 and 1913 over 11m. people entered the United States, and at a time of 'a remarkable advance in real investment and income the index number of the full-time real wages of unskilled workers in manufacturing fell from 114 in 1897-9 to 101 in 1910-13. There was a premium on processes needing a relatively large quantity of low-grade labour;

industries adopting these processes expanded rapidly, their products fell in price, and a number of them found that they no longer required protective tariffs.'[28]

It is often supposed that the large inflow of unskilled workers in the later nineteenth century encouraged the adoption in industry of methods of production which economized in scarce skills and made possible maximum utilization of unskilled labour. No doubt this occurred; but it is important to notice that a high degree of mechanization, mass production, and standardization of product had been a marked feature of certain American industries even before 1850 (e.g. furniture, ploughs, screws, files, nails, biscuits, locks, clocks, small arms, nuts and bolts, and sewing-machines). Habakkuk has argued that before 1850 it was the scarcity, and high wages, of *unskilled* labour that encouraged manufacturers to adopt capital-intensive techniques. It was the simple operations that could be performed by unskilled labour that were most easily mechanized; and the high labour productivity in agriculture, resulting from abundance of land, tended to keep unskilled labour scarce and expensive in industry. Intensive utilization of machinery, and early replacement by superior machines, together with the development before the Civil War of firms making highly specialized machine tools, encouraged a growing trend towards large-scale mass-production methods in American industry.[29] Experience in the use of machinery showed where new machines might be profitably introduced in other processes. Thus the great influx of unskilled labour in the later nineteenth century was absorbed, in part, by an industrial system which had long experience of the use of machinery, and was well able to exploit the cheapness of the new labour supply. Indeed, one might suppose that the cheapness of unskilled labour at this period would have retarded the progress of industrial techniques. In fact, cheap labour added to industrial profits and so encouraged further capital expansion, while much of the cheap immigrant labour was absorbed by non-manufacturing industries that as yet made relatively little use of machinery—railroads, mining, building and construction, transport, and the service industries.

Immigrants were herded in sub-standard housing with bad health conditions, and were concentrated in ethnic groups in the large cities, or often made up the whole population of mining camps and cities of recent growth, such as the steel town of Gary, Indiana.

While illiteracy among the native Americans fell to negligible proportions after 1880 (except in the South), among the foreign-born a
constant level of about 12-13 per cent illiteracy was found down to the
1920s, largely because of the high proportion of illiterates among
such 'new' immigrants as the Poles, Italians, and Slavs. The proportion of the foreign-born unable to speak English was as high as
22·8 per cent in 1910. However, the view that immigrants added
greatly to the level of crime in the United States had no foundation
in the statistics of prison inmates.[30]

Returning to the specifically British emigration, there remains to
be considered the effects of the outflow on the British economy. There
is evidence that the upswings of emigration coincided with upswings
of capital exports (as in 1870-3, 1881-8, and 1903-13). The two
flows, no doubt, were inter-related. New investment opportunities
abroad attracted British capital, and the increased employment
which followed attracted immigrants; in time, the demands arising
from an increased labour force might provide further outlets for
capital. But how serious for the British economy was the loss of this
capital and labour?

Ashworth has pointed out that the British national income was
growing rapidly in the late nineteenth century, and that although
the proportion being saved was rather smaller than in the peak years
of the early seventies, it was possible for the absolute amount of new
investment to continue to increase. Fluctuations in the level of investment had much more effect on the foreign capital market than
on domestic capital formation. And, although net lending abroad
accounted for 43 per cent of total net investment between 1870 and
1913, 'it was possible to maintain a fairly steady growth in the
amount of capital used within the United Kingdom . . . the amount
of domestic capital per occupied person must have been at least half
as much again in 1914 as it was in 1870, and probably more. That
was in itself a substantial contribution to a transformation of productive methods, a greater efficiency of business, and a more comfortable material condition of society.'[31]

Between 1871 and 1911 Britain experienced a net loss of nearly
2m. people by migration (i.e. taking into account the return of
former emigrants and the increased immigration from Europe, especially of Jews who fled the revival of anti-Semitism). Furthermore,
the people lost were predominantly young adults from the most

active section of the labour force. On the other hand, as Ashworth notes, the young adults were becoming relatively more numerous, although the loss of young men abroad upset the sex ratio, contributed to the gradual long-term decline in the rate of population growth, and stimulated the employment of women. As a whole, the loss of people by emigration was cushioned by the, as yet, still high rate of population growth—the loss of the 2m. was much more than offset by the natural increase of some 18m.[32]

Lack of, or imperfect, statistics, together with the great number of variables involved, make it impossible to be very definite about the precise influences of the movement of factors at this time. We cannot even very satisfactorily distinguish the British element in the world movements of labour and capital. Both the advantages of the flows for the American economy, and the disadvantages for the British economy, can easily be exaggerated, and may well have been only of marginal significance. But, more widely, the movement of factors was clearly a major and essential element in the growth of an international multilateral trading system that was vital for the economic growth of the pre-1914 world.

Notes

1   ASHWORTH, W., *An Economic History of England: 1870-1939* (1960), pp. 139-41.

2   ASHWORTH, *op. cit.*, pp. 144-6.

3   *Ibid.*, pp. 143-6.

4   SAUL, S. B., 'The Export Economy 1870-1914', in Studies in the British Economy 1870-1914 (ed. J. Saville), *Yorks. Bull. of Econ. and Social Research* 17, 1 (1965), pp. 6-8.

4a   WILLIAMSON, H. F. (ed.), *The Growth of the American Economy* (Englewood Cliffs, N.J., 2nd ed. 1951), pp. 545-50.

5   SAUL, *op. cit.*, p. 7.

6   ASHWORTH, *op. cit.*, p. 154.

7   *Ibid.*, p. 160.

8   ASHWORTH, *op. cit.*, pp. 161-2; SAUL, S. B., *Studies in British Overseas Trade 1870-1914* (Liverpool U.P. 1960), pp. 57-65.

9   See JONES, *op. cit.*, pp. 168-71, for a survey of the tariff changes.

10   GIDEONSE, MAX, in *The Growth of the American Economy* (ed. Harold F. Williamson, 2nd ed. 1951), p. 537.

11   CAIRNCROSS, A. K., *Home and Foreign Investment* 1870-1913 (Cambridge, 1953), pp. 98-102.

12   Royal Institute of International Affairs, *The Problem of International Investment* (1937), pp. 144-60.

13   IMLAH, A. H., *Economic Elements in the Pax Britannica* (Harvard, 1958), pp. 72-5.

14   IMLAH, *op. cit.*, pp. 73-5.

15   ASHWORTH, *op. cit.*, pp. 141, 159.

16   CAIRNCROSS, *op. cit.*, pp. 188-95.

17   See for example SAMUEL, A. M., 'Has Foreign Investment Paid?' *Economic Journal* (1930).

18   HABAKKUK, H. J., 'Fluctuations in House-building in Britain and U.S.A. in the Nineteenth Century', *Jour. Ec. Hist.* XXII (1962), pp. 224-5.

19   See FORD, A. G., 'Overseas Lending and Internal Fluctuations 1870-1914', *Yorks. Bull. of Econ. and Social Research* 17, 1 (1965), pp. 21-30.

20   SIGSWORTH, E. M. and BLACKMAN, JANET, 'The Home Boom of the 1890s', *ibid.*, pp. 96-7.

21   ALDCROFT, D. H., 'The Entrepreneur and the British Economy 1870-1914', *Econ. Hist. Rev.* 2nd ser. XVII (1964-5), p. 132.

22   THOMAS, BRINLEY, *Migration and Economic Growth* (Cambridge, 1954), pp. 61-2.

23   *Ibid.*, p. 143.

24   JEROME, HARRY, *Migration and Business Cycles* (New York, Nat. Bureau of Econ. Research, 1926), p. 208.

25   THOMAS, *op. cit.*, pp. 92-4.

26   *Ibid.*, pp. 160-3.

27   See DAVIE, M. R., *World Immigration* (New York, 1936), pp. 223-35, 282-4.

28   THOMAS, *op. cit.*, p. 165.

29   HABAKKUK, H. J., *American and British Technology in the Nineteenth Century* (Cambridge, 1962), pp. 96, 104-6, 126-7.

30   DAVIE, *op. cit.*

31   ASHWORTH, *op. cit.*, pp. 184-5.

32   *Ibid.*, p. 191.

Suggestions for further reading

Texts

ASHWORTH, W., *Economic History of England 1870-1939* (1960), ch. 6-8. *The International Economy since 1850* (2nd ed., 1962), ch. 7.

WILLIAMSON, H. F. (ed.), *The Growth of the American Economy* (Englewood Cliffs, N.J., 2nd ed., 1951), ch. 27.

Specialized works

CAIRNCROSS, A. K., *Home and Foreign Investment 1870-1913* (Cambridge, 1953).

HALL, A. R. (ed.), *The Export of Capital from Britain 1870-1914* (1968).

HANDLIN, OSCAR, *The Uprooted* (New York, 1951).

IMLAH, A. H., *Economic Elements in the Pax Britannica* (Harvard U.P., 1958).

JONES, M. A., *American Immigration* (U. of Chicago P., 1960).

Royal Institute of International Affairs, *The Problem of International Investment* (1937).

SAUL, S. B., *Studies in British Overseas Trade 1870-1914* (Liverpool U.P., 1960). 'The Export Economy *1870-1914*', in *Studies in the British Economy* 1870-1914 (ed. J. Saville), *York. Bull. of Econ. and Social Research* 17, (1965).

SPENCE, C. C., *British Investments in the American Mining Frontier* (Cornell, U.P., 1958).

THOMAS, BRINLEY, *Migration and Economic Growth* (Cambridge, 1954).

WOODRUFF, W., *Impact of Western Man; a Study of Europe's role in the World Economy, 1750-1960* (1966).

YEARLEY, C. K., *Britons in American Labour: A History of the Influence of U.K. immigrants on American Labour 1820-1914* (Baltimore, Johns Hopkins Press, 1957).

5   The money and capital markets

1 Britain

a **The currency** In 1850 the British currency was superior to the American in both general acceptability and stability of value. Since 1816 Great Britain had been on the Gold Standard, with silver and copper used for the subsidiary coinage. Gold sovereigns were of unlimited legal tender but the silver coinage was legal tender only for amounts up to 40 shillings. From 1821 onwards the notes of the Bank of England were fully convertible into gold; but throughout the years until 1914 the golden sovereign was the standard of value and one of the principal means of payment. In 1835 the last significant Parliamentary move to establish a bi-metallic standard (with silver in as privileged a position as gold) was a complete failure. Thereafter monometallism was virtually unchallenged in Britain.

The importance of the sovereign was increased through the fact that after 1826 the issuance of bank notes in denominations under £5 was illegal. On the other hand, from the same date, the Bank of England began to open branches in the provinces and by this means spread the circulation of its notes of £5 denomination and above.

Thus, by 1850 the notes of the central bank were becoming generally known and acceptable throughout the kingdom, in contrast with the situation twenty-five years earlier when they scarcely circulated beyond London and Lancashire. A law of 1833, which made Bank of England notes legal tender, and the practice of the Bank's branches of offering special concessions to country banks which replaced their own note issues by those of the Bank of England, helped to bring about a quick decline in the relative importance of country bank-note issues. Some joint-stock banks also issued notes, but this side of their business was less important than their acceptance of deposits. In any case, bank-notes were rapidly becoming 'the mere small change of the ledger';[1] all large transactions were settled by cheque. In 1844 207 private and seventy-two joint-stock banks were issuing notes to a total value of over £8m. compared with the £21m.

of the Bank of England. By 1914 the aggregate circulation of the seven private and four joint-stock banks that still clung to the privilege of note issue had fallen to £401,719. Seven years later the process of banking amalgamation had finally eliminated the note issues of both private and joint-stock banks (other than the Bank of England).

TABLE 14

Notes held by the public to the nearest £'000 1844-1920, and nearest £m. 1930-9

	Bank of England	Country	Scottish
	£	£	£
1844	21,216	8,175	2,951
1850	19,448	6,330	3,225
1860	21,252	6,450	4,228
1870	23,327	4,910	4,933
1880	26,915	3,440	5,538
1890	24,561	2,350	6,296
1900	29,366	1,243	7,946
1910	28,300	197	7,074
1920	102,770	170	28,953
	£m		£m
1930	358·7	—	21·4
1939	507·3	—	24·7

Source: *British Historical Statistics*, p. 450.

As a result of war-time inflation after 1914 bank notes achieved a renewed importance. To take the place of the rapidly disappearing sovereigns and half-sovereigns, Treasury notes for 10*s*. and £1 were issued from 1914 to 1928, when they were replaced by notes of similar denomination of the Bank of England.

The British public throughout the entire period were thus fortunate is escaping the confusion arising from bi-metallism, such as occurred in the United States in the 1860s, and the disasters of run-away inflation as experienced in Central Europe in the early 1920s.

b **Commercial banking** Apart from specialized concerns such as the discount houses, British commercial banking in 1850 was carried out by two main types of institution, the country bank and the joint-stock bank. The country banks, which were generally older established than their joint-stock rivals, were limited by law to not more than six partners. Many of them had been founded during the years of war between 1793 and 1815, when there was a scarcity of coins from the Mint and also of Bank of England notes. Their main function was to issue notes and to make short-term advances to their business customers. Their stability was under suspicion since sixty-three of them had failed in the financial panic of 1825-6, and a further eighty-two were forced to close during the years 1839-43. It was widely believed that their instability sprang from their unlimited right of note issue before 1844, a right restrained only by their liability to pay stamp duty and their concern to maintain liquidity. Between 1844 and 1924, 189 of them were absorbed by joint-stock banks whilst a further eighty disappeared through amalgamation with other country banks. The gradual concentration of the note issue in the Bank of England, as provided for under the Bank Charter Act of 1844, and the growing use of the cheque for settlement of accounts were decreasing their importance. Their numbers shrank to four dozen in 1914, and to only two in 1923.

Joint-stock banking (outside a 65 mile radius from the City of London) had been permitted for the first time in England and Wales in 1826, though it had been legal before this in Scotland. The Bank Charter Act of 1833 permitted the establishment of joint-stock banks in London but denied them the right of note issue within that area. Joint-stock banking was further encouraged by legislation of 1858 and 1862 which permitted such banks to limit the liability of their shareholders, by their admission to the Bankers' Clearing House in 1854, and by the introduction in 1879 of 'reserve liability' (by which shareholders were liable in the event of the failure of the bank to pay the difference between the amount they had paid up and the nominal amount of their subscription). Thus encouraged, the number of joint-stock banks rose to a peak in the early 1870s, stayed at this level for more than a decade, and then started to decline as the amalgamation movement gathered momentum in the closing years of the century.

Branch banking developed earlier in Great Britain than it did in America. One important reason for this difference was that when joint-stock banks appeared on the scene in England in the second quarter of the nineteenth century they needed both to divert customers from the country banks and to create new banking business. Branches were opened in areas hitherto lacking in banking facilities. The number of branch offices of joint-stock and private banks rose nearly eight-fold between 1844 and 1924, or from 1,032 to 8,081. In consequence of these developments the danger of bank failures through a commercial crisis confined to one part of the country only, was minimized. One lesson of the financial panics which occurred in such years as 1825, 1847, 1857, and 1866 was that the small local bank was much less likely to survive than was an institution national in its scope. Furthermore, the public was much better served. In 1851 there was one branch office to every 19,921 of the population; in 1923 there was one to every 4,689.

TABLE 15

Total bank offices of joint-stock and private banks in England and Wales 1858-1921

	Offices	*Offices in relation to population*
1858 (estimate)	1,195	1 to 16,644
1872	1,779	1 to 12,766
1881	2,413	1 to 11,283
1891	3,383	1 to 7,788
1901	4,762	1 to 6,787
1911	6,267	1 to 5,630
1921	7,644	1 to 4,972

Source: J. Sykes, *The Amalgamation Movement in English Banking*, 1825-1924 (1926), p. 113.

Another means by which joint-stock banks attracted more customers was by offering generous interest payments on deposits. Although this policy helped to tap idle reserves of cash and to generate the banking habit, it had its dangers. The fiercer the competition for customers the greater was the interest paid on deposits and the more imperative was the bank's need to employ every available penny profitably. Loans at call or short notice to bill brokers or discount houses were greatly stimulated. The increased influence of the discount houses in the London money market marched in step with the growing importance of the joint-stock banks which, because of the urgent need to earn money for their deposit allowances, sometimes encouraged trading in bills of dubious security. When in 1877 the

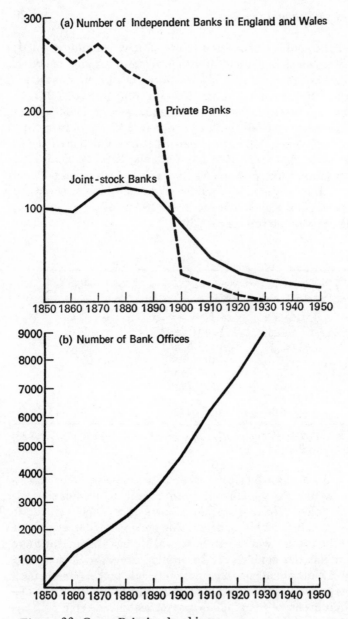

Figure 22. Great Britain: banking.
a Number of independent banks in England and Wales 1850-1950
b Number of bank offices 1850-1950

banks finally agreed to end the practice of paying interest on deposits, one of the unstable influences in the British banking system was removed.

From the 1890s onwards industrial concentration was gathering momentum, and the increasing capitalization of the typical business firm demanded a corresponding growth in the resources of banks. In 1901 the Chairman of the Buckinghamshire and Oxfordshire Bank, justifying an amalgamation proposal to the bank's shareholders, said 'We have had to refuse business which was too much for our limit.' By 1914 the process of amalgamation and financial concentration had proceeded so far that each of the twenty largest joint-stock banks had more than a hundred offices while the three largest had over 500 each. By 1922 there were only thirty-nine British banks (in contrast with over 30,000 separate institutions in the United States), and the 'Big Five' joint-stock banks owned 6,800 out of a total of 9,650 branches.[2]

TABLE 16

Amalgamations in banking: England and Wales, 1844-61–1903-24

	Private bank with private bank	Joint-stock bank with joint-stock bank	Joint-stock bank by private bank	Private bank by joint-stock bank	Total
1844-61	11	10	—	23	44
1862-89	31	40	1	66	138
1890-1902	37	51	1	64	153
1903-24	1	58	2	36	97

Source: J. Sykes, *The Amalgamation Movement in English Banking*, 1825-1924 (1926), p. 97.

c **Central banking** The Bank of England was founded in 1694 principally as a convenient means of financing the war against France, and not primarily with the intention of its functioning as a central bank. Even as late as 1850 the directors of the Bank were by no means fully aware that their responsibility to make the Bank a lender of last resort and a regulator of national credit policy ought to take precedence over considerations of maximizing the financial return for the shareholders. Only gradually in the forty years after

1844 did the Bank emerge as an effective instrument of credit control.

The Bank Charter Act of 1844 which was the great legislative landmark of the nineteenth century, has been described as 'less a Bank Act than a Bank Note Act'[3] One of the main purposes of the measure was to provide for the eventual concentration of the note issue in the Bank of England and to limit its size to the value of the bullion reserve, with the exception of a small fiduciary issue backed by Government securities. For other aspects of banking, as distinct from the note issue, it was thought wise to allow the directors complete freedom to conduct business in the same way as any other commercial bank. Any idea of the *discretionary* regulation of the nation's credit was remote from the thinking of the cabinet and of the Bank's directors in 1844. Richard Cobden expressed the consensus of opinion at the time when he said:

'I hold all idea of regulating the currency to be an absurdity . . . the currency should regulate itself: it must be regulated by the trade and commerce of the world: I would neither allow the Bank of England nor any private bank to have what is called the management of the currency. . . . I would never contemplate any remedial measure which is left to the discretion of individuals.'[4] When asked in 1847: 'Do you consider that the Act . . . relieved you entirely from any responsibility as regarded the circulation?' the Governor of the Bank replied: 'Entirely.'[5]

One lesson which had yet to be learned was that the rule of thumb increase or decrease in the note issue to match the augmentation or depletion of the Bank's bullion reserve was no substitute for a managed credit policy, since the volume of commercial bank deposits was far more influential on prices and the level of business activity than was the value of notes issued. A drain of gold from the Bank might arise from 'external' or 'internal' causes which had very little to do with the size of the country's note issue. In the second place, the directors of the Bank had yet to appreciate the need for a more positive use of bank rate and open-market policy in order to check an over-expansion of credit sufficiently early to prevent subsequent financial panic.

In the commercial crises of 1847, 1857, and 1866 the Bank was subject to runs which threatened the bullion reserve. On all three occasions the Governor was given permission to increase the fiduciary issue beyond the limits laid down in the Act of 1844, and in 1857 it proved necessary to print some of the extra notes authorized. These experiences made the management of the Bank more cautious in making advances to customers in periods of boom. After 1848 Bank Rate (i.e. the rate at which the Bank would discount first-class bills of exchange) was generally above, rather than below, the market rate of discount, and from 1858 the Bank gave accommodation to those who were not its regular customers only on quarterly settlement dates.

However, these measures of caution, while making the Bank's own position more secure, weakened its ability to influence the market. Commercial customers naturally preferred to borrow money from the discount houses and commercial banks rather than from the Bank of England, whose scrutiny of the borrower's means and intentions was now more thorough and whose charges were generally higher. In consequence, between 1833 and 1873 the ratio of the Bank's deposits to those of all other banks fell from one-third to less than one-twentieth.[6]

The Bank eventually gained effective control over the money market by changes in its business practices and not by any change in the law. Thus from 1878 the Bank formalized a practice that had already become common of allowing its regular customers to borrow at the market rate of discount irrespective of the level of Bank Rate. This change not only ensured that the Bank did not lose any more custom to rival banks and to the discount houses, but also served to emphasize that Bank Rate was a penal rate, a danger signal to the whole money market. At the same time the Bank let it be known that it was willing to advance money at all times and to all credit-worthy borrowers but only at the Bank Rate, which was generally higher than the market rate. The issuance of Treasury bills after the passing of the Treasury Bills Act, 1877, provided the Bank with an additional instrument with which to control the credit situation. To reinforce a rise in the Bank Rate, the Bank's agents, Messrs. Mullins and Marshall, would be instructed to sell Treasury Bills in the open market, a measure which would cause depletion of the commercial banks' cash reserves and therefore a tightening of the general credit situation. Such measures ensured that the bill market would never get too independent of the Bank.[7] To emphasize still more the importance of an increase in the Bank Rate as a warning signal, after

1880 increases in the Bank Rate were made in steps of one per cent rather than one half of one per cent.

The changed situation in the London money market is illustrated in the contrast between the events of 1860-6 and the Baring crisis of 1890. In 1860 the largest discount house in the city, Messrs. Overend and Gurney, were at loggerheads with the Bank and had withdrawn a huge deposit at an inconvenient time as a fighting protest against the Bank's policy of not discounting for the bill brokers.[8] In 1866, when Overend and Gurney Ltd. failed, there followed 'the wildest panic' in which all the commercial banks 'were intent on saving themselves, and had no spare funds for any other purpose'.[9] In the autumn of 1890 it was known that although the firm of Baring Brothers was not insolvent, it had liabilities of about £34m., a large part of which could not be met in the short run. To save the firm and prevent a panic which would otherwise have made that of 1866 pale into insignificance, the Bank of England, in co-operation with the joint-stock and private banks, launched a reserve fund which eventually reached the impressive total of £18m. Baring Brothers was, by this means, saved from liquidation and was eventually able to pay its creditors 20/- in the pound. The whole episode was 'a striking demonstration of the change in relations between the Bank and the banks since the eighteen-eighties.' It marked 'the appearance of a new spirit in the money market'.[10]

It has frequently been the subject of awed comment that by the end of the nineteenth century the Bank was able to exercise control over the money market despite the strait jacket of the Bank Charter Act of 1844, and while using only a 'thin film of gold' as reserve. The explanation for the survival of the Act lies in the greatly increased use of the cheque as against the sovereign or the Bank of England note as a means of payment. By the 1890s more than 95 per cent (by value) of payments were made by cheque. On the other hand, increased gold supplies from California and Australia, in the 1850s, and from South Africa and the Klondike after the 1890s, helped to avert a breakdown of the metallic reserve of the Bank.

Thus by the outbreak of the First World War the Bank was the undisputed leader of the London money market even though it conducted but a small fraction of the volume of business undertaken by the joint-stock banks and discount houses. Such a position had been brought about through the gradual growth of confidence in its leadership and the gradual modification of its business policies within the framework of the Bank Charter Act.

d **The banks and the provision of capital for industry** Owing largely to the longer period of growth of industry and the greater abundance of capital resources in relation to demand, British industrial firms were less dependent on the banks for their long-term capital needs than were industrial concerns in America. In the early days of British industrialization the country banks had made long-term advances to newly established firms from time to time. Thus the banking firm of Parr, Lyons and Co. of Warrington aided the file-making business of Peter Stubbs (mainly by means of overdrafts), and Arkwright's cotton spinning factories obtained some of their capital from Toplis's bank, of which Arkwright himself was one of the partners. But throughout the nineteenth century the principal function of the banks was to 'finance the *movement* of goods and the holding of stocks rather than their production'.[11] The situation was well described by the historian of the English capital market when he wrote:

A substantial part of the free resources of the country is placed under the control of the banks in the form of lodgements on current and deposit accounts. The greater part of this, it would seem, is employed in financing commercial processes originating in the continuous replacement of the streams of materials passing through the successive stages of production. Some part of the remainder is applied each year to the extension of stocks, machinery, plant and buildings.

For more substantial capital improvements the banks were not an important source of supply:

The predominant methods by which business men in this country are supplied with the resources they require to extend their operations are those where the economic distance to be bridged is small, where capital has not 'far to go', where the sources of demand and supply are connected by personal or business ties, or in the limit are identical. It is supplied mainly . . . by way of partnership, in that broad sense of the term in which it includes private joint-stock companies; by way of borrowing from personal and business friends; and, above all, in the form of the persistent re-investment of profits by which small businesses are continually growing into large undertakings in almost all branches of industry and trade.[12]

Even as late as 1914 neither the banks nor the stock exchanges were the principal sources of supply of long-term capital to industry. Although the stock exchanges were the means of mobilization of capital for railways, Government issues, public utilities, and some trading corporations, 'at least half the additions to capital of industrial concerns in Britain came from undistributed profits'.[13]

One major difference between the two countries was that in England capital was, broadly speaking, as easy to obtain in one part of the country as in another. By the 1850s there was a national capital market made possible by the growth of the joint-stock banks and the discount houses, and by the use of the inland bill (now declining in importance) and the cheque. The surplus funds which were available in late autumn from the farming districts, say, of East Anglia, were channelled either through the country banks' London agents or through the branches of the joint-stock banks to industrial Lancashire, Yorkshire, and the Midlands to finance the day-to-day needs of business firms. By contrast, there was no national capital market in America until the 1920s. Before then, capital was more expensive and more difficult to obtain in the South and West than it was in New England and the Middle Atlantic states.[14]

e **London as a centre of international finance**   In 1858 it was correctly asserted that 'the trade of the world could hardly be carried on without the intervention of English credit . . . a man in Boston cannot buy a cargo of tea in Canton without getting a credit from Messrs. Matheson or Messrs. Baring'.[15] Even at that date Britain's involvement in world finance was no novelty. In 1818 the Duke of Richelieu claimed that there were six powers in Europe, 'Great Britain, France, Austria, Prussia, Russia, and the Baring Brothers.'[16]

However, the coming of the ocean-going steamship, the laying of the transatlantic cable in 1866, and the opening of the Suez Canal and the first transcontinental railway in America three years later, greatly increased the opportunities for financing international trade and lending. In the later 1860s the decision of important groups of foreign merchant bankers to make London the centre of their operations for loan and acceptance business helped still more to strengthen its position as 'the undisputed centre of the world's transactions'.[17] After the Franco-Prussian War had undermined the position of the Paris money market, London became the one important free market for buying and selling gold. When Treasury bills became available in the 1870s continental bankers, to an increasing extent, took to holding a stock of bills in London as a quick means of realizing gold in an emergency. Although these developments gave rise to valuable earnings which contributed handsomely to the British balance of payments, they also brought new dangers. By the end of the century the London money market 'had become primarily an instrument of external finance and only secondarily one of domestic finance'.[18] Already in 1873 Walter Bagehot had urged, in his masterpiece *Lombard Street*, that the Bank should carry a larger gold reserve to meet the eventuality of a sudden foreign drain. In 1907 the emergency Bagehot had foreseen was demonstrated when a sudden, greatly increased, demand for gold from America forced up the Bank Rate from $4\frac{1}{2}$-7 per cent within ten days.

Another drawback was that considerations of international finance tended to take precedence over the needs of domestic industry and employment. In 1931 it was pointed out that 'in some respects the city was more highly organized to provide capital to foreign investors than to British industry'.[19] The historian of the steel industry believed that the structure of the British capital market was one of the two chief reasons for the failure to produce new, high capacity, plants in the British steel industry.[20]

Nevertheless the consensus of opinion amongst economists was that the advantage of a situation in which London was the centre of the international Gold Standard far outweighed any drawbacks to British industry. It was a viewpoint which was encouraged by the quick recovery from the crisis of 1907, and the achievement, before 1914, of new records in the volume and value of British overseas trade.

2 America

a **The currency**   Whereas for the greater part of the nineteenth century Britain was on a single (gold) standard, the American Government attempted to maintain a bimetallic one. Although it was held that the double standard would be conducive to a greater stability of prices, it proved impossible to keep both gold and silver in circulation simultaneously, gold being undervalued at the mint, and therefore out of circulation, before 1834; and silver undervalued and tending to disappear from circulation thereafter. The system was abandoned temporarily between 1873 and 1878, and finally after the passing of the Currency (Gold Standard) Act in 1900 when America joined the majority of economically advanced nations on the Gold Standard.

Despite the fact that there was a Federal Mint from 1792 onwards, insufficient coins were minted before the Civil War to meet the monetary needs of the nation. Before 1834 Spanish silver coins and French five franc silver pieces were more frequently used for small payments than were the gold eagles ($10), half eagles, and quarter eagles, or the silver dollars, half dollars, quarter dollars, dimes, and half dimes of the United States Mint. Not until 1857 was a law finally passed ending the legal tender status of all foreign coins. The consequence of the coexistence of these different coinages was that it was necessary to make calculations in three currencies, one decimal, another based on eighths, quarters, and halves, and a third on twelfths and twentieths. Even so, it is doubtful whether such incentives to agility in mental arithmetic proved such 'an inevitable drag on business' as some historians have claimed.[21]

To make up for the shortage of coin and to earn themselves a profit, the banks chartered by the Comptrollers in the states printed such a large variety of notes of differing denominations that they created an environment ideally suited to the operations of the counterfeiter. In 1862 it was reported that the nation's 1,500 banks produced 253 different kinds of notes for which no known counterfeits existed; but unauthorized imitations of 1,861 types of notes, and improper alterations to a further 3,039 issues were known. In addition, 1,685 kinds of purely spurious notes were in circulation. Each banker and merchant was thus obliged to make frequent reference to works like Bicknell's 'Counterfeit Detector and Bank Note List' to glean some guidance on the authenticity and market value of the notes that were offered to him. But this was not the only precaution taken: 'He scrutinized the worn and dirty scrap for two or three minutes, regarding it as more probably "good" if it was worn and dirty than if it was clean, because these features were proof of a long and successful circulation. He turned it up to the light and looked through it, because it was the custom of banks to file the notes on slender pins which made holes through them. If there were many such holes the note had been often in banks and its genuineness was ratified.'[22]

The outbreak of the Civil War, with the greatly increased demands of the Government for goods and services and the comparatively sudden disappearance from circulation of over $25m. of silver, produced an acute shortage of small currency. Although the Treasury began issuing notes of $5 denomination and above, known subsequently as 'Greenbacks', there was still a shortage of smaller denominations. Indeed, the public began using postage stamps for small payments. On 17 July 1862 the Union Government announced that from 1 August U.S. postage stamps were to be receivable for Government dues in amounts less than $5 and redeemable in Greenbacks at all Treasury offices. Later ungummed 'stamps' were issued as notes, but from October 1863 this, 'the worst form of currency ever used by a civilized people',[23] was gradually withdrawn from circulation.

Under the National Bank Act of 1863 the federally authorized National Banks began the issue of a uniform paper currency—national bank notes—which it was hoped would quickly supersede the issues of the state chartered banks. However, it was not until Congress imposed a tax of 10 per cent on the issues of state banks after 1865 that the new notes rapidly replaced all rival paper currencies. After the passing of the Federal Reserve Act in 1913, Federal Reserve notes and the notes of the twelve Federal Reserve Banks circulated alongside the currency of the National Banks, but after 1935 arrangements were made for the more rapid replacements of the National Banks issues by Federal Reserve notes which had become, by the end of the decade, the only important paper money in the country.

Lest the student of the American currency of the nineteenth century should become too obsessed with its inconvenience to the business community, the opinion of a modern historian is worth quoting: 'Economists nowadays are prone to stress the importance of a sound and stable money . . . for both developed and developing nations. Yet it is a striking fact that virtually every example on record of rapid and successful industrialization has taken place in spite of a grossly deficient or badly disorganized hand to hand circulation.'[24]

In particular, it is worth remembering that the British currency was in an unsatisfactory state in the closing years of the eighteenth century during the early stages of rapid industrialization, and that the deficiences of the American currency did not preclude a rate of economic growth much more rapid than that of Britain's.

b **Commercial banking**   Apart from the First (1791-1811) and Second (1816-36) Banks of the United States, which fulfilled some of the functions of central banks, there were two chief types of commercial bank before the Civil War: the state chartered banks, and the non-corporate banks which existed under free banking laws. The attitude of state legislatures ranged from extreme laxity of regulation to outright prohibition of all banking operations. In 1852 banking was completely illegal in seven states, was a state monopoly in Indiana and Missouri, and in New York was permitted without the need of special incorporation under 'free banking' laws. Although by 1862 fourteen states had followed the example of New York, most states adhered to the plan of granting charters of incorporation to banks functioning within their frontiers. Some states, such as Louisiana, had a well-deserved reputation for their sound banking laws.

Commercial interests in America displayed a remarkable ingenuity in finding somehow a means of payment for goods and services, despite the absence of a reliable currency and the intermittent prohibition of all banking activities in a number of states. Thus, in the 1850s, at a time when the government both of Wisconsin and of Illinois declared the practice of banking illegal, the deposit certificates of the Wisconsin Marine and Fire Insurance Company were circulated as money.

Partly in consequence of the inadequacy of the metallic reserve, 'wildcat' banking became a well-known feature of American business in the nineteenth century. The notes of such banks were redeemable only at the head offices, which were deliberately located 'out among the wild cats' to ensure that very few claims for metallic currency were in fact made, even though the notes circulated only at a substantial discount. The excessive fiduciary issues of such banks, and the laxity of control exercised over them by some of the states, have both been subject to criticism. 'There is little doubt, however, that the easy money policy that found almost universal expression in banking institutions led to a more rapid economic development than would have occurred under a more conservative regime. The ability to create credit without much regard to specie reserves made

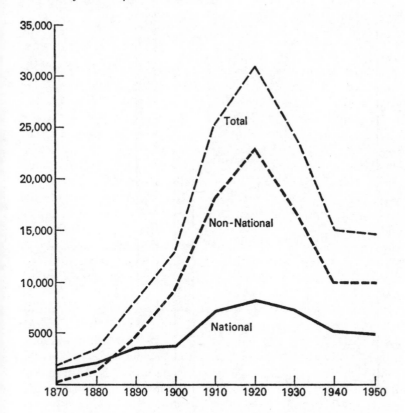

Figure 23. U.S.A.: banking. Number of national and non-national
banks 1870-1950

possible the promotion of large numbers of undertakings that would
otherwise have been delayed. This development did not take place
without some losses of economic efficiency.'[25]

If wildcat banking was not a wholly unmitigated evil, the virtual
absence of branch banking in America was an undoubted element of
insecurity. In 1900 only eighty-seven of the 13,053 banks in the
country were not unit banks, and they possessed between them but
119 branch offices. It was assumed that the National Banks set up
from 1863 had no right to establish branches, and it was not until
November 1918 that Congress passed the Consolidation Act, for the
first time permitting the merger of two or more National Banks.

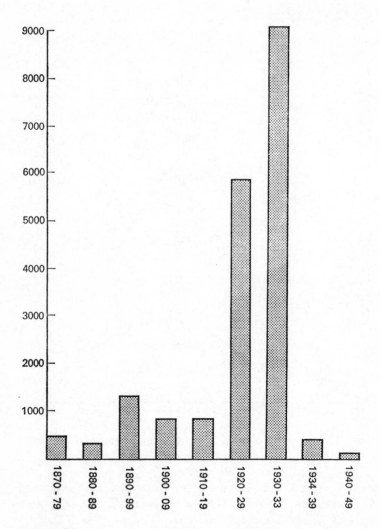

Figure 24. U.S.A.: banking. Number of bank suspensions
1870-9–1940-9

The McFadden Branch Banking Act in 1927 authorized the establishment of branches by the National Banks, provided that the states
within which they functioned allowed it. Since branch banking was
specifically forbidden in twenty-two states, it is not surprising that
progress was not sufficiently rapid to prevent the widespread failures

characteristic of a unit banking system. Between 1864 and 1933 no less than 15,110 banks closed their doors.

TABLE 17

Branch banking in the United States 1900-50

	No. of banks operating branches	No. of branches
1900	87	119
1910	292	548
1920	530	1,281
1930	751	3,522
1940	1,040	3,531
1950	1,354	4,721

Source: *Historical Statistics of the United States, Colonial Times to 1957.*

In the absence of a branch banking network the banks in the country deposited spare funds with 'correspondent' banks in major commercial cities. Under the National Banking Act of 1864 country banks given a National charter were permitted to keep part of their reserves in National Banks in any one of seventeen major commercial cities. National Banks in the City of New York gained the lion's share of such reserves. Though designed, in part, to increase security, the arrangement tended rather to aggravate financial panics. To attract custom the 'correspondent' banks undertook to pay interest on the deposits they received, an obligation which made imperative the profitable employment of idle funds by lending money at call or short notice largely for speculative investment. In the late summer and fall when funds were required to move the harvest, large withdrawals of country bank deposits embarrassed the correspondent banks. The financial panics of 1873, 1884, 1893, and 1907 were aggravated by such deposit withdrawals following upon earlier speculative manias.

By simplifying ,the clearance of notes and cheques, clearing agencies such as the Suffolk Bank in Boston (1815-58), the New York Clearing House (from 1853), and the five others in existence in 1860, helped to overcome some of the disadvantages of unit banking.

c **Central banking** Between 1836 and 1914 the United States possessed no central bank. The two experiments made between 1791 and 1836 though, in the main, well-conducted and largely successful, aroused the resentment of banking interests in the states. After President Jackson had vetoed the renewal of the Charter of the Second Bank of the United States in 1832, Government funds were transferred to a number of 'pet' state banks which, however, used them speculatively in the subsequent boom of 1833-7. The losses in the commercial crisis which followed helped to convince the Federal Government to withdraw its funds entirely from the influence of the commercial banks. Under the Independent Treasury System in continuous operation from 1847 to 1921, Government funds, including receipts from taxes, were kept in a series of 'strong boxes' distributed throughout the country. Although one historian of the Independent Treasury considered that, given the existence of 'irresponsible' state banks, its establishment was justifiable and necessary for the safe keeping of Government funds,[26] the system operated to tighten credit unduly in times of Government revenue surpluses—which included most of the years between 1865 and 1913. On the other hand, in times of trade depression, the requirement that government dues should be paid in specie, tended to delay recovery by making more difficult the expansion of credit. As customs receipts rose between May and September each year and specie was paid in to the Independent Treasuries, the banks became less able to meet the usual fall demand for money to move the crops. In times of crisis, therefore, it proved necessary for the Treasury Department to come to the aid of the banks by the purchase of Government bonds and the depositing of surplus funds. The principle of the scheme was further undermined in the National Banking Act of 1863, a product of the Civil War emergency, which allowed National Banks to act as depositories of public moneys and as agents of the Government.

With the chartering of National Banks by the Comptroller of the Currency and Secretary of the Treasury under the Act of 1863, the Government hoped that the new institutions would outnumber and dominate the state banks. Under the blow of the heavy tax on state bank-note issues, it appeared for a time as if this was likely to happen. But the success of the National Bank-notes tended to divert the state banks towards deposit banking—a field in which they enjoyed commercial advantages over the National Banks, especially in real estate loans, and in 1892 they became more numerous than the National Banks for the first time since 1865. They have retained their lead both in numbers and in volume of deposits—though not always in capital assets—ever since. Thus there was no prospect of effective central control over banking policy via the National Banks.

TABLE 18

Banks in the United States:
Number and assets in millions of dollars 1870-1950

	National banks	Assets $m	Non- national	Assets $m
1870	1,612	1,566	325 (est.)	215
1880	2,076	2,036	1,279	1,364
1890	3,484	3,062	4,717	3,296
1900	3,731	1,944	9,322	6,444
1910	7,138	9,892	18,013	13,030
1920	8,024	23,267	22,885	29,827
1930	7,247	28,828	17,026	45,462
1940	5,164	36,816	9,912	42,913
1950	4,971	89,691	9,705	89,474

Source: *Historical Statistics of the U.S., Colonial Times to 1957*. pp. 62-8.

Nor was there much prospect of profiting from the English experience, regarded as different and irrelevant. British and American trade union leaders exchanged views: but amongst American bankers 'there is little evidence of interchange of ideas'[27] with their opposite numbers in Britain before the First World War. Rather it was the bitter experience of wholesale bank failures in the commercial crises of 1893 and 1907 that helped to convince both the banking community and Congress of the need for reform. The panic of 1907, which did most to stimulate criticism, has been described as an 'exclusively banking' one. Foreign bankers at this time were coming to regard the United States as 'a great financial nuisance'.[28]

In its *Report*, the National Monetary Commission which made a full investigation into the American banking system between 1908 and 1912, deplored the inelasticity of the note issue; the inadequacy of the cheque clearing system; the helplessness of individual banks in meeting emergencies in the absence of branch banking; and the drawbacks of a system in which the Federal Treasury operated independently of the banking system.

Congress had to reconcile the evident need for a central bank to exercise a more flexible control over currency and credit with the fear of monopoly and invasion of states' rights by an all-powerful federal body. Under the Federal Reserve Act of 1913 it provided for the establishment of up to twelve regional Federal Reserve Banks, to which all National Banks were obliged, and all state banks invited, to affiliate. The member banks provided the capital and a majority of the directorate of the Federal Reserve Bank of their district. To supervise the whole there was set up the Federal Reserve Board of seven members: the Secretary of the Treasury, the Comptroller of the Currency, and five other persons nominated by the President.

In so far as the Act made possible a more elastic currency, the Federal Reserve Notes, established a central control of discount rate and gold supply, and provided a flexible reserve of credit (rather than a pool of member banks' money), it marked an important advance towards effective central banking. The Federal Reserve Bank finally replaced the Independent Treasuries as the depository for Government funds. But the Act was weak in failing to provide stronger inducements to the state banks to affiliate, and by 1917 only thirty-seven of them had done so. It did nothing directly to encourage the growth of branch banking. The plan to relate the issue of Federal Reserve Notes to the value of good commercial bills discounted encouraged undue expansion of credit in commercial booms and an undesirable contraction of credit during recessions. Although the United States now had a central bank, the record crop of bank failures in the years 1929-33 was sufficient evidence of the inadequacy of the new instrument and of the policies for central bank control over credit. Not until the New Deal in the 1930s were these shortcomings made good.

d **The banks and the provision of capital for industry** During the nineteenth century in America, as in Britain, the greater part of the long-term capital needs of industry was met by the ploughing back of profits. The banks' principal task was to find the short-term funds for financing day-to-day production and the movement of goods. Apart from the Civil War period, the American businessman went virtually untaxed, there being no permanent income tax until after 1913. However, both the problems of westward expansion and the newness of much of the nation's industry made the problem of raising an adequate supply of capital a more difficult one than it was in Britain. 'The longer a firm exists before it is forced to obtain additional capital, the more likely it is that it can generate the necessary finance internally. Other things being equal, therefore, the longer and more continuous industrial history of Britain should have made it easier for firms to acquire finance without resorting to the capital markets. Although the evidence is sketchy what there is does suggest that this was, in fact, the case. . . . The histories of indivi- dual English firms show a much more marked dependence upon internal finance than their American counterparts.'[29]

America did not have the benefit of a truly national capital market until well into the twentieth century. As late as the 1870s there still existed a number of relatively small and partially isolated short-term markets. The rates charged for the borrowing of capital varied as much as 10 per cent between New York and California. There is also much evidence that the immobility of capital seriously retarded economic growth in the South.

Because of the relative shortage of long-term capital for American industry in the second half of the nineteenth century (even though most industries were for the greater part self-financed) there was a greater dependence on bank loans, particularly in the case of the newer industries, than was the case in Britain. In the early 1860s, John D. Rockefeller 'wore out the knees of his pants begging credit of the banks'.[30] Later, the Standard Oil Company which he formed had financial backing from the Cleveland banks, the Merchant National, Commercial National, and Second National. Likewise, the Aluminum Company of America was given loans by the banker, Andrew Mellon, who thereby acquired a controlling interest in the company's stock. Most of the successful meat packing firms, includ- ing Armours and Swifts, were dependent on bank loans for capital during their early years. Between the Civil War and the First World War banks provided $1,000m. of the $10,000m. of railroad bonds raised. Before about 1880 the state banks were not directly important as a source of farm mortgage credit but they frequently acted as agents for wealthy individuals, insurance companies, and savings banks from the more affluent regions such as the North East.

From the mid 1870s onwards a new class of investment bankers, of whom J. P. Morgan was an outstanding example, played an important part in the refinancing and consolidation of major industries. Notable among these undertakings was the reorganization of the Erie and other railroads in the 1890s, and the formation of the United States Steel Corporation in 1901. Some of these investment houses had branched out into international finance before 1914, but this aspect of banking became much more important after the outbreak of the First World War.

As industry became longer established and wealthier its dependence on the banks for long-term capital declined. As early as 1885 Rockefeller declared that Standard Oil 'should have its own money and be independent of the street', but most large industrial firms approached financial independence at a later date. In the twentieth century the large majority of American firms no longer relied on banks or even the stock market for new capital. Between 1900 and 1956 ploughed-back profits formed nearly 90 per cent of gross capital formation.[31]

3 Summary and conclusions

By the middle of the nineteenth century Britain had been on the gold standard for three decades and the gold sovereign was internationally recognized as a much prized currency, widely acceptable, and of stable value. At the same time America depended on a hotchpotch of currencies including French and Spanish coins, the coinage of the United States Mint, and the notes, of greatly varying reliability, of around 1,500 commercial banks. Whilst such a bewildering situation made commercial calculations more complicated and provided ample opportunity for fraud, there is no evidence that it seriously impeded the rate of economic growth. In any case, in both countries notes and coin paled into relative insignificance as a means of payment compared with cheques, which were used for making over 90 per cent of payments (by value) in 1890.

In both countries a rapidly increasing proportion of commercial banking was being undertaken by joint-stock banks, though throughout the century the English country (partnership) banks played a more significant part in commercial transactions than did the unincorporated banks in America. Joint-stock banks were legal throughout Britain from 1833 onwards. In America there were widespread differences between the states but banks either functioned under 'free banking' laws of the state legislatures or under charters granted by the state Comptroller of the Currency. In both countries banking competition encouraged the practice of giving generous deposit allowances. This was unfortunate as it encouraged rash lending and the circulation of bills of dubious or even fraudulent character. It is a measure of the earlier maturity of British banking that the practice was brought to an end in 1877 by agreement among the joint-stock banks, whilst in America the practice was only brought to an end after legislation banning it had been passed in 1933.

For political and constitutional reasons, as well as commercial ones, there was very little branch banking in America until the 1930s. By contrast the 'Big Five' English joint-stock banks had established an impressive network of branches by 1914, and the situation was one of much greater security than existed across the Atlantic. Furthermore, the English banks in the course of the second half of the nineteenth century looked upon the Bank of England as lender of last resort. Until 1914 American banks had no comparable refuge.

In the third quarter of the nineteenth century the banking and commercial community in Britain was learning how to make proper use of the central bank already in its midst. No new legislation was needed to modify the practices of the Bank of England in order to make them those of a modern lender of last resort. The banking and commercial community in America, meanwhile, had yet to learn that such an institution was needed for the smooth working of the country's banking system. The lesson was not fully learnt after the financial panic of 1907 had brought many failures, and the National Monetary Commission had exposed the manifold weaknesses of the banking system. The Federal Reserve Bank in 1914 possessed some of the powers of a central bank but it lacked such control over the money market as was possessed by the Bank of England in London. It was twenty years before new legislation filled in some very important gaps in the powers exercised by the Federal Reserve Board (later renamed the Board of Governors of the Federal Reserve Bank.)

In both countries the principal task of the commercial banks has been to meet the short-term needs of industry for the day-to-day production and movement of goods. The long term capital needs of industry were generally met by the ploughing back of profits, by bringing in wealthy partners, or by making private arrangements for loans. However, since most American industry was more recently established and had had a shorter time in which to accumulate capital it was to a greater extent, in its formative period, dependent on long-term loans from the banks. This dependence was overcome in the case of most industries by the early years of the present century.

Notes

1 NEWMARCH, WILLIAM, quoted in J. H. Clapham, *Economic History of Modern Britain* II (Cambridge, 1932), p. 234.

2 *Banking and Trade Financing in the United Kingdom*, U.S. Dept. of Commerce Trade Information Bulletin No. 636, p. 10.

3 AVEBURY, LORD, quoted in Clapham, *op. cit.* I (Cambridge, 1926), p. 521.

4 Quoted in FETTER, F. W., *The Development of British Monetary Orthodoxy, 1797-1875* (Cambridge, Mass., 1965), p. 176.

5 CLAPHAM, *op. cit.*, I, p. 525.

6 MORGAN, E. V., *The Theory and Practice of Central Banking 1797-1913* (Cambridge, 1943), p. 192.

7 SAYERS, R. S., *Central Banking after Bagehot* (Oxford, 1957), p. 10 *et. seq.*

8 CLAPHAM, *op. cit.*, II, p. 375.

9 KING, W. T. C., *History of the London Discount Market* (1936), p. 243.

10 FEAVEARYEAR, A., *The Pound Sterling* (2nd ed., Oxford, 1963), p. 328; KING, *op. cit.*, p. 308.

11 CHECKLAND, S. G., *The Rise of English Industrial Society 1815-1885* (1964), p. 202.

12 LAVINGTON, F., *The English Capital Market* (1921). pp. 280-1.

13 CAIRNCROSS, A. K., *Home and Foreign Investment, 1870-1914* (Cambridge, 1953), p. 98.

14 DAVIS, LANCE, 'The Capital Markets and Industrial Concentration', *Econ. Hist. Rev.*, 2nd ser. XIX (1966), pp. 256 *et seq.*

15 KING, *op. cit.*, p. 265.

16 HIDY, R. W. and M., *The House of Baring in American Trade and Finance* (Harvard U.P., 1949), p. 64.

17 CHECKLAND, *op. cit.*, p. 205.

18 KING, *op. cit.*, p. 271.

19 *Committee on Finance and Industry* (Macmillan Committee). *Report* (1931), Cmd. 3897, para. 397.

20 BURN, D. L., *Economic History of Steelmaking* (Cambridge, 1940), pp. 250-4.

21 CAROTHERS, NEIL, *Fractional Money* (New York, 1930), p. 83.

22 HEPBURN, A. B., *A History of the Currency of the United States* (New York, 1924), p. 163.

23 CAROTHERS, *op. cit.*, p. 174.

24 RONDO CAMERON, 'Theoretical Bases of a Comparative Study of the Role of Financial Institutions in the Early Stages of Industrialization', *Second International Conference of Economic History* (Paris, 1962), p. 579.

25 WILLIAMSON, H. F., in Williamson (ed.), *The Growth of the American Economy* (1958 ed.), p. 253.

26 KINLEY, D., *The Independent Treasury of the United States* (Boston, 1893), p. 39.

27 MINTS, L. W., *A History of Banking Theory in Great Britain and the United States* (Chicago, 1945), p. 255.

28 STUDENSKI, P. and KROOSS, H., *Financial History of the United States* (New York, 2nd ed., 1963), p. 252.

29 DAVIS, *loc. cit.*, p. 259.

30 TRESCOTT, P. B., *Financing American Enterprise* (New York and Evanston, 1963), p. 72.

31 KUZNETS, S., *Capital in the American Economy: Its Formation and Financing* (Princeton U.P., 1961), p. 264.

Suggestions for further reading

Texts:

ASHWORTH, W., *An Economic History of England 1870-1939* (1960), ch. 7.

JONES, G. P. and POOL, A. G., *A Hundred Years of Economic Development* (1940), ch. 12.

ROBERTSON, R. M., *History of the American Economy* (New York, 2nd ed., 1964), ch. 7, 13, 20.

WILLIAMSON, H. F., *Growth of the American Economy* (Englewood Cliffs, N. J., 2nd ed., 1951), ch. 13, 14, 28, 29.

Specialized works:

FEAVEARYEAR, A., *The Pound Sterling* (2nd ed. revised by E. V. Morgan, Oxford, 1963), ch. 10-13.

DAVIS, LANCE, 'The Capital Markets and Industrial Concentration', *Econ. Hist. Rev.* 2nd ser. XIX (1966).

KING, W. T. C., *History of the London Discount Market* (1936), ch. 4-9.

KUZNETS, S., *Capital in the American Economy: Its Formation and Financing* (Princeton U.P., 1961).

SAYERS, R. S., *Central Banking after Bagehot* (Oxford, 1957).

STUDENSKI, P. and KROOSS, H., *Financial History of the United States* (New York, 2nd ed., 1963).

SYKES, J., *The Amalgamation Movement in English Banking 1825-1924* (1926), pp. 8-93.

TRESCOTT, P. B., *Financing American Enterprise: the Story of Commercial Banking* (New York and Evanston, 1963).

1 Britain: old industries and new

a **The staple industries** In the span of years between 1850 and 1914 British industry, and the British export trade, were dominated by the great staple industries, cotton, coal, iron and steel, and shipbuilding. At their peak in 1913 these four industries employed some two million people, or over 10 per cent of the working force. The output figures below are evidence of their very considerable growth and importance:

TABLE 19

Output of British staple industries 1850-4–1909-13

	Cotton Raw cotton consumption	*Coal* Output	*Iron/steel* Output of pig iron	*Shipbuilding* Sailing ships	Steam-ships
	m. lb	*m. tons*	*'000 tons*	*'000 tons*	*'000 tons*
1850-4	705	62·5 (1854-8)	3,398 (1854-8)	134·1	115·4
1870-4	1,198	121·3	6,378	100·9	295·5
1890-4	1,583	180·3	7,285	155·6	461·5
1909-13	1,934	269·6	9,616	28·5	751·9

Source: *Abstract of British Historical Statistics*

These four industries, in many ways the basis of industrial change before 1880, were by the end of the nineteenth century beginning to show signs of hardening of the arteries. Cotton was dominated by small family firms, and in 1884 under a fifth of the 1,642 firms in spinning and weaving were organized as joint-stock companies. Even when joint-stock organization became the rule, it was the private form that was often adopted, which meant that family control was

retained and the firm was debarred from raising new capital from
the market. Techniques were slow to change, with only limited
adoption of ring-spinning, automatic looms, and electric power. It
was true, however, that the older forms of machinery were better
suited to the medium and fine yarns and cloths in which Lancashire
and its highly skilled operatives specialized, unlike the concentration
elsewhere, particularly in America, on the coarser cloths with
machines that made possible a higher output from a less skilled
labour force. The continued availability of overseas markets for the
Lancashire products, despite tariffs and the growth of cotton manufacturing in the United States, Europe, India, Japan, and elsewhere,
perhaps encouraged a degree of complacency, and the big expansion
of Lancashire's capacity in 1905-7 (when ninety-five new mills were
added in two years), still made use of the conventional methods. In
1913 cotton accounted for nearly a quarter of Britain's home-produced exports and employed some 620,000 people.[1]

Coal-mining was, of course, the rock on which British industrial
power rested. Originally concerned almost entirely with the home
market, after 1850 the increase in the world-wide use of steam
power and the widespread growth of steam shipping, together with
the British mines' easy access to ports and cheap shipping, encouraged the development of a large export trade. Exports took 15
per cent of total production in 1880, and about a third by 1913.
While new mines were opened and output grew rapidly, the multiplicity of coal companies made for inefficient exploitation of the
fields; and with the working-out of the better seams and the primi-
tive nature of coal-getting methods and crude systems of underground haulage, productivity per man-year declined. From a peak of
319 tons in the 1880s it fell to only 257 tons in 1908-13. Nevertheless, down to the First World War coal kept its dominance as the
source of power in the British economy, with electricity (really a
more economical use of coal) and oil obtaining no more than a toe-
hold in the market. Employment in coal rose rapidly as output increased, rising from 687,000 in 1898 to 1,107,000 in 1913, and it has
been argued that the falling productivity of the miners owed something to this large influx of new, inexperienced labour, as well as to
some reduction in the miners' effort and an increase in voluntary
absenteeism.[2]

The great inventions of Bessemer, Siemens, and Gilchrist-Thomas revolutionized steel-making in the second half of the nineteenth century, although the conservatism of British ironmasters delayed the adoption of the Bessemer and Siemens processes, and the ease of importing high-grade ores obviated the use of the Gilchrist-Thomas process which was popular with continental steel-makers using local low-grade ores. Cheap steel replaced iron in ships, railways, bridges, engines, and many other uses, and output grew rapidly, although much less rapidly than in Germany and the United States. British firms were as slow to adopt the post-1880 technical improvements as they had been to accept the earlier ones, and the industry, in common with many others in Britain, remained one where practical experience was more highly regarded than scientific knowledge.

'By 1914 Britain was producing less than half as much steel as Germany and less than one quarter as much as the United States. . . . Moreover, whereas in 1875 Britain had imported but 150,000 tons of iron and steel, a quantity equivalent to about 8 per cent of her exports of iron and steel at that time, by 1913 her imports, amounting to 2,231,000 tons, were equivalent to 45 per cent of her exports. Almost incredibly, on the eve of the First World War, Britain had become the world's largest importer of iron and steel.'[3] The most recent expert opinions hold that Britain's technological lag and relatively high costs of production were the consequence of slow growth and foreign competition in the home market, rather than the deficiencies of British steelmakers.[4] As an exporter, 'Britain held her share of the world trade in iron and steel reasonably well to 1909. . . . The most disappointing period was to come when from 1909 to 1913 . . . (Britain's) share of world exports fell from 40 per cent to 33·8 per cent and in 1912 and 1913 for the first time German exports exceeded British.'[5]

Like iron and steel, shipbuilding saw a revolution in the nature of the main product in the second half of the nineteenth century, as iron, and later steel, steamships replaced the sailing vessel. Long experience in the use of steam power, technical improvements in marine propulsion, developed coal and iron industries, together with a large overseas trade, enabled British shipbuilding and shipowners to assume a position of world dominance which was very largely maintained until the First World War. Between 1860 and 1911 Britain's share of total world merchant shipping tonnage remained at some 33-36 per cent, although in this period world tonnage rose from

13·3m. tons to 34·6m. tons. Owing to a policy of selling off older ships to other nations, 'by the early twentieth century British ships were carrying around one-half the seaborne trade of the world whilst in the twenty-five years before the war we built two-thirds of the new ships that were launched.'[6]

In the 1870s there appeared the triple-expansion engine, and new pioneering engineering firms developed high-speed engines for powering hydraulic capstans, force pumps, air compressors, etc., 'with a degree of standardization and inter-changeability which was superior to anything known in the United States'. The supreme advance was the Parsons steam turbine (together with the Parsons generator designed to match the high speed of the turbine), a development which led to the use of the turbine for large-scale generating purposes, and eventually for ship propulsion. The major shipbuilding firms, however, neglected the diesel engine which appeared at about the same time as the Parsons steam turbine was used for ships, partly through conservatism and partly because the construction of diesel engines required a higher degree of technical skill than did steam engines.[7]

b **The new industries**   Alongside these large and well-established industries, and others such as building, railways, and the clothing trades, some young and as yet fairly insignificant newcomers were appearing. By 1913 the invention of the internal combustion engine had led to a considerable number of small firms producing the modest total of 34,000 motor-cars a year for the custom of the well-to-do, and at that date some 260,000 vehicles were licensed. Many of the early motor firms developed from the making or repair of bicycles, a new industry of the 1880s, but others sprang from the manufacture of sewing machines and various branches of engineering. There was a high failure rate, and few firms developed as large producers. The majority were specialists in highly individual vehicles, with an emphasis on technical perfection rather than large-scale production. Labour productivity was low, and the industry lagged about five years behind American output and methods. 'Up to 1914 no British firm managed to exceed one car per man per annum. The largest, Wolseley, in 1913 used 4,000 workers for 3,000 cars and Austin with about 1,900 workers must have averaged about the same.'[8]

The later nineteenth century was a great age for new methods of production, a greater range of products, and greater use of by-products (e.g. fertilizers) in chemicals. Advances in chemicals were important in cheapening paper (and thus, with improved printing methods, helped to create the popular press), but the developments of artificial textiles and plastics were mainly important only after 1920. Chemical knowledge lay behind the making of alloys and hardened steels for use in high-speed machine tools and armaments, and was basic also to the rubber industry, with its growing range of products from clothing and footwear to tyres and fittings for railway rolling stock.

By 1913 Britain was the third most important producer of chemicals after the United States and Germany, producing 11 per cent of all chemicals compared with 34 per cent for the United States and 24 per cent for Germany. Britain produced some 50 per cent of soda-ash, 13 per cent of sulphuric acid, and 12 per cent of chemical nitrogen, but only 3 per cent of dyestuffs. Total British output (by volume) rose by 48 per cent between 1900 and 1913, and the labour force climbed from 81,000 in 1881 to 201,000 in 1911, but in organic chemicals and electro-chemicals Britain lost ground to America and Germany. The technological record was a mixed one: conservatism in some fields such as the Leblanc soda industry, synthetic dyestuffs, and super-phosphates, was offset by progressiveness in soaps, paints, some fertilizers and heavy chemicals, coal-tar intermediates, and explosives. Exports of chemicals grew more slowly than total exports after the 1870s, while imports increased faster than total imports, reflecting in part national specialization within chemicals, and Britain's neglect of research and development and a concentration on products that were growing only slowly in international trade.[9]

In some other new fields—electricity generation and electrical engineering, and scientific and optical instruments, for example—Britain also tended to lag behind. This, however, was not necessarily a sign of failing enterprise and industrial conservatism. In each case there were specific if not entirely convincing reasons: a comprehensive system of railways and urban public transport made the motor-car a luxury rather than a necessity; cheap coal, and the widespread use of gas for lighting and cooking, limited the market for electricity; dyestuffs and instruments could be readily imported from Germany.

The First World War did much to change this situation, and inter-war conditions made for rapid growth in these and other industries. Nevertheless, the relatively slow development in Britain before 1914 of industries that grew much more rapidly elsewhere does raise the question of the influence exerted by an economy whose general rate of growth had slowed down, a question which we take up in a later section.

2 The United States: the rise of a great industrial power

a **Industrial growth before the Civil War**   In 1850 the American economy was predominantly concerned with primary production and over 60 per cent of the labour force was engaged in agriculture. By 1910 the proportion in agriculture had fallen to 30 per cent, while employment in manufacturing, mining, and building had come to account for about the same proportion of the labour force: in the interim the United States had become easily the world's leading industrial nation, with nearly 36 per cent of world manufacturing output. Estimates of manufacturing production show a six-fold increase between 1860 and the end of the century, and a further doubling between then and 1913.[10] Between 1870 and 1920 United States manufacturing output rose over ten-fold, while the corresponding figure for the United Kingdom showed a less than three-fold increase.[11] These are the measures of the enormously rapid industrialization of the economy.

The process had in fact begun in the 1830s, and by 1860 the United States was already the world's second most important industrial power. This early development was based partly on the processing of a wide variety of agricultural produce and timber, and partly on the manufacture of a range of industrial commodities in large demand: cotton and woollen goods, boots and shoes, clothing, leather goods. Already in 1860 115,000 people were engaged in the cotton industry, while iron employed as many as 49,000, and the production of machinery 41,000. Cotton textiles were the centre of this early stage of industrial development, influencing the growth of clothing manufacture and the production of textile machinery. Already by 1860 there were nearly 1,100 establishments in cotton manufacturing, housing 5·2m. spindles and consuming 422·7m. lb of cotton.

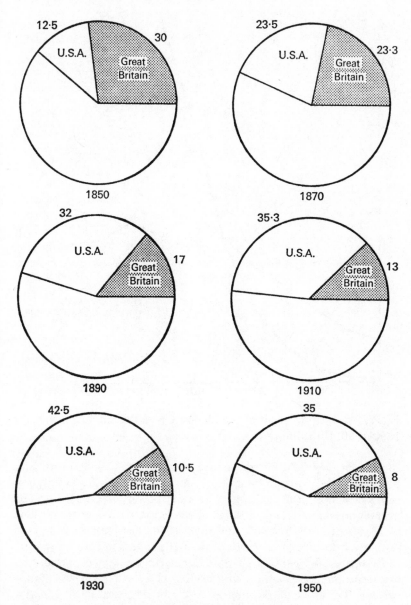

Figure 25. Industrial output: percentages of world total, Great Britain and U.S.A. 1850-1950

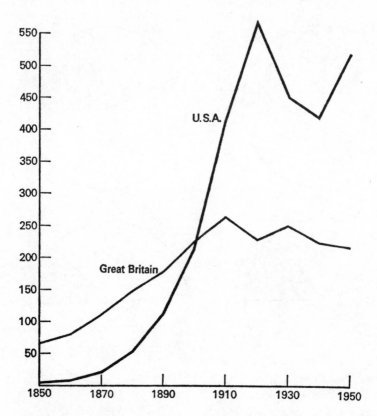

Figure 26. Bituminous coal production Great Britain and U.S.A.
1850-1950, (in millions of tons)

The development of an industrial complex in the north-east
depended partly on the location of natural resources (especially for
iron production), the availability of water power, and the growth of
near-by markets. The population of the North-east rose from 3·9m.
in 1810 to 11·4m. by 1860, and until 1850 represented the largest
(although declining) proportion of total population: 54·6 per cent
in 1810, and 36·5 per cent in 1860. Furthermore, large urban centres
of consumption appeared in the leading cities of New York, Philadelphia, Boston, and Baltimore. Also important was the concentration in the North-east of the shipping and foreign trade markets.
These provided the basis of a distribution network for home-pro-

Figure 27. Pig iron production Great Britain and U.S.A. 1850-1950, (in millions of tons)

duced goods as well as imports, and the ports of the North-east were also the centres of immigration and hence of a supply of (largely unskilled) labour. In the 1840s there was a rapid expansion of markets through transport developments, and the great increase in the eastward flow of western produce forced eastern farmers of marginal lands to seek alternative employment, and so expanded the industrial labour force. The capital market, too, developed in the North-east largely to serve the needs of shipping and trade, but subsequently concerned itself with the development of the textile industry and railroads.[12]

A remarkable feature of the industrial growth was the ability of American industrialists to overcome the handicaps of higher wages and dearer capital. They had the advantages, of course, of closer proximity to the market and a degree of tariff protection, but in the

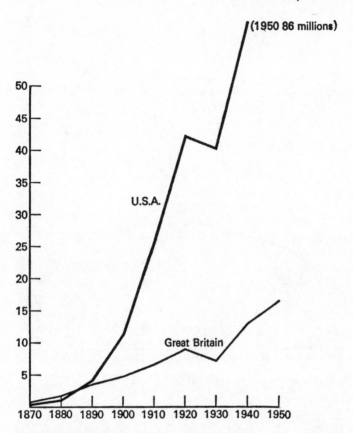

Figure 28. Steel production Great Britain and U.S.A. 1870-1950, (in millions of tons)

main they offset their higher costs by increased productivity. Much American industry was concerned with humdrum everyday commodities in widespread use—screws, files, nails, nuts and bolts, locks, clocks and watches, furniture, agricultural implements, footwear, and clothing—which lent themselves to standardization and mass-production techniques. In the iron industry stoves were as important a product as rails. American industrialists had the initial advantage of being able to draw upon an existing reservoir of techniques as well as the skilled labour and capital of Europe, particularly Britain, and to this they added the further advantages of a high natural capacity

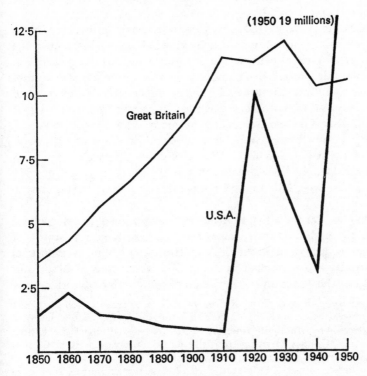

Figure 29. Shipping: registered merchant vessels Great Britain and U.S.A. 1850-1950, (in millions of tons)

for invention, enterprise, and adaptability. By the 1850s America was already leading Britain in mechanization, standardization, and mass production in a variety of fields, as was remarked by two groups of English technicians who visited the country at this time. The growth of the market and the scarcity of labour made for capital-intensive methods of production, and capital itself was economized by intensive operation of machines and rapid incorporation of the latest improvements. 'Because of the scarcity of labour, the introduction of new machines and techniques did not threaten the jobs of workers; without displacing anyone they increased labour productivity, and possibly brought some increases in wages. Numerous changes in production methods originated in the ingenuity of working men themselves.'[13]

Government also played some part in industrial growth by financing transport improvements which extended the market, and by the provision of public utilities and insurance and banking facilities. Particularly important in some areas were the promotional activities of state, county, and municipal governments in the development of inland navigation, turnpikes and road improvements, toll bridges, and railroads. The markets created by the westward expansion could be tapped first through water transport and subsequently railroads. By 1860 the population of the West (including the present-day Midwest) was 11·8m., and exceeded that of the north-east, and in 1853 merchandise worth $94m. was shipped to the western states via the Erie Canal.[14]

It has been argued, too, that the early extension of a basic general education in the western states, together with the appearance of technical colleges and mechanics' institutes, contributed to industrial productivity. The English visitors, Whitworth and Wallis, commented in the 1850s on the provision of compulsory education

by which some three months of ever year must be spent at school by the young operative . . . (and so gave) the foundation for that widespread intelligence which prevails amongst the factory operatives of the United States. . . . Quickly learning from the skilful European artisans thrown amongst them by emigration, or imported as instructors, with minds, as already stated, prepared by sound practical education, the Americans have laid the foundation of a wide-spread system of manufacturing operations, the influence of which cannot be calculated upon, and are daily improving upon the lessons obtained from their older and more experienced compeers of Europe.[15]

And D. C. North has stated that 'the investment in human capital was a critical factor both in innovations and in the relative ease with which they could spread. The primary source of the quality of the labour force and entrepreneurial talent was the widespread free education system in the north-east, although the skills of English and German immigrants were an important supplement.' In 1850 the ratio of the American school population to the total population was 20·4 (New England 25·7), compared with 14·3 for Britain (1851).[16] Education thus gave direction to the pervasive mechanical aptitude and capacity for innovation produced by the economic and physical environment.

b **Industrial growth after the Civil War**   After the Civil War, with
a continued expansion of the home market, industry widened both
geographically and in terms of range of products. The national
market, upon which American industrial growth was concentrated,
trebled in size with a growth of population from 31 to 91m. between 1860 and 1910. Moreover, the real incomes of consumers
were improving rapidly with the growth of manufacturing and the
shift of resources out of primary production into industry. The *per
capita* real product grew from $223 in 1869-73 to $632 in 1912-16.[17]
Estimates of real wages in manufacturing show increases of about
50 per cent for 1860-90, and a further rise of about a third between
1890 and 1913.[18] The growth of the labour force arose from the high
natural rate of population increase plus the massive immigration,
while imports of capital expanded greatly, but even so were dwarfed by
the capital generated by the profits and savings of the home economy.

The great widening in range of the products of American industry
owed much to technology, little to tariffs. Tariff protection was
important in enabling certain industries to obtain an initial grip
upon the home market; the American tinplate industry, for
example, made rapid progress once British imports were kept out by
tariff protection. Within a short space, however, American industry
as a whole was technologically ahead of that of Europe, and with the
natural advantages of abundant raw materials, easier access to the
market, and a closer knowledge of market trends, required no help
from protection. The tariff was more important as a political force
than an economic one. The American steel industry, for example,
soon outstripped its European rivals, and output per man-year in American blast furnaces rose over thirty-fold between 1850 and 1914.[19]

Indeed, by the end of the nineteenth century the British market
was being invaded by American goods. The manufacturing in
Britain of boots and shoes was modernized through American influences, the British bicycle boom was based upon American
machine tools, and the discovery in America of high-speed steel
(1898) gave stimulus to the British machine-tool industry. In electrical engineering the British made use of American patents for arc-
lighting and water-tube boilers, while the early electric trams and
equipment for the underground railways were imported from the
United States. American industry, in fact, developed along two
main lines: the production of iron and steel products, machinery'

machine tools, and railroad equipment to meet the needs of the rapidly changing industrial technology and advances in transport, and secondly the mass-production of consumer goods, including durables such as stoves, cookers, sewing-machines, and iceboxes, to meet the needs of increasingly urbanized consumers enjoying higher living standards. Thus, in terms of the proportion of manufacturing employment engaged, textiles and leather goods fell away, while iron and steel, transport equipment, lumber and lumber products, and printing and publishing, all grew.[20] Coal, the basis of nineteenth-century industry, increased in output from a mere 4m. tons in 1850 to a massive 478m. tons in 1913, when coal mining employed 572,000.

With these changes in industry, and also with the opening of remote resources, the building of railroad repair shops at focal points, and the westward shift of the balance of population, there followed considerable inter-regional shifts in manufacturing employment. New England and the Middle Atlantic regions, which in 1859 had 71·5 per cent of manufacturing employment, had in 1914 only 52·7 per cent, New England's decline being particularly marked. In the same period the Great Lakes region rose from 12·1 to 23·7 per cent, the south-east from 9·8 to 13·1 per cent, the Plains from 2·3 to 5·1 per cent, and the Far West from 1·5 (1869) to 3·3 per cent. Among the more important industrial changes in location was the move of steel-making from the Pittsburgh area in the direction of the Great Lakes, reflecting the decline of coal as a governing force in costs. Cleveland and Chicago became great centres of steel production. And around steel the related processing and manufacturing industries grouped themselves, those producing castings, rails, plates, rods, pipes, tubing, steamships, locomotives, chains, axles, wheels, and eventually motor vehicles. This vast complex of industries formed the base for 'the continuing relative dominance of manufacturing in the area roughly bounded by Chicago on the west, and from Washington to Boston in the east. Even as late as mid-twentieth century, this area still contains 68 per cent of United States' manufacturing and has 43 per cent of the United States' population despite the fact that it has only 7·7 per cent of the total area of the United States.'[21]

Other geographical shifts included the movement of lumbering from the East to the Great Lakes, and then as this region was cut over to the South and the Far West. Petroleum moved out of the Mid-west into the South-west and Far West, while copper mining shifted from Michigan into Montana and Arizona. The industrial progress of the South was a remarkable development in view of its dominant agricultural specialization and unprogressive social structure, and a standard of living that in 1929 was only 47 per cent of the national level. But the attractions of a cheap and tractable labour force were important considerations for northern investors, while the proximity of raw cotton and tobacco, minerals, oil, and timber were obviously significant in the growth of industries concerned with the processing and manufacturing of goods based on these raw materials.

c **The Civil War as a turning-point**   How important was the Civil War as a 'catalyst' of industrial growth? The traditional view was that the war, by stimulating new industries and greater use of machinery, by encouraging entrepreneurs with fat war contracts, and by swelling the growth of industrial capital by means of high wartime profits and inflation, provided industry with a great, far-reaching stimulus. This view has been challenged by T. C. Cochran, who argues that the statistical evidence now available does not support it. In fact the statistical series show that the decade of the Civil War saw either no increases, or less than average increases, in the rate of growth of major industries, and in other indices of the economy. Thus Gallman's figures for value added by manufacture give the following results:

TABLE 20

U.S.: value added by manufacture (constant 1879 dollars)
1839-49–1879-89

Percentage increases

1839-49	155
1849-59	76
1859-69	25
1869-79	82
1879-89	112

It will be seen from these figures that the increase during the Civil War decade was much lower than in any other between the 1840s and the 1880s. Figures for individual industries tend to support this conclusion: the rate of growth of coal output seems to have been little affected by the war, while cotton consumed in manufacturing fell by 6 per cent in the decade of the 1860s. The woollen industry's output was stimulated by the wartime demand for uniforms, but fell again after the war, while the figures for both civil construction and the volume of business activity were below normal in the war years, as also was the level of immigration for obvious reasons. The wartime growth of railroad mileage was also very small, and bank loans were lower in 1866 than in 1860.[22]

Cochran's iconoclastic intervention has sparked off a lively debate. On the one hand, Ralph Andreano has pointed out that Cochran's statistical evidence is not entirely conclusive. The rate of growth of value added by manufacturing was falling in the 1850s—before the war—while the rate for the 1870s was higher than that for the 1850s. Further, figures quoted for the whole decade of the 1860s may be misleading since it remains uncertain whether the poor statistical performance of the decade as a whole was typical of the war years. There is also the question of whether the war had the effect of bringing about significant structural changes in the pattern of industrial output.

On the other hand, the speakers at a 1964 conference on economic change in the Civil War era were unanimous in holding that the effects of the war on a variety of aspects of the economy—commercial banking, foreign investment in American enterprise, the international market for agricultural commodities, government-business relations, science and technology, and the organization of manufacturing and transport—were in general fairly limited. Stress was placed on the emergence of important pre-war trends on which the war had largely only a temporary influence. In particular, Alfred D. Chandler Jr. emphasized the significance of the great development of the railroad system in the 1850s, with its consequences for the centralizing of the investment market in New York City and the development of a new and greatly advanced administrative structure in American business. Together with the telegraph and the steamship, the railroads, he argues, led to the widespread adoption of the factory system with its mass-production methods, which had been gradually developing in a limited number of industries in the preceding two decades.[23]

At present the balance of opinion seems to be against the old view of the Civil War as an important turning-point, but there are many unsolved questions, especially concerning the war's long-term effects. To what extent, for example, did the transfer of incomes to business-men through wartime inflation and the earning of easy profits play a major part in the high rate of industrial growth achieved in the late 1870s and 1880s? To what extent did the banking reforms and tariff increases of the war period aid subsequent business expansion? It is relevant here, Cochran points out, to note that pre-war industrial growth did not appear to be unduly checked by lack of capital, low tariffs, or a weak banking system. In any case, the reforms were only partial: as late as 1875, 40 per cent of the banks were still outside the national bank system; and while the large wartime issues of Federal bonds provided a wider base for credit transactions and a more active security market, few industrial shares were marketed before the 1880s. It is possible, as has been suggested, that the combination of the high protective tariffs brought in during the war, with the expansionist western policy associated with the Homestead Act and the building of western railroads with the aid of Federal land grants, 'turned America inwards' and encouraged a greater attention to the exploitation of America's natural resources, and so reduced the out-ward-looking interest in foreign trade. Such a trend was inevitable, however, given the lure of western resources and the growth of American industrial supremacy on the basis of a rapidly expanding home market and a superior level of technology.

In general, the post-war industrial growth was the logical sequel to the pre-war industrial developments; it does not need the 'catalyst' view of the Civil War to explain it. As Cochran remarks, American industrial growth was already firmly established in the years between 1843 and 1857, 'the first long period without a major depression, after railroads, canals, and steamboats had opened a national market'.[24] And, he reminds us,

those who write of the war creating a national market tied together by railroads under-estimate both the achievements of the two decades before the war and the ongoing trends of the economy. . . . By the late 1850s the United States was a rapidly maturing industrial state with its major cities connected by rail, its major industries selling in a national market and blessed or cursed with financiers, security flotations, stock markets and all the other appurtenances of industrial capitalism.[25]

d **Industrial concentration**   An outstanding feature of the post-war industrial growth was the increasing concentration of the control of business operations in the hands of a limited number of relatively large industrial firms. This tendency towards concentration, first noticeable in railroads, also developed rapidly after 1870 in mining, processing, and manufacturing. Between 1890 and 1905, especially, the rate of consolidation was so rapid as to give rise to the label 'the merger movement'.

It is necessary here to distinguish between the factors affecting the size of individual plant or unit of production, and those which affected the size of business unit, the unit of ownership. The size of the productive unit was influenced primarily by the size of the market, the nature of the product and of the productive process itself, and how far these lent themselves to production methods offering economies of scale with consequent reductions in unit cost. Economies of scale were for technological reasons particularly valuable in steel, shipbuilding and shipping, chemicals, textiles, clothing, and boots and shoes. In America the rapid growth in the size of the market and its homogeneous character, together with an early acceptance of standardization and mass-production methods, made economies of scale more readily attainable than in Europe, and this is one reason why the 'merger movement' went much further in America than elsewhere.

The growth of the business unit and of combinations such as pools and trusts, on the other hand, was largely due to attempts to reduce competition and insecurity, the importance of creating integrated marketing organizations as the market expanded, and attempts to gain some degree of control over prices, and so improve profits. Vertical integration, in which control was extended backward from the manufacturing process to earlier stages of production and the supply of raw materials, and forward to embrace distribution and retail outlets, was undertaken mainly to reduce dependence on other firms and to bring all the stages of production and distribution under a unified control. Horizontal integration, however, involved unified control over a number of originally independent firms all at the same stage of production. This type of combination might be formed in order to reduce competition and raise prices, or where concentration of production in the plants of the most efficient producers reduced costs—the process known as rationalization.[26]

It is significant that in both Britain and America the most active period of amalgamation and combination came in the 1890s at the end of a long period of falling prices and profits, and considerably after the introduction of joint-stock legislation and the widening of the capital market to indicate new classes of investors. In Britain the merger movement was much more limited than in the United States. It was prominent particularly in railways, banking, chemicals, cement, wallpaper, and sewing thread, but in large, old-established industries such as textiles and coal mining there was relatively little sign of large-scale combination. Where there were mergers they were often defensive, as in steel, and as late as 1907 there were still over 100 blast-furnace companies and ninety-five steel firms in Britain. It is noticeable that more of the largest British firms were concerned with the production of consumers' goods, such as beer and tobacco, rather than producers' goods, contrary to the typical American development. Further, and again contrary to the best American business practice, when British firms combined there was a tendency for administrative weaknesses to prejudice the advantages gained by combination. Management remained only loosely central-ized as family control remained, and the organization was cluttered by unnecessarily large numbers of directors retained from the management of the formerly separate businesses that made up the combine. What was often lacking was first-class—and ruthless—administrative ability, a 'Napoleon in organization'.[27]

Even the biggest British firms were much smaller than their American counterparts. As a relevant factor it may be pointed out that the British home market grew less rapidly than did the Ameri-can, the population less than doubling between 1860 and 1910, when the American population nearly trebled in size. Furthermore, the British home market was probably less homogeneous in character than the American, with a more class-conscious society discriminat-ing carefully in the type of goods bought. British staple industries relied heavily on overseas markets in a period when the rate of growth of exports was slowing down. Further, British overseas markets were various and changing, and offered less scope for stan-dardization of products. It may be also that the selling of goods abroad through separate merchant houses removed British indus-trialists from direct contact with their markets and again reduced the possibilities of mass-producing a more limited range of goods.

The dominance in the British staple industries of the small family firm, more concerned with keeping the business in the hands of the original owners than with rapid expansion, was also of significance. As late as 1885 limited companies accounted for only a very small proportion of business organizations of importance. While British firms moved rapidly towards the joint-stock form of organization after 1885 (the number of companies rose from under 10,000 to nearly 63,000 between that date and 1914), in the older industries, as distinct from chemicals, electricity, motor vehicles, and cycles, many small firms adopted the private form of joint-stock company.[28] In this the number of shareholders was limited, and capital could not be raised in the market; equally it was made difficult for outsiders to gain control of the company. Such firms continued to expand by the old practice of ploughing back profits into the business. 'Among such enterprises, some, like Huntley & Palmer, Crosse & Blackwell, J. & J. Colman, Pilkington Brothers, and Harland & Wolff, were extremely efficient and became very large, despite the fact that they were entirely private on the very eve of the First World War. But the great majority remained relatively small family firms, jealous of their heritage. . . .' They were often highly specialized, not only in type of product but also in equipment and entrepreneurial resources, and this contributed to a limited view of market possibilities and formed a barrier to expansion. In 1915 the average capital per British company was only £41,000.[29]

The ability of British firms to find their capital from internal sources is one of the major differences between British and American industrial growth in the later nineteenth century. Lance Davis has pointed out that the growth of American industry, with its great geographical shifts, its development of new products by new firms, and its adoption of large-scale plant offering economies of scale, placed much greater strains on industrial finance than did the less exuberant growth of British industry. Many British firms were of course old-established and the development in Britain of new industrial areas was relatively limited, while a significant proportion of industrial growth took the form of the expansion of already existing industries; further, the changes in technology and the introduction of large-scale production methods were both much less marked than in American industry. British firms had a long tradition of financing expansion from their profits, and a slower rate of growth made it convenient to continue this practice. Moreover, the capital market for industrial securities developed earlier than in the United States where 'there was almost no market for industrial securities until the last few years of the nineteenth century.'[30]

Davis argues that when innovations made the American steel industry capital-intensive, growth depended on the energies of great steel financiers, Carnegie and J. P. Morgan. Similarly, Armour and Swift were able to take advantages of the opportunities of creating a new large-scale meat-packing industry, based on the introduction of the refrigerated railroad car in the 1880s, because of their personal sources of finance and their intimate connections with the commercial banking system. The growth of new technology in the petroleum industry in the 1860s and 1870s offered considerable economies of scale but also posed problems of finance. Again, it was men with personal contacts in banking circles that were first in the field, and thus Rockefeller was able to build up his great Standard Oil empire which, by the 1880s, 'with its almost monopolistic access to the formal capital markets became something of a financial institution itself.'[31]

Chandler argues that the major industrial innovation was in organization and management, the introduction of new integrated methods of industrial organization and marketing techniques, a fundamental change which developed mainly after 1880 and was the product of the industrialists themselves rather than the financiers. He agrees with Davis, however, in seeing the era before 1897 as that in which industrialists with access to finance played a key part in combinations. After 1897, when the emphasis shifted to production of producers' goods, outside bankers and financiers were more in evidence.[32] Of the ninety-two largest combinations in 1904, seventy-eight controlled 50 per cent or more of the industries, fifty-seven controlled 60 per cent or more, and twenty-six controlled 80 per cent or more. Typically these new large firms took the form of holding companies, frequently dominated by the investment bankers and financiers who had taken the lead in their promotion. In the labyrinthine financial manoeuvres there was a strong speculative element: it was almost as if the great speculative urge which had hitherto played so large a part in western expansion and the opening up of new lands and natural resources, had now been transferred to business enterprise, the shift in speculative activity coinciding with the more mature stage now reached by the economy. It is therefore not so extraordinary that the merger movements were concentrated in growth industries, and were especially prominent in periods of rapid growth of the economy as a whole.[33] Thus it appears that it was the more rapid growth of the American economy, and not merely the greater size of the home market, that was the major factor in the disparity between the development of concentration in America and Britain.

The American movement owed something, too, to the Federal patent law, which enabled firms to control through purchase of patents the strategic industrial processes and exclude competitors for considerable periods. Further, the company laws of certain states, such as New Jersey, West Virginia, and Delaware, directly encouraged the establishment of monopolies. To these legal advantages, dominant firms added later monopolistic control of raw materials (frequently obtained through the Federal land laws and land grants), and preferential railroad rates and similar commercial advantages that accrued to the powerful business. Aggressive policies, such as fierce price wars undertaken to drive out weaker competitors, also featured in the rise of the leading firms. Even the Sherman Anti-Trust Act of 1890, which forbade agreements, cartels, and pools, was interpreted by the courts as permitting actual merger or combination of firms. The Sherman Act, originally designed to appease the farmers' hostility to big business, was too vaguely drawn to provide an effective check upon the growth of combinations, and until Theodore Roosevelt's term of office beginning in 1905 little was achieved under its provisions. Even after 1905 the attempts to restore competition by bringing more cases to the courts proved of limited success, despite the forced dissolution of the Standard Oil Company in 1911; and the Clayton Act of 1914 and establishment of the Federal Trade Commission formed no more than feeble extensions of the Sherman Act. Gradually it became clear that the courts would dissolve existing mergers only in exceptional circumstances. Concentration was regarded as an established fact of economic life, and size in itself was not to be regarded as an offence; only where there was evidence of present attempts to exclude competition and 'intent to monopolize' could the law be invoked.

The tariff was once held to be 'the mother of all trusts': this was said specifically of the Dingley Tariff Act of 1897 which imposed an average level of 57 per cent, the highest of the century. However, except for one or two instances, such as the American Sugar Refining Company, it is as difficult to measure the importance of tariff protection for the American merger movement as it is to determine the significance of free trade for the more limited degree of combination in Britain. It is quite clear, however, that in areas where mass-production methods were inappropriate, the market was small and local, or a specialized product was best produced by a small firm, the small business could survive and multiply. In 1880 there were 1·2m. small enterprises, in 1950 as many as 5·4m.; and New York state and New York City, Connecticut, New Jersey, and Pennsylvania were important centres for specialized firms of clothing manufacturers, small metal goods, clocks and watches, hardware, woollens, silk and knitted goods, carpets, hosiery, cameras, electric lamps, and many other varieties of consumer goods. Thus it was possible for small concerns both to fill old roles and find new niches in the consumer goods industries, and many of them, such as Kodak and Elgin, became in time large businesses alongside the giants in steel, railroads, and engineering.

3 The retardation of the British economy

a **The statistics** In recent years historians have concerned themselves with the phenomenon of the retardation of the British economy in the later nineteenth century, and the factors that may lie behind it. That there was some slowing down in the rate of growth is common ground, but the questions of just when the main change in trend occurred, the extent of the deceleration, its significance, and its causes, are the subject of debate.

Undoubtedly the economy was growing in terms of output, employment, and foreign trade, but the indices, while not entirely in agreement, do suggest that a serious fall in the rate of growth occurred either in the 1870s or in the 1890s. R. C. O. Matthews's figures below obscure the question of exactly when the retardation began because he shows only one average rate of growth for the whole period 1856-99. However, his figures do bring out the point that the average rate of growth has been higher since the 1920s than in the half-century before 1914, and that the early years of the twentieth century were particularly bad ones for economic growth:

TABLE 21

Annual percentage rate of U.K. growth of real G.N.P.
1856-99–1948-62

1856-99	2·0
1899-1913	1·1
1924-37	2·3
1948-62	2·5

Source: R. C. O. Matthews, 'Some Aspects of Post-War Growth in the British Economy in Relation to Historical Experience', *Manchester Statistical Society* (Nov. 1964), p. 3.

D. J. Coppock has argued, however, that while the early twentieth century was a period of actual cessation of growth, the break in trend—or 'climacteric'—in the rate of growth came with the secular price fall of the last quarter of the century, that is with the 'Great Depression' of 1873-96. His figures are as follows:

TABLE 22

Average annual rates of growth: Britain 1819-25–1847-53 to
1870-74–1893-97

	%
1819-25–1847-53	3·5
1847-53–1866-74	3·0
1866-74–1890-9	1·9
1870-4–1893-7	1·5

Source: D. J. Coppock, 'British Industrial Growth during the "Great Depression" (1873-96): a Pessimist's View', *Econ. Hist. Rev.* XVII (1964-5), p. 389.

It would appear from these figures, therefore, that both the 1870s and the 1890s saw a shift to a lower rate of growth. But it should be noticed that A. E. Musson has criticized Coppock's figures for over-emphasizing the deceleration during the 'Great Depression' period, since Coppock has compared the boom conditions of the early 1870s with the slump conditions of the middle 1890s. In Musson's view the 'Great Depression' of 1873-96 did not mark such a dramatic change as Coppock suggests: it 'was not a great trough, but part of a longer-term process of deceleration lasting up to the First World War.'[34] This problem of timing is indeed difficult to resolve, and as D. H. Aldcroft has pointed out, 'the retardation or deceleration is by no means continuous or identical for all the main variables.'[35] A selection of the figures will illustrate this point:

TABLE 23

Average annual rates of growth: Britain 1860-1913–1900-13

	Industrial Production	Industrial Productivity	Exports
	%	%	%
1860-1913	2·1	0·7	2·8
1860-70	2·9	1·1	3·2
1870-80	2·3	1·2	2·8
1880-90	1·6	0·5	2·9
1890-1900	2·8	0·2	0·4
1900-13	1·6	0·2	5·4

Source: D. H. Aldcroft (ed.), *The Development of British Industry and Foreign Competition* 1875-1914 (1968), p. 13.

The relatively poor performance of the British economy comes out more strongly when placed against that of the United States and Germany:

TABLE 24

Long-term rates of growth (per cent per annum) 1870-71–1913

	U.K.	U.S.A.	Germany
Industrial Production	2·1	4·7	4·1
Industrial Productivity	0·6	1·5	2·6
Exports (1880-1913)	2·2	4·3	4·3

Source: D. H. Aldcroft (ed.), *The Development of British Industry and Foreign Competition* 1875-1914 (1968), p. 13.

These figures certainly suggest that Britain's economic pace was flagging in the forty years before 1914, but international statistical comparisons are notoriously difficult to make, and percentage changes are particularly suspect when the absolute levels in the base period are widely different. A. E. Musson has argued that especially relevant here is a country's stage of economic growth, and that rates of growth tend to be high when countries are in the early stages of industrialization (as were the United States and Germany), and are naturally lower when they have reached a more mature stage (as had Britain).[36]

It might even be urged that some of the various indices of industrial growth (for example the large increases in output of steel, coal, and textiles), and of employment and real incomes, show there to have been little wrong with the British economy in the later nineteenth century. Total industrial horse power, for example, more than doubled from 900,000 to 2·3m. between 1870 and 1896;[37] unemployment fluctuated in the long term between only 4·2 per cent of the labour force (1894-1913) and 5·7 per cent (1876-95) although it went higher in bad years (e.g. to 7·0 per cent in 1884-9);[38] and some estimates show real incomes as rising by 1·6 per cent per annum between 1860 and 1913.[39] The period was evidently one of progress, but it also seems clear that it was progress at a generally slower rate, and one disturbing factor was the failure of Britain to keep ahead in innovation and technology, and even to lag badly in the adoption of new inventions and techniques developed elsewhere.

b **The causes of retardation**   Among the various factors that have been discussed as relevant to this situation are the size and direction of British overseas trade, the changing direction of capital investment, and the tendency among British industrialists towards complacency and conservatism with a consequent neglect of research and development. Let us briefly take these points in turn.

As world competition in manufactures increased in the later nineteenth century, Britain's share of the world market fell from over 40 per cent in 1880 to 30 per cent in 1913. At the same time Germany's share rose from 19 to 26·5 per cent, and the American from 3 to over 12 per cent. In part, Aldcroft argues, 'Britain's trade difficulties were self-generated, that is they stemmed from internal deficiencies within her own industrial structure'—particularly the narrow base provided by an industrial structure that was concentrated heavily on a few traditional industries.

In 1907 three industries, coal-mining, iron and steel and textiles, accounted for 46 per cent of the net industrial output and supplied 70 per cent of all exports. . . . Even within individual industries the export base was sometimes extremely narrow. In the iron and steel industry, for example, galvanized and tinplate sheets accounted for 40 per cent of the growth of iron and steel exports in the decade prior to the first world war. . . . [Furthermore] in comparison with Germany and the United States, a higher proportion of Britain's trade in manufactures was concentrated in declining export sectors.[40]

But how far was the decline in the rate of growth of exports due to increased competition from other industrial countries and to tariffs, and how far to weaknesses in the British industrial base? The export performance of Germany suggests that tariffs were not in fact an insuperable obstacle and that it was possible despite increased competition to gain and expand markets. It seems, therefore, that the chain of causation was not from a poor performance in exports that led in turn to a low rate of capital accumulation and hence a low rate of economic growth; rather, it ran from conservatism and lack of rapid diversification in British industry to too narrow and unchanging a range of exports that, in turn, limited the growth of British trade. In the case of new products the export weakness may have been intensified by the slow rate of growth of the home economy which, it has been argued, did not provide a sound home market on which to base a large-scale export effort. Saul points out that the influence of foreign trade on the British economy was at its peak in the 1870s and 1880s (when the ratio of foreign trade to national income was nearly 30 per cent), and 'that with an economy so heavily export orientated as the British, exports must be a limiting factor in the rate of economic growth . . .' But, he asks,

why do we not stress more the impact of growth upon exports? The fact that over the last seventy years at least there has been a close correlation between a country's share of world manufacturing production and its share in world markets strongly suggests that growth of itself leads to higher productivity in the export sector. It is generally agreed, too, that with only rare exceptions—Swiss watches and precision instruments for example— industrial countries have developed exports only on the basis of the home market and that this tendency was increased towards the end of the nineteenth century by the risks involved as the size of initial capital outlays grew. If, as seems to be true, one of Britain's weaknesses was her inability to develop exports of new engineering products, the fault must surely lie in the inability of the home market—for whatever reason—to provide the necessary jumping-off ground.[41]

If, as Saul argues so persuasively, the problem lay in the development of the home economy, then what form did this problem take?
Some writers hold the view that the check to real income which
occurred in the 'climacteric' of the 1890s was due to the decline in
influence of the great nineteenth-century innovations of steam and
steel, resulting in a decline in investment and industrial productivity. H. W. Richardson considers that the chief factor in the retardation of industrial growth was a 'discontinuity in the flow of major
innovations'.[42] Ashworth gives more emphasis to the less productive
directions taken by capital investment in the late Victorian economy.
Apart from the fact that the absence of shift working meant that
optimum use was not made of industrial plant, much of the new
capital investment that was undertaken showed a low return in
output and productivity, for example the building of dormitory
suburbs, seaside resorts, and the extension of railways to suburban
areas and thinly-populated rural districts. Government expenditure
on social services rose from 1·9 per cent of G.N.P. in 1890 to 2·6 per
cent in 1900, and 4·1 per cent in 1913, and 'a social situation may
have arisen in which certain necessary lines of action were bound to
reduce the measurable rate of economic growth'. Much of this expenditure was on education and health, but from the point of view of
yielding an economic return could have been better applied; for
example, education was not sufficiently technical in character.[43]

Yet other writers have seen in the slowing down of the British
economy and its technological lag 'rigidity and ossification, the
characteristics of an old economy . . .', involving a sociological explanation which lays technical deficiencies at the door of British
entrepreneurs. The English social structure and public opinion, it is
argued, 'were less favourable than the American to entrepreneurship, less favourable both to the recruitment of ability and to full
exertion of ability once recruited'.[44]

In the United States, there was no long-established class system to impede
social mobility. The possibility of rising to the top was believed to be greater
than anywhere else in the world, and probably was so in fact. This belief
in an open avenue to wealth was one of the main reasons for the amount of
ability devoted to entrepreneurship in the United States. Moreover, in the
United States, there were few competitors to business success as a source
of social prestige. There was no large and powerful bureaucracy, no heredi-
tary aristocracy. There was no professional military class and soldiers
were not held in high esteem. Horatio Alger, the hero of the American

success story, wanted to be a business man, not a general or a civil servant
or a great landowner. The men of ambition and ability turned naturally to
business, not only because of the gains which might be made there—
though they were sometimes certainly enormous—but because business
men, a Rockefeller or a Pierrepont Morgan, were the leading men of the
country. . . .

In England, as, of course, in other countries of Western Europe conditions were more complicated. There existed a strongly entrenched social
system which limited social mobility, a social system inherited from pre-
industrial times when landowners were the ruling groups. Moreover, there
were sources of power and prestige besides business. Landownership,
bureaucracy, the army and the professions were all powerful competitors of
business for the services of the able men. There was therefore a haemor-
rhage of capital and ability from industry and trade into land ownership
and politics. Robert Peel and Gladstone both came of entrepreneurial
families, but their abilities were devoted to politics not to industry and
trade.[45]

Thus in England birth and family, education, behaviour, manners,
and accent determined social status, not success in business. Moreover, English entrepreneurs were likely to be of the second and third
generation, and more likely than their fathers or grandfathers to
interest themselves in society, politics, and leisure pursuits. Their
liberal education did not fit them to comprehend the growing technical complexity of industrial processes, and their attitude to scientific
research was at best apathetic.[46] Nevertheless, as Habakkuk points
out, there was a 'curious patchiness' about English business performance, with remarkable technical progress in some branches of
industry, while there is as yet no clear evidence for the importance
in industrial progress of education and scientific knowledge, nor for
the view that British industrialists were notably less well-prepared
for the more scientific age that was developing.[47]

Furthermore, Charles Wilson has reminded us that notable enterprise and invention in the late Victorian economy was being devoted
to new developments in light industry, particularly the manufacture
of foodstuffs, and to commerce and retail trade, witness 'the Levers,
the Boots, the Harrods, Whiteleys and Lewises'—as also such new
household names as Cadbury, Rowntree, Player's, Bovril, Lipton,
and Beecham. Historians, Wilson, complains, have concerned themselves overmuch with 'spectacular technological innovation and
massive investment as the indispensable condition of economic
growth', and have neglected the important shift towards a new and

different kind of economy. Aldcroft's dictum that 'Britain's relatively poor economic performance can be attributed largely to the failure of the British entrepreneur to respond to the challenge of changed conditions' appears thus as only a half-truth which may apply to certain branches of certain older industries; in Wilson's view enterprise 'responded in these years to the prospects offered by the mass demand for consumer (and other) goods in a context of rising real incomes'.[48]

In the older industries it may have been that Britain's early start in industrialization had by the later nineteenth century some adverse effects upon growth. It is true, of course, that at some point the first starter has to replace industrial plant and then has the opportunity of becoming the technological leader again, but the process is complicated by the fact that changes in one industry or component of plant may involve complementary changes in the size, location, or processes of other industries or plant (e.g. larger ships required larger docks). In an already old-established industrial complex the existing layout of communications, transport, and facilities, and of individual firms' buildings, may severely limit the capacity of a firm to introduce innovations. Thus 'the size and layout of an old textile mill imposed restrictions on the choice of techniques which were not present in one newly built in knowledge of the most recent techniques'. The adoption of new developments was further complicated by the high degree of specialization in British industry, which while certainly promoting mechanization also split up the control of lengthy processes of manufacture and limited the ability of the firm to innovate.[49] However, it has been argued that the extent of Britain's 'early start' over America and Germany was not in fact so very great, and that the problem of replacing obsolete plant was made the less resolvable by the unwillingness of entrepreneurs to accept either the conversion costs involved or the subsequent advantages.[50]

Industrial enterprise in Britain was necessarily influenced, too, by the supply and cost of factors of production. Cheap coal (and hence cheap gas) discouraged attempts to economize in fuel and delayed the introduction of electricity and oil, cheap capital deterred industrialists from maximizing the returns from plant, and cheap labour retarded the mechanization of coal mines, cotton factories, steelworks, and railways.[51] Habakkuk lays particular stress upon differences in labour costs when comparing British industrial development with American.

While there are indications that British labour was becoming less cheap (and was certainly dearer than on the continent), it was never really scarce. In America the higher cost of labour compelled manufacturers to raise the productivity of their workers by intensive use of labour-saving machinery. English manufacturers (and workers, too), on the other hand, were influenced in their attitudes to mechanization by long experience of cheap labour. Not only were industrialists apathetic towards labour-saving devices, they were also reluctant to pay the higher earnings which such devices warranted once adopted. There was a strong tendency to see wages as related to a man's position in the social scale, a kind of 'social norm' for wages which inhibited the idea of productivity payments.[52] Trade unions, too, were inclined to conservative attitudes towards the protection of members' jobs, although it is difficult to say how far this may have influenced the incentive for entrepreneurs to innovate.[53] The influence of cheap labour should not be exaggerated, however. Very often the persistence of old methods in British industry owed much to natural conditions (as in coal-mining) or to the peculiarities of the market (as in the wide variety of steel rails used in Britain)[54]— while the warning note given by Charles Wilson about the ample evidence of new enterprise in light industry and commerce must also be kept in mind.

Most important, probably, was the size, nature, and—particularly —the rate of growth of the market. The American economy was not only large, well-protected by tariffs, and homogeneous in the character of its market, thus offering scope for standardization and mass-production techniques—it was also growing rapidly, through exploitation of huge natural resources, the shift from agriculture to industry, and immigration, among other factors. Long experience in producing labour-saving devices had developed in America a pool and range of mechanical engineering skills which enabled new ideas (often borrowed from Europe) to be rapidly put into practical use.[55] The highly specialized machine tool industry 'played the role of a transmission centre in the diffusion of the new technology'.[56]

The market prospects for British manufacturers were less favourable after the 1870s. Exports grew less rapidly, partly because of tariffs, while that proportion of British trade that went to underdeveloped countries offered little incentive for the adoption of advanced techniques. The home market was open, of course, to foreign competition, and it was also less favourable to standardization and mass-production because of the less homogeneous nature of the demand arising from a more class-divided society. With a less rapidly growing market there were fewer opportunities for adding to already large industrial capacity, and hence less inducement to adopt new methods. With less prospects for growth, too, the outlook for enterprising businessmen and innovators of genius was less rewarding; while falling prices and profit margins sapped confidence, and the squeeze of profits between prices and costs stimulated not improved technology but wage cuts.[57]

It may be, as has often been suggested, that ideological influences were more favourable to growth in developing countries such as the United States and Germany than in Britain:

In the U.S.A. the need to open up the vast natural resources of the country had aroused general feelings of buoyancy and optimism. In addition immigration provided an emotional dynamism. For the Europeans who had taken the momentous step of tearing up their roots and migrating to America had an immensely strong incentive when they got there to prove their decision right by ensuring, through hard work, that they did in fact better themselves. In Britain, on the other hand, the mid-Victorian pride in her industrial leadership—a pride which had its basis in fact, but which developed a life of its own and acquired an ideological character—was blighted by doubts in the depressions of the 1870s and 80s; and such ideological movements as there were in Britain in the decades before 1914—imperialism and socialism for example,—were not particularly favourable to economic effort.[58]

But, Habakkuk concludes, it is not necessary to invoke these unmeasurable non-economic influences in order to explain the differences in technical progress between Britain and the United States in the later nineteenth century:

Such lags as there were in the adoption of new methods in British industry can be adequately explained by economic circumstances, by the complexity of her industrial structure and the slow growth of her output, and ultimately by her early and long-sustained start as an industrial power.[59]

Notes

1 TYSON, R. E., 'The Cotton Industry' in Derek H. Aldcroft (ed.), *The Development of British Industry and Foreign Competition 1875-1914* (1968), pp. 100, 121-2.

2 TAYLOR, A. J., 'The Coal Industry', in Aldcroft, *op. cit.*, pp. 46, 50-3.

3 PAYNE, P. L., 'Iron and Steel Manufactures' in Aldcroft, *op. cit.*, p. 75.
4 *Ibid.*, p. 97.

5 SAUL, S. B., 'The Export Economy, 1870-1914', in *Yorks. Bull. of Econ. and Social Research*, 17, 1 (1965), p. 15.

6 ALDCROFT, D. H., 'The Mercantile Marine', in Aldcroft, *op. cit.*, pp. 326-8.

7 SAUL, S. B., 'The Engineering Industry', in Aldcroft, *op. cit.*, 206, 219-20.

8 SAUL, S. B., 'The Motor Industry in Britain to 1914', *Business History* V, 1 (1962), pp. 26, 41-4.

9 RICHARDSON, H. W., 'Chemicals', in Aldcroft, *op. cit.*, pp. 278-80, 291-2, 298.

10 *Historical Statistics of the United States*, p. 409.

11 FRANKEL, M., *British and American Manufacturing Productivity* (Urbana, Ill., 1957), p. 81.

12 NORTH, D. C., 'Industrialization in the United States', in *Cambridge Economic History of Europe* VI, Part II (ed. M. Postan and H. J. Habakkuk, Cambridge, 1965), pp. 682-5, 687-90.

13 BRUCHEY, S., *The Roots of American Economic Growth 1607-1861*, pp. 159-64.

14 GOODRICH, CARTER quoted by BRUCHEY, *op. cit.*, pp. 82, 156.

15 Quoted by NORTH, *loc. cit.*, p. 692.

16 Quoted by BRUCHEY, *op. cit.*, p. 187; NORTH, D. C., *Growth and Welfare in the American Past* (Englewood Cliffs, N. J., 1966), p. 85.

17 NORTH, *loc. cit.*, p. 703.

18 LONG. CLARENCE D., *Wages and Earnings in the United States 1860-1890* (National Bureau of Economic Research, Princeton U.P., 1960), p. 61; REES, ALBERT, *Real Wages in Manufacturing, 1890-1914* (National Bureau of Economic Research, Princeton U.P., 1961), p. 120.

19 SAUL, S. B., 'The American Impact on British Industry 1895-1914', *Business History* III (1960), pp. 19-20, 22-3, 26, 30-1.

20 NORTH, *loc. cit.*, pp. 693-4. See also Alfred D. Chandler, Jr., 'The Beginnings of Big Business in American Industry', in Ralph L. Andreano (ed.) *New Views on American Economic Development* (Cambridge, Mass., 1965), pp. 277-81.

21 *Ibid.*, pp. 697-702.

22 COCHRAN, T. C., 'Did the Civil War retard Industrialization?' *Mississippi Valley Historical Review*, 48 (1961-2), pp. 197-205.

23 ANDREANO, RALPH L. (ed.) *New Views on American Economic Development* (Cambridge, Mass., 1965), pp. 246-50; GILCHRIST, DAVID T.

and LEWIS, DAVID W., *Economic Change in the Civil War Era* (Eleutherian Mills-Hagley Foundation, Greenville, Delaware, 1965), pp. 142, 148-9.

24   COCHRAN, T. C., 'Did the Civil War retard Industrialization?' *Mississippi Valley Historical Review*, 48 (1961-2), pp. 197-205.

25   *Ibid.*, pp. 209-10.

26   For a valuable discussion of the various motives behind horizontal and vertical forms of integration see CHANDLER, *loc. cit.*, pp. 282-9, 292-300.

27   PAYNE, P. L., 'The Emergence of the Large-Scale Company in Great Britain, 1870-1914', *Econ. Hist. Rev.* 2nd ser. XX (1967), pp. 534-6.

28   ASHWORTH, W., *An Economic History of England: 1870-1939* (1960), pp. 94-5.

29   PAYNE, *loc. cit.*, pp. 525-6, ASHWORTH, *op. cit.*, p. 95.

30   DAVIS, LANCE, 'The Capital Markets and Concentration: the United States and the United Kingdom, a Comparative Study', *Econ. Hist. Rev.*, 2nd ser. XIX (1966), pp. 256-62.

31   *Ibid.*, pp. 264-6.

32   CHANDLER, *loc. cit.*, pp. 282-90, 300.

33   NELSON, R., *Merger Movements in American Industry, 1895-1956* (Princeton, 1959), pp. 104, 129-31.

34   MUSSON, A. E., 'British Industrial Growth, 1873-96: a Balanced View', *Econ. Hist. Rev.*, 2nd ser. XVII (1964-5), pp. 397-8.

35   ALDCROFT, D. H. (ed.), *The Development of British Industry and Foreign Competition 1875-1914* (1968), p. 12.

36   MUSSON, *loc. cit.*, p. 400.

37   *Ibid.*, p. 399.

38   ASHWORTH, W., 'The Late Victorian Economy', *Economica* n.s., XXXIII (Feb., 1966), p. 18.

39   ALDCROFT, *op. cit.*, p. 13. Mr. Coppock has pointed out that revised estimates by Feinstein show a rate of growth of real income of only 0·9 per cent between 1856-65 and 1890-9, and a cessation of growth between 1899 and 1913: COPPOCK, *loc. cit.*, p. 395.

40   ALDCROFT, *op. cit.*, pp. 21, 23.

41   SAUL, S. B., 'The Export Economy 1870-1914', in *Yorks. Bull. of Econ. and Social Research*, 17, 1 (1965), pp. 11-12.

42   See PHELPS BROWN, E. H., and HANDFIELD JONES, S. J., 'The Climacteric of the 1890s: a Study in the Expanding Economy', *Oxford Economic Papers* n.s. IV (1952); RICHARDSON, H. W., 'Retardation in Britain's Industrial Growth, 1870-1913', *Scot. Journal of Political Economy* XII (1965), p. 128.

43   ASHWORTH, W., *loc. cit.*, pp. 19-23, 28-32.

44 HABAKKUK, H. J., *American and British Technology in the Nineteenth Century* (Cambridge, 1962), pp. 189-90.

45 *Ibid.*, pp. 190-1. It might be pointed out here that the high degree of social mobility in the United States did not apply to negroes.

46 For a discussion of British conservatism in management, neglect of science and education see, LEVINE, A. L. *Industrial Retardation in Britain 1880-1914* (1967), pp. 57-76.

47 HABAKKUK, *op. cit.*, pp. 191-4.

48 WILSON, CHARLES, 'Economy and Society in Late Victorian Britain', *Econ. Hist. Rev.*, 2nd ser. XVIII (1965-6), pp. 189-98. ALDCROFT, D. H., 'The Entrepreneur and the British Economy, 1870-1914' *Econ. Hist. Rev.*, 2nd ser. XVII (1964-5), p. 113.

49 HABAKKUK, *op. cit.*, p. 218.

50 LEVINE, *op. cit.*, pp. 121-5.

51 ALDCROFT, D. H., 'Technical Progress and British Enterprise, 1875-1914', *Business History* VIII (1966), pp. 128-31.

52 LEVINE, *op. cit.*, pp. 77-8.

53 *Ibid.*, pp. 79-101, 147.

54 HABAKKUK, *op. cit.*, pp. 194-201.

55 *Ibid.*, pp. 201-2.

56 ROSENBERG, N., 'Technological Change in the Machine Tool Industry, 1840-1910', *Jour. Ec. Hist.* XXIII, 4 (1963), pp. 425-6.

57 HABAKKUK, *op. cit.*, pp. 205-13; ALDCROFT, 'Technical Progress', pp. 134, 138-9.

58 HABAKKUK, *op. cit.*, pp. 219-20.

59 *Ibid.*, p. 220.

Suggestions for further reading

Texts

ASHWORTH, W., *An Economic History of England: 1870-1939* (1960), ch. 4.

JONES, P. D'A., *An Economic History of the United States since 1783* (1956), ch. 7.

WILLIAMSON, HAROLD F. (ed.), *The Growth of the American Economy* (Englewood Cliffs, N. J., 2nd ed., 1951), ch. 24-5, 31-2.

Specialized works

ALDCROFT, D. H. (ed.), *The Development of British Industry and Foreign Competition 1875-1914* (1968).

ALLEN, FREDERICK LEWIS, *The Big Change* (New York, Bantam Book ed., 1961).

ANDREANO, RALPH L. (ed.), *New Views on American Economic Development* (Camb., Mass., 1965).

ASHWORTH, W., 'The Late Victorian Economy' *Economica* n.s. XXXIII (Feb., 1966).

BRUCHEY, S., *The Roots of American Economic Growth 1607-1861* (1965).

COCHRAN, T. C., 'Did the Civil War retard Industrialization?' *Mississippi Valley Historical Review* 48 (1961-2.)

GILCHRIST, DAVID T. and LEWIS, W. DAVID, *Economic Change in the Civil War Era* (Eleutherian Mills-Hagley Foundation, Greenville, Delaware, 1965).

HABAKKUK, H. J., *American and British Technology in the Nineteenth Century* (Cambridge, 1962).

KENDRICK, J. W., *Productivity Trends in the United States* (National Bureau of Economic Research, Oxford, 1962).

LEVINE, A. L., *Industrial Retardation in Britain 1880-1914* (1967).

NELSON, R., *Merger Movements in American Industry, 1895-1956* (Princeton, 1959).

NORTH, D. C., 'Industrialization in the United States', in *Cambridge Economic History of Europe* VI, Part II (ed. M. Postan and H. J. Habakkuk, Cambridge, 1965).

PAYNE, P. L., 'The emergence of the Large Scale Company in Great Britain, 1870-1914', *Econ. Hist. Rev.*, 2nd ser., XX (1967), p. 519.

POLLARD, SIDNEY and CROSSLEY, DAVID W., *The Wealth of Britain 1085-1966* (1968), ch. 6.

SAUL, S. B., 'The Export Economy 1870-1914', *Yorks. Bull. of Econ. and Social Research*, 17, 1 (1965).

WILSON, CHARLES, 'Economy and Society in Late Victorian Britain', *Econ. Hist. Rev.*, 2nd ser. XVIII (1965-6).

1 Britain

a **The extent and effectiveness of trade unions in 1850**   With some important exceptions, such as the cotton textile industry, few British industries in 1850 were organized on a large scale. The typical establishment was still the small family business or partnership, the men employed often personally known to their employer. Local variations in wage rates and conditions of service still survived, for although railway building during the two previous decades had greatly speeded communications, inland travel was still expensive in relation to working-class incomes.

These facts help to explain why national trade unions of an enduring character were in their infancy in the 1850s, and why such a small proportion of wage earners were trade unionists. Although it is not possible to give an exact figure (since the Labour Department of the Board of Trade was not set up until 1886, and did not publish comprehensive figures of trade union membership until 1892), it is certain that only a small proportion of wage earners were enrolled in trade unions in the third quarter of the nineteenth century. If the opinion of a trade union leader in 1867 that 'there were never at any time more than a quarter of a million members' is correct, less than 5 per cent of the wage earners were trade unionists.

Union membership was very unequally distributed between the trades: the engineers, cotton spinners, printers, and stone masons were among the best organized, the strength of the miners' trade unions fluctuated violently, while agricultural labourers, railwaymen, and transport workers were virtually without organization.

b **1850-75: advances in organization and legal status**   During the third quarter of the nineteenth century real progress was made in the organization, legal position, and social standing of British unions. If the objectives of the movement were more limited and practical, and the leadership more cautious, than had been the case in the preceding quarter century, there was solid achievement in laying the foundation for the more spectacular and broadly based advance of the concluding years of the century.

The organizations which achieved the greatest influence in these years were the 'New Model' unions of skilled craftsmen, of which the prototype was the Amalgamated Society of Engineers, formed in 1851 through the merging of a number of smaller, mainly local, craft unions. The outstanding features of this new organization were the centralization of its funds, the appointment of a full-time permanent general secretary, and the provision of liberal friendly society benefits. Each of these policies had been followed by different unions before 1851; what was new was their simultaneous adoption by the one organization.

Partly because they were so heavily committed to pay friendly society benefits to their members, but also because their views were often more orthodox on economic questions than was the case with the earlier generations of trade unionists, the leaders of the New Model unions were reluctant to call their members out on strike. As one of the best-known of the General Secretaries expressed it, strikes were regarded as a 'dernier ressort'. It was not that the strike weapon was abandoned—another General Secretary, Daniel Guile of the Ironfounders, said in 1867 that he considered strikes 'a negative good'. Nevertheless, between 1851 and 1859 inclusive, the Amalgamated Society of Engineers spent £2,987,993 on friendly society benefits and only £86,664 on industrial disputes, most of the latter expenditure incurred in supporting members locked out by the employers in 1852.

Whilst the 'amalgamated' form of organization served mainly to further the interests of the labour aristocracy of skilled craftsmen, who formed some 11 per cent of the total labour force and whose wage rates were often double those of their unskilled assistants, some amalgamated unions were formed to serve all workers in a single trade and were used as instruments of militant struggle. The Amalgamated Association of Miners, founded in 1869, though a highly centralized body, was inclined to the left in its policy, and during its brief existence of six years spent the greater part of its resources in support of strikes in the coalfields of South Wales and Lancashire.

In common with their American contemporaries, trade union leaders in these years had as a foremost objective the shortening of the working day and the elimination of systematic overtime. It was held to be morally indefensible for a man to be obliged to work in excess of the 'normal' ten-hour day in order to maintain himself and his family. It was on this issue that the engineers were locked out in 1852. Seven years later, the London building trade workers attempted, by means of a strike, to reduce the working day to nine hours. Although failing in this objective, they successfully defeated the attempt of the employers to make repudiation of trade union membership a condition of employment. It was not until the trade boom of the early 1870s that any substantial success was achieved by the nine-hours movement.

Courageous but only partially successful attempts were made to establish unions in hitherto unorganized employments. Joseph Arch's National Agricultural Labourers Union, formed in 1872, quickly recruited a membership of 100,000, but as quickly lost most of it when East Anglian farmers organized a lock-out of unionists in 1874. Another union formed in 1872, the Amalgamated Society of Railway Servants, also found it hard to survive. Both farm labourers and railwaymen were difficult to organize because of the scattered nature of this employment, the debilitating effects of the tied cottage system, and the anti-union paternalism of the farmers and railway directors.

The most impressive successes achieved by labour at this time were in the political and legal spheres. Through such organizations as the Northern Reform Union in Manchester and the National Reform League in London, leading trade unionists in the 1860s joined forces with middle-class radicals in demanding manhood suffrage and voting by secret ballot. On 23 July 1866 a crowd of between 100,000 and 200,000 persons, demonstrating in favour of manhood suffrage, forced its way into Hyde Park, London in defiance of a police ban, tearing up miles of iron railings as it advanced. In demanding the franchise, British workmen were heartened by the knowledge that wage-earners (other than negroes) in America had more political rights and greater economic opportunities than they did. John Bright, the foremost radical M.P., told his audiences that the American working man had the advantage of 'a free church, a free school, free land, a free vote, and a free career for the child of the humblest born in the land'.[1] Through the combined influence of British trade union agitation and the American example, the demand for reform proved irresistible, and the Reform Bill, which extended the franchise to many of the skilled artisans, though not to the unskilled labourers, became law on 15 August 1867. After its enactment the influence of organized labour in Parliament was much enhanced, partly because, for the first time, a handful of working men became M.P.s, but mainly through the fact that in a number of parliamentary constituencies candidates needed the votes of artisans to secure election. After 1872 the Ballot Act ensured that the working man could exercise the franchise with less danger of victimization by his employer or landlord.

The trade union leaders were not slow to exploit the new opportunities open to them after 1867. The Trades Union Congress, a loose federation of national trade unions and trades councils, first summoned in 1868 in Manchester, set up in the following year a Parliamentary Committee, which soon became active in lobbying M.P.s and questioning Parliamentary candidates on matters which concerned the unions.

Half-way through the nineteenth century the legal status of the trade union was still very precarious. As a result of Acts passed in 1824 and 1825 repealing the Combination Laws, trade unions, as such, were no longer illegal. But this did not mean that they were accorded a recognized place in society. By the iron law of wages, one of the widely accepted economic doctrines of the day, unions were held to be incapable of raising the real wages of their members except at the expense of other workers. The deportation of the six Tolpuddle labourers in 1834 had revealed that, despite the legislation of the previous decade, other measures were still available for prosecuting trade unionists.

However, for more than a decade after the passing of the Friendly Societies Act in 1855 it was assumed that the unions had legal protection for their funds. This belief was shattered in 1867 in the case Hornby v. Close, in which the Boilermakers Society failed to recover £24 wrongfully withheld by the treasurer of its Bradford branch, Lord Chief Justice Cockburn declaring that a trade union was an unlawful society, in restraint of trade, and therefore not able to obtain legal protection for its funds.

One of the great issues which occupied the attention of the labour movement was the injustice of the Master and Servant laws under which a workman who broke his contract of employment was held to have committed a criminal offence and was liable to imprisonment for up to three months, whilst an employer, accused of a similar offence, was tried under civil law and was punishable only by a fine. Largely through the initiative of the Glasgow Trades Council a national campaign for a revision of the law was launched at a Trade Union Conference in London in 1864.

Union leaders had an opportunity of airing their views on these issues when called as witnesses before the Royal Commission on Trade Unions in 1867. Robert Applegarth of the Amalgamated Society of Carpenters and Joiners and other members of the Junta— the general secretaries of the principal 'amalgamated' unions with head offices in London—created a very favourable impression by their obvious integrity and respectability. It is therefore not surprising that the Report of the Royal Commission, published in 1869, recommended full legal recognition of trade unions even though it took an unfavourable attitude towards picketing. In 1871 the Gladstone Government accepted the Commission's advice and passed the Trade Union Act which gave legal status to the Unions, and also the Criminal Law Amendment Act which severely hamstrung the activities of pickets in an industrial dispute and made the 'watching and besetting' or 'persistently following' of blacklegs a criminal offence.

In the General Election of 1874 candidates were closely questioned on their attitude to the Master and Servant Laws and the Criminal Law Amendment Act. Since the replies of most of the Conservatives were regarded as more satisfactory than those given by the Liberals, it is believed that working-class votes made a significant contribution to the return of a Conservative administration. Certainly by two laws passed in the following year the interests of trade unionists were substantially advanced. By the Employers and Workmen Act matters were placed on a footing of greater equality, since a breach of contract by either was to be treated as a civil offence. Under the Conspiracy and Protection of Property Act the conduct of a strike was less fraught with danger in that peaceful picketing was now legalized.

Thus, by their sustained effort on both the industrial and parliamentary fronts, union leaders had paved the way for the greater achievements of the new generation of leaders in the last years of the nineteenth century.

c **The British Labour Movement 1875-1914** By the later 1870s, with the onset of the Great Depression, increasing dissatisfaction was expressed with the policies of the leadership of the 'New Model' unions. Confronted with the falling prices and narrowing profit margins characteristic of these years, employers demanded wage reductions in an effort to lower production costs. Union leaders were in a dilemma. If they resisted these encroachments by means of strikes, their ability to pay their friendly society benefits might be impaired: if they failed to resist, the soundness of the 'New Model' policies of industrial conciliation would be increasingly questioned. Even when resisting they frequently failed to prevent wage reductions, as was the case with the stonemasons in 1877, and the cotton operatives in the following year. By 1886, Tom Mann, a leader of the younger generation of engineers, was bemoaning the fact that 'the true unionist policy of aggression' was 'entirely lost sight of', and that the average unionist was 'a man with a fossilized intellect'. A year later John Burns, another engineer, complained that the unions had degenerated into 'mere middle class or upper class rate reducing institutions'. As the part played by machinery and mass production techniques in industry increased, the craft exclusiveness of some of the unions such as the Boilermakers, was seen to be increasingly inappropriate. The unskilled were not content to be excluded from the benefits of trade unionism indefinitely, and this impatience was increased after many of them—though not all—were given the parliamentary franchise for the first time in 1884.

The characteristics of the 'New Unionism'—which came into prominence with the London Dock strike in the late summer of 1889 but which had its origins at least as far back as 1886—were the recruitment of many types of workers not previously organized, the emphasis on general rather than craft unionism, and the use of militant industrial tactics. The movement was encouraged by the Socialist revival of the 1880s and 1890s, a development marked by the foundation of the Social Democratic Federation and the Fabian Society in 1884, and of the Independent Labour Party in 1893. The part played by members of the S.D.F. in organizing the unskilled helps to explain the greater emphasis of the new unionism on state intervention, both to secure the eight-hour day and to establish public ownership of basic industries, though it is understandable that unions composed of poorly paid men would eschew the large contribution and liberal benefits characteristic of the craft unions and would emphasize instead the role of the state in welfare services.

Three remarkable successes in industrial organizations in 1888-9 helped to establish the New Unionism at a time when an industrial boom and consequent labour shortage made the conditions for advance favourable. The first, in 1888, was the successful strike of the poorly paid and hitherto unorganized match girls employed at Bryant and May's factory in London. Secondly, in the spring of 1889, the London gasworkers, organized by Will Thorne, succeeded without a strike in reducing the working shift from twelve to eight hours a day. Finally, in August and September of the same year came the successful strike of the London dockers for a minimum payment of 6*d.* an hour, a minimum of four hours employment when taken on, and payment for overtime at 8*d.* an hour.

Whilst it is true that many of the gains in union membership were lost in the succeeding industrial slump of 1891-2, the inspiration brought by the spectacular successes of 1888-9 helped to recruit 300,000 men into unions of the unskilled and to increase total union membership from about 750,000 in 1889 to 1,500,000 in 1892, and 2,000,000 in 1900. The changes in policy introduced by the new unions often induced modifications in the rules of the older craft-style unions. Thus, urged on by Tom Mann, the Amalgamated Society of Engineers introduced less exclusive conditions of membership in 1892.

An important consequence of the spread of organization to the unskilled was the increased importance of picketing in industrial disputes. Where strikes were conducted by skilled artisans the scarcity value of their labour was some guarantee against their easy replacement; but where disputes involved unskilled labour, especially in times of trade depression and unemployment, their effectiveness might well depend upon the ability of pickets to exclude blackleg labour. The more vigorous the picketing necessary to render the stoppage complete the more criticism the unions were bound to incur from the press and the courts. Thus in the closing years of the nineteenth century the unionists' comfortable belief that the legislation of the 1870s had given immunity from prosecution for damages and had upheld the right to picket was undermined in a series of hostile court decisions.

One outstanding difference between the unions in Britain and America has been the organizational link between most of the British unions and the Labour Party, a link which has been a salient feature of the political scene in the U.K. for more than sixty years. By contrast, the American unions have carefully avoided such close ties with either of the main political parties and have been reluctant to sponsor one of their own. That the British unions took the path they did was largely in consequence of the Taff Vale judgement in 1901 and the Osborne judgement in 1909.

Ever since the reform of the franchise in 1867 some trade unionists had sat in Parliament, but until 1900, they had almost invariably been sponsored by the Liberal Party and hence had become known as 'Lib-Labs'. It was an arrangement which never pleased the Socialists who, in September 1899, persuaded the T.U.C. to summon a conference of those interested in independent labour representation in Parliament. However, when the Labour Representation Committee, formed in February 1900, invited affiliations from trade unions, the response was at first a meagre one. After a year, only sixty-five organizations with a total membership of 469,000 had affiliated. Then came the Taff Vale Railway strike of August 1900 and the Law Lords' judgement in the Taff Vale case in the following year. The A.S.R.S., which had conducted the strike, was held liable for damages amounting to £23,000. After some hesitation during which the full significance of the judgement became appreciated, the union leaders were convinced that only a change in the law would provide satisfactory conditions for the functioning of trade unions. Since neither the Liberal Party nor the Conservative Party was in any great hurry to propose new legislation, the unions were won over to the case for independent representation. By 1903-4 the L.R.C. had secured the affiliation of 165 trade unions with a combined membership of nearly a million. In the general election of 1906, using the financial support given by the unions and benefiting from a non-aggression pact with the Liberals, the L.R.C. was successful in electing twenty-nine of its candidates. The Parliamentary Labour Party had been born.

One of the first tasks of the new Parliament was to pass the Trade Disputes Act (1906) which again legalized peaceful picketing and exempted the unions from claims for damages arising from industrial disputes. By this new law British unions acquired a legal standing such as American unions achieved only after 1935.

The union policy of support for the newly formed Labour Party was not without its critics. Walter V. Osborne, Walthamstow branch secretary of the A.S.R.S., had such strong objections to it that he sued his own union. The case was taken to the Law Lords who, in December 1909, ruled that expenditure of union funds on political objects was *ultra vires* the Acts of 1871 and 1876. At one blow the principal source of income for Labour M.Ps—subsistence allowances from the unions—was denied them. Parliament eased the situation by passing a Commons resolution in 1911 authorizing the payment of M.P.s by the state. By the Trade Union Act of 1913, where the majority of the members approved a union's political objects, it could spend money for political purposes provided the individual member was free to 'contract out' of making such payments.

Thus whilst the Taff Vale judgement convinced the trade union sector of the labour movement of the value of an (independent) Labour Party in Parliament, the Osborne judgement made the Socialists appreciate more keenly the financial value of trade union affiliation. This marriage of convenience contracted at the beginning of the century has stood the test of time.

Stimulated by the example of the Industrial Workers of the World, an American syndicalist movement founded in Chicago in 1905, rank-and-file opinion in Britain increasingly favoured the formation of industrial unions to recruit into one organization all the employees of an industry so that they might more effectively match the strength of the employers' federations, which were growing in number and influence. The National Union of Railwaymen, formed in 1913 through the merging of three smaller unions, came nearest to a practical expression of this new ideal. Syndicalist influence was also to be seen in the formation between 1913 and 1915 of the Triple Industrial Alliance of miners, railwaymen, and transport workers to secure co-operative action in industrial disputes.

d **Industrial relations in wartime Britain 1914-18** Although at the meetings of the Socialist International held before 1914, British leaders had given support to anti-war resolutions, in the emergency of the summer of 1914 a wave of patriotism swept the country. The support which most of the trade union leaders gave to the war effort was manifested at the Treasury conferences held early in 1915 at which the dilution of labour and the industrial truce were accepted 'for the duration'. On both sides of the Atlantic the full co-operation of labour leaders was, indeed, regarded as essential for the successful prosecution of the war. This gave trade union leaders a greatly enhanced status. In Britain Arthur Henderson of the Ironfounders and G. N. Barnes of the Amalgamated Society of Engineers were given Cabinet office. To many other younger and less well-known trade union leaders the war provided the opportunity for the exercise of administrative ability in a wider sphere. Thus Ernest Bevin served on the Port and Transit Executive Committee, where his gifts as an organizer were given full scope.

The circumstances of the war also greatly encouraged the process of trade union consolidation. When the rapid rise in the cost of living made imperative the negotiation of war bonuses as supplements to basic wage rates, it was found convenient—especially in the case of the miners and the railwaymen—to do this at a national rather than a regional level. Inevitably, the influence of the general secretaries who negotiated these settlements was greatly enhanced. Consolidation was still further encouraged with the passing of the Trade Union (Amalgamation) Act of 1917 which made easier the merging of two or more unions. Through it such trade union giants as the Amalgamated Engineering Union (1921) and the Transport and General Workers Union (1922) came into being soon after the war.

In both Britain and America the bargaining strength of the unions was increased, not only by the wartime scarcity of labour, but also by rapidly rising trade union membership. In Britain the number of trade unionists grew from 4,150,000, in 1914 to 7,926,000 in 1919, whilst in the U.S.A. the rate of growth (from 2,687,000 to 4,125,000 over the same period) was only slightly lower.

Such a rapid growth brought its problems of adjustment. In Britain, partly because the gulf between the national leaders and the rank and file tended to widen, and because problems of labour dilution could best be solved at workshop level, the shop stewards gained increased influence. They dominated the labour scene in areas like the Clydeside and led a number of successful unofficial strikes.

e **British labour between the wars** On both sides of the Atlantic 1919 was a year of great industrial unrest. During the period of industrial truce, the trade unions had marked time in respect of demands for a shorter working week and other improvements in working conditions. At the same time the war brought a growing awareness of the potential industrial and political power of labour. Inevitably, with the coming of peace, a backlog of demands was submitted by the unions. On the other hand the outstanding objective of many employers was the removal of wartime government restraints and a return to 'normalcy'. In a competitive post-war world, so it was argued, wage rates as well as other production costs would have to come down.

In Britain trade unionists came to regard the response to the miners claims for improved wages, a six-hour day, and public ownership of the industry as a touchstone of the intentions of both Government and the employing class. In face of a threat by the miners to go on strike in support of their demands Lloyd George played for time. He appointed Sir John Sankey as Chairman of a Royal Commission on the Coal Mining Industry and allowed the miners to nominate half its members. But when the Commission failed to agree on the future structure of the industry (although a majority of its members favoured enlargement of public control), the Government thought itself absolved of the responsibility to act. The miners felt themselves betrayed. They were further disillusioned when their Triple Alliance partners, the railwaymen and the transport workers, on 'Black Friday', 15 April 1921, failed to back them up in a strike fought against the replacement of national by district wage agreements. One reason for this breakdown in industrial solidarity was that the railwaymen, by their strike of September 1919, had persuaded the Government to postpone wage reductions which had been contemplated. Thus having won their own battle, some of the railwaymen were less enthusiastic to join forces with the miners. However, after Britain returned to the Gold Standard in April 1925 and coal exports slumped, trouble flared up again in the mining industry. In this new crisis, prompted no doubt, by an uneasy conscience about the 'betrayal' on 'Black Friday', the railwaymen and transport workers decided to support the miners in their resistance to wage reductions. On 30 July 1925—'Red Friday'—the Government, faced with this display of trade union solidarity, took the easy way out and granted a nine months' subsidy to the industry as well as appointing another Royal Commission, this time under the chairmanship of Sir Herbert Samuel, to make recommendations for the reorganization of the industry.

These measures led neither to any fundamental improvement in the management of the industry nor to any revival of demand for coal. When the subsidy came to an end, therefore, the mine owners declared their intention of introducing substantial reductions in wages.

A conference of trade union delegates held in London on 29 April 1926 authorized the General Council of the T.U.C. (a body which replaced the old Parliamentary Committee in 1921) to try to negotiate a settlement with the Government; but when the Cabinet decided to break off these talks on 3 May the General Strike in support of the miners was ordered to start on the following day. On the ninth day of the strike the negotiating committee of the T.U.C. called again at No. 10 Downing Street and agreed unconditionally to order a return to work. They did so, not because the strike was weakening to any appreciable extent, but because they had no intention of overthrowing the Government and they feared that, if the struggle continued, control of the movement might pass out of their hands. Although the T.U.C.'s order calling off the strike was generally obeyed, the miners fought on until they drifted back to work, defeated and impoverished, in November 1926.

In many respects the General Strike was a decisive turning point in the history of British labour. In the first place, the industrial power of the unions was eroded by the Trade Disputes and Trade Unions Act of 1927—a direct outcome of the strike—which declared general and sympathetic strikes illegal and placed new curbs on the unions' rights to picket in industrial disputes. Secondly, by the same Act, the resources of the Labour Party were curtailed through the requirement that in future 'contracting in' to the unions' political funds was to replace 'contracting out'. In consequence of this change the Labour Party's income from trade union affiliations quickly fell by one-third of its 1926 level. Thirdly, in the backwash of disillusionment which followed the General Strike, and in a situation of continuing heavy unemployment, the decline in trade union membership, which had begun in 1921, was accelerated. Unions affiliated to the T.U.C. which had over $5\frac{1}{2}$m. members in December 1925 had less than $4\frac{1}{2}$m. seven years later. Lastly, by contrast with the unrest of the years 1919-26, the remaining years before the outbreak of the Second World War formed a period of comparative industrial peace. In January 1926 trade union funds exceeded £$12\frac{1}{2}$m.; in January 1927 they had fallen to £$8\frac{1}{2}$m., and the bulk of this sum, consisting of friendly benefit funds, was not available for financing industrial disputes. Since it took many of the larger unions the best part of a decade to recoup the funds expended in May 1926, it is not surprising that in the ten years 1927-36 inclusive, the number of days work lost through industrial disputes was just under one-eighth of the working days lost in the years 1917-26 inclusive.

Nevertheless, it is arguable that the difficulties experienced by British trade unions through most of the inter-war years were nothing like as great as those experienced by American labour. Despite the General Strike, there was after 1926 'no general employers' offensive against the trade unions'[2]. Some of the employers, in fact, drew the lesson from the General Strike that a policy of full union recognition and co-operation with labour would be more fruitful than one of conflict. In 1928 Sir Alfred Mond (later Lord Melchett) of Imperial Chemical Industries, initiated discussions with Ben Turner (later Sir Ben Turner), Chairman of the T.U.C. General Council, on harmonizing the interests of labour and capital. Although the practical outcome of the discussions was very limited, and although there was sustained left-wing criticism of the policy of some of the leaders of the T.U.C., the Mond-Turner talks were symbolical of the more sober mood which prevailed in the British Labour Movement in the 1930s.

2 America

a **Reasons for the weakness of the unions in the nineteenth century** A recent historian of nineteenth-century America has written: 'Until the 1850s, the colonels and captains of American economic life were merchants, land speculators, transport promoters, iron masters, millers, lumbermen. Manufacturers were still hardly distinguishable from the labouring class from which they emerged.'[3]

Since this was the case, it is not surprising that before the Civil War trade unions were organized mainly on a local basis, had a small and rapidly fluctuating membership, and were all too prone to quick extinction in years of commercial crisis such as 1837 and 1857. Not until the third quarter of the century, when a national transport network was created, was there established something like a national economy on which a national trade union movement could be based.

But the rapid industrialization after 1850 provided no guarantee that a strong trade union movement would emerge. Abram S. Hewitt who was familiar with industrial conditions in the middle Atlantic states in America, told the Royal Commission on Trade Unions in London in 1867 that he considered the organizations in America 'rather crude', with 'no single organization reaching so widely over the country there as it appears to do here'.[4]

One important reason for this difference was that, despite the many acknowledged hardships of the nineteenth-century wage-earner, America remained as it had been described by William Penn in the seventeenth century, 'a good poor man's country'. Throughout our period real wages in America were generally higher than those in comparable trades in England. At least to the large immigrant community, accustomed to lower standards of living, a strong trade union movement must have appeared less essential in the New World than in the Old.

Furthermore, the American worker enjoyed a more assured status in society than did his British contemporary. Unless he had a black skin, he had acquired the franchise at least since the late 1820s, and he was often better educated. In the 1860s in Britain the increased influence of the trade unions was associated with a political campaign to give the working man the vote: it assumed the character of a crusade of emancipation. The American labour movement lacked such a stimulus. Fear of the competition of negro labour prevented an uninhibited campaign for negro enfranchisement.

In respect of the law, however, American trade unionists had a longer and harder battle to establish favourable conditions for collective bargaining. The effect of the Cordwainer Cases (1806-15) in Philadelphia and elsewhere was similar to the English Combination Laws (1799-1800) in that both treated trade union activity as illegal because it was in restraint of trade. Similarly, a broad comparison may be made between the case Commonwealth (Mass.) *v.* Hunt in 1842 and the British Acts of 1824 and 1825 which repealed the Combination Laws, in that both made possible a limited sphere of legal activity for the unions. Thereafter the tendency was for the law in America to operate increasingly to the detriment of unions, whilst in Britain the area of legalized activity widened despite important temporary setbacks.

In both state and federal courts sympathetic strikes, picketing by strangers, boycotts (as in the Danbury Hatters Case 1902-8), and secondary boycotts (as in the Duplex Printing Press Case, 1921) were all declared illegal. At the same time the Supreme Court, in the case Hitchman Coal and Coke Co. *v.* Mitchell (1917), upheld 'Yellow Dog' contracts (i.e. contracts requiring renunciation of union membership as a condition of employment). Through such cases as Lochner *v.* New York (1905) attempts to ameliorate arduous working conditions by means of legislation were often hamstrung; but on the other hand, by 1914 the Supreme Court had established the constitutionality of the Workmen's Compensation Laws of several states.

The unions' most formidable legal obstacle from the 1870s onwards was undoubtedly the use by employers and the state of the injunction to prevent the use of the strike weapon. In the famous Pullman strike of July 1894 a Federal injunction was issued forbidding Eugene Debs' American Railway Union from engaging in any action which would hamper the business of twenty-three specified railroads. Since compliance with the injunction would in any case have broken the strike, the union leaders defied it. Their imprisonment quickly followed. The rank and file of the strikers, deprived of leadership and direction, returned to work defeated and demoralized. Only after the Norris-LaGuardia Act in 1932 was the use of the injunction forbidden in industrial disputes.

Even the Federal Anti-Trust legislation—notably the Sherman Anti-Trust Act of 1890 and the Clayton Act of 1914—was more frequently and effectively invoked against trade unions than against trusts. American employers—a parvenu class in comparison with their English counterparts—were intolerant of any interference by trade unions in the conduct of their businesses. They employed detective agencies whose 'labour spies' ensured that militant unionists were sacked and blacklisted. To break the strike in its Homestead works in 1892 the Carnegie Steel Company hired 300 armed Pinkerton agents. Their arrival on the scene was resisted by the strikers and twelve men were killed in the pitched battle which followed. As late as 1935 an estimated total of 40,000 labour spies were employed by American firms which paid $80m. a year to 230 different detective agencies for their services.[5]

b **Labour unions in America before 1914** It would be a mistake to attribute the low membership figures of American unions solely

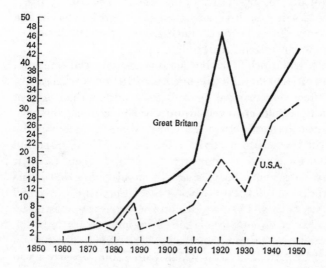

Figure 30. Great Britain and U.S.A.: membership of trade unions 1850-1950; trade union membership as a percentage of gainfully employed labour 1850-1950

to the hostility of employers and the courts. Through faulty leadership and inappropriate organization the unions were themselves partly responsible for their ineffectiveness. The National Labour Union (1866-72) after achieving some successes in the campaign for an eight-hour day, was rent asunder by conflicts over the admission of women and negroes to membership, monetary reforms, and the respective merits of political action and 'pure and simple' trade unionism.

Uriah S. Stephens, who founded the Noble and Holy Order of the Knights of Labour in Philadelphia in 1869, decided to keep the new organization secret and highly centralized in order to minimize blacklisting and emphasize solidarity. But it was not until the movement came into the open after 1879 that it acquired a mass membership. Its successful conduct of strikes on the Kansas Pacific and other railroads in 1884 led to a sudden growth of its membership from 52,000 in 1884 to a peak of over 700,000 in 1886. However, the order proved incapable of organizing these new members successfully. Terrence W. Powderly, who succeeded Stephens as Grand Master Workman in 1879, favoured the organization of district assemblies on an industrial or regional, rather than a craft, basis. Some of the movement's organizers, however, believed that the grouping of men on craft lines would be more successful. Hence the order became a hotch-potch of craft, industrial, and mixed assemblies. As a federation it was unable to protect the interests of craftsmen (with some exceptions such as the window glass workers) or of the unskilled. Moreover, Powderly's interests lay in political action. He favoured the boycott rather than the strike. Disillusionment quickly followed the failure of a strike he had been unable to prevent on the Southwestern Railway in the spring of 1886, and membership slumped from 510,000 in 1887 to 100,000 in 1890. By the end of the century the movement had virtually disappeared.

The founders of the American Federation of Labour, which was established in 1886, had a strong preference for craft rather than industrial unionism. Wishing to avoid the extreme fluctuations in union membership characteristic of the preceding twenty years, they favoured chartering for admission to the Federation only unions rich enough to provide generous friendly society benefits—a striking comparison with the new model unions in Britain. Workers joining such unions would then consider it worth while maintaining con-

tinuous membership: there was no *individual* membership to the
A.F.L. The leaders consciously emulated the junta-led unions in
Britain. Samuel Gompers, who was president of the A.F.L. from
1886 to 1924 (with one break in 1894), wrote in his autobiography
that before revising the rules of his union, the International Cigar
Makers, he had gathered all the information he could get 'on the
benefits provided by British Trade Unions'.[6]

Of those affiliated to the A.F.L. the most successfully organized
craftsmen were the carpenters and cigar makers. Industrial unions
such as the United Mine Workers were not excluded, though their
presence in the Federation was exceptional. Once a union was
chartered it was given exclusive jurisdiction to organize workers in
that trade, a policy which often caused resentment among unions not
favoured with a charter. One important group of unions, the Railway Brotherhoods, maintained a tradition of independence. Some of
these believed that they did not require the assistance of the Federation to exploit their scarcity value.

British trade unionists came to believe in the benefits of political
action: Samuel Gompers' experience was different. In the 1870s he
tried at both state and federal level to secure legislation to protect
the interests of the cigar makers. All his efforts were fruitless. The
federal measure was blocked by a lobby of manufacturers and the
state legislation was declared unconstitutional by the courts. From
then on he advocated 'pure and simple' unionism—a policy of
limited industrial aims to be achieved by the bargaining strength of
the unions—and he won over the A.F.L. to his way of thinking.
Increasingly after 1900 union leaders in Britain co-operated with
the socialists. Gompers fought against them, opposing public ownership of the means of production and state intervention to shorten the
working day, regulate wages, or provide social security benefits.
There were other reasons why American unions did not affiliate to a
political party of the left. The American socialist movement was split
between the supporters of the Socialist Labour Party (1878) and
the Socialist Party of America (1900), while the Anarchists gained
supporters in Chicago and the mining camps of the west. Many
immigrants found the immediate practical benefits of voting the
Democratic ticket as instructed by the Tammany Hall bosses more
attractive than the promises of a better future made by socialist
orators.

TABLE 25

Membership of British and American trade unions, 1850-1950

Great Britain				U.S.A.			
	A Total gainfully employed labour force (excluding agriculture) ('000s)	B T.U. membership ('000s)	C 'B' as a percentage of 'A'		D Total gainfully employed labour force (excluding agriculture) ('000s)	E T.U. membership ('000s)	F 'E' as a percentage of 'D'
Year				Year			
1851	7,367	—	—	1850	2,775	200 (1853)	7·2
1861	8,578	191	2·3	1860	4,470	—	—
1871	10,101	289	2·9	1870	6,010	300	5·0
1881	11,106	507 (1882)	4·6	1880	8,685	200	2·3
						(1,000, 1887)	9·0
1891	12,997	1,596 (1892)	12·1	1890	12,570	400	3·2
1901	14,714	2,025	13·7	1900	18,150	868	4·8
1911	17,187	3,139	18·2	1910	25,140	2,140	8·5
		8,347 (1920)	46·6				
1921	17,906	6,632	37·0	1920	27,088	5,048	18·6
1931	19,702	4,624	23·5	1930	29,143	3,393	11·7
1941	—	6,542	—	1940	32,058	8,717	27·2
1951	21,391	9,235	43·1	1950	44,758	14,300	31·9

Sources: *For Great Britain: Statistical Tables and Report on Trade Unions*, pp. 1887, LXXXIX. Mitchell and Deane: *Abstract of British Historical Statistics*, pp. 60-1 and 68. Cole, G. D. H., *A Short History of the British Working Class Movement, 1787-1947* (1948), p. 275. For the U.S.A.: *Historical Statistics of the United States* (1960), pp. 72-3, 98. Rayback, J. G. *A History of American Labour* (New York, 1959), p. 104, 118, 156, 163. Wolman, L. *The Growth of American Trade Unions* (New York, 1924), p. 21. Figures for the years before 1890 are approximate only.

As mass-production methods increasingly supplanted individual craftsmanship in the two decades before the First World War, the appropriateness of the policies of A.F.L. leadership was increasingly questioned. Craft union distinctions rapidly lost their meaning. The organizers of the Industrial Workers of the World (known as the I.W.W. or 'Wobblies') maintained from its foundation in 1905, that only by creating one big industrial union in each industry could the growing power of capital be matched by that of labour. Despite some successes amongst immigrant textile workers in New England, migratory workers, and western miners, membership was always small. The movement was weakened by the split between its political and industrial syndicalist wing after 1908. Nevertheless by their 'free speech' campaigns and their exposure of inhuman working conditions in many industries the Wobblies gave 'a tremendous spiritual impetus to the progressive movement'.[7]

c **American labour 1914-32.** In America, as in Britain, the bargaining strength of the trade unions was greatly increased in wartime because of growing labour shortages. Although the U.S.A. did not enter the war until 1917, the munitions, shipbuilding, and other industries were exceptionally busy from early in 1915 fulfilling orders from the allied governments. The supply of labour became less elastic with the enlistment of 4m. men after the declaration of war, and the fall of total immigration in the years 1915-18 inclusive to less than the figure for the one year 1914. Between 1914 and 1918 the number of civilians employed by the Federal Government rose from 401,887 to 854,500, a development strengthening the hand of the A.F.L. which participated in collective bargaining in most sections of Government employment. Exploiting these circumstances to their advantage, trade unions increased their membership from 2·7m. in 1914 to a peak of 5·1m. in 1920. Since the Government was concerned to maintain continuous production and employers' profits were inflated, it is not surprising that in the war industries wage rates were advanced with little difficulty. In manufacturing, transport, and coal mining real wages rose by 20 per cent between 1914 and 1918.

With the majority of unions in the A.F.L. wholeheartedly behind the war effort trade union leaders in America, like their counterparts in Britain, assumed new responsibilities in Government agencies.

On the War Labour Board, established early in 1918, five nominees of the A.F.L. sat opposite five representatives of industry and sought a peaceful settlement of industrial disputes on the basis of the acceptance of collective bargaining by the employers and of the industrial truce by the unions.

A glance at Table 25 reveals that throughout the 1920s the membership of American trade unions was falling. During the war Gompers had viewed with equanimity the growth of company or 'yellow dog' unions in the belief that after the armistice they would assert their independence of the employers. It proved otherwise. With the slackening of demand for labour after 1920 the employers' hold over their men increased. By profit sharing, welfare schemes, and high wages—including the well-known $5 a day at Ford's factories—they succeeded in keeping the majority of wage-earners out of the trade unions. Further, most judgements of the Supreme Court in the 1920s hampered trade union activity. In the case Bedford Cut Stone Coy. *v.* Journeyman Stone Cutters Association (1927) the 'yellow dog' contract was upheld and attempts to defeat it by means of a boycott declared illegal.

d **American labour under the New Deal and after.** In the six years between 1932 and 1937 the prospects and influence of American trade unions were transformed. New Federal legislation, upheld by the Supreme Court, provided the favourable environment; radical changes in union organization and policy helped labour to exploit the new situation to its advantage.

The Norris-La Guardia Act passed by the Republican Administration in 1932, greatly restricted the use of the injunction in labour disputes, legalized picketing, and outlawed 'yellow dog' contracts. In the New Deal era, section 7a of the National Industrial Recovery Act of 1933 gave powerful support to the unions by recognizing the right of employees 'to organize and bargain collectively through unions of their own choosing'. In this and other new deal measures concerning labour, Roosevelt's main objective was to spread employment and increase purchasing power. Strengthening the trade unions was an incidental rather than a primary aim of policy. Of outstanding importance was the National Labour Relations (Wagner) Act of 1935 which established a National Labour Relations Board for the purpose of supervising elections held by employees to determine who should represent them in negotiations with employers. It was also the duty of the board to ensure that employers did negotiate with the workers' representatives and that they did not resort to any of the 'unfair labour practices' specified in the act. The unions' efforts to improve working conditions were supported by the provision of the Walsh-Healy Public Contracts Act (1936), which established the eight-hour day and minimum wage rates for all Government contract work, and the Fair Labour Standards Act (1938), which improved the rewards of many poorly paid workers. Although some of the most powerful employers for a time refused to recognize the Wagner Act, its terms were upheld by the Supreme Court in the case National Labour Board *v.* Jones and Laughlin Steel Corporation in 1937.

Meanwhile, at the annual convention of the A.F.L. held at Atlantic City in November 1935, the attempt of John Lewis of the United Mineworkers to persuade the delegates to sponsor a campaign for organizing the mass-production industries on the basis of industrial unionism was frustrated by the opposition of 'old guard' leaders William Green and 'Big Bill' Hutcheson. Seven union leaders then joined Lewis in forming a Committee for Industrial Organization on 9 November 1935 to unionize such important industries as automobiles, rubber, and steel.

The year before the C.I.O. was formed the President of the A.F.L., William Green, had declared: 'We do not want to charter the riff-raff or good for nothings, or those for whom we cannot make wages or conditions, unless we are compelled to do so by other organizations offering to charter them under any conditions.' After 1935 the A.F.L. *was* compelled to organize the 'riff-raff' (i.e. the unskilled) because of the success of the 'sit down' strikes of the C.I.O.—led by the United Rubber Workers in 1936 and United Automobile Workers (in General Motors) in 1937, and the recognition of another C.I.O. body, the Steel Workers Organizing Committee, by the United States Steel Corporation in 1938. By 1940 the A.F.L., by organizing such unskilled groups as teamsters, machinists, and hotel workers, had increased its affiliated membership to 4,200,000, a figure which included a larger number of unskilled than did the C.I.O.'s 3,600,000.

Because of the outstanding successes of the American labour movement between 1933 and 1940, the advances made between December 1941 and 1945 when America was at war seemed less spectacular than concessions won in the First World War. Among the outstanding events of the years of the Second World War were 'no strikes' and 'no lock-outs' pledges given to Roosevelt by the principal leaders of the unions and of business; the creation of a War Labour Board (on which prominent union leaders were represented) to deal with all disputes which could not be settled by collective bargaining; and a maintenence of membership agreement by which those already members of trade unions had to retain their membership if they wished to keep their jobs.

Since eleven million persons were enlisted into the armed forces, and demand for war equipment greatly exceeded that of the First World War, a labour shortage enhanced the bargaining position of the unions, which increased their membership from 9m. in 1939 to 14·8m. in 1945. In the post-war period the tide of public opinion and of legislation tended to flow against the unions. The Taft-Hartley Act of 1947 banned the closed shop and imposed an 80-day 'cooling off' period (before a strike would be legal) in industries where strikes were likely to imperil health or national safety.

3 Summary and conclusions

This chapter has shown that an effective trade union movement appeared at a later date in America than it did in Britain. Part of the explanation of this difference lies in the different deployment of labour in the two countries. In the New World, the abundance of fertile land provided increasing opportunity for agricultural employment and it was not until 1880 that the number of industrial workers exceeded the number working on farms, and not until 1890 that the Census authorities stated that they could no longer trace a clearly discernible frontier of settlement. The scarcity of labour in America helped to stimulate the introduction of labour-saving inventions and increase the productivity, and often in consequence the wages, of labour. In Britain, land was scarce and labour relatively abundant. The entrepreneur had little inducement to innovate where labour was cheap, and in consequence the productivity of labour did not rise as rapidly as it did in America. Despite the imperfections of the early British census returns, it is clear that, at least by 1830, more adult males were employed in 'trade, manufactures and handicrafts' than were employed solely in agriculture. It is easier to organize men congregated in urban factories and workshops than it is to unionize a scattered agricultural labour force. The earlier predominance of the urban industrial worker in Britain therefore helps to explain the earlier growth of its trade union movement.

Through the period from the Civil War to the First World War the proportion of foreign-born to the total population of the United States was never less than 13·2 per cent or more than 14·5 per cent. This posed a problem of assimilation of greater magnitude than that experienced by Great Britain through the immigration of coloured peoples in the 1950s. Since the majority of the immigrants congregated in the large cities and industrial districts, language barriers made trade union organization unusually difficult, especially after 1890 when the proportion of Latin and Slav peoples among the immigrants rapidly increased. The U.S. Immigration Commission reported in 1910 that in twenty-one of the principal industries of the United States 57·9 per cent of the employees were foreign-born. Whilst it was true that after 1865, an extraordinarily large proportion of the founders, organizers, and executives of American trade unions had been born abroad',[8] it was also a fact that immigrant labour was frequently brought in to crush strikes, as was the case in the Pennsylvania coalfield in the 1870s and 1880s. These facts help to explain the advocacy of immigration restriction by the Knights of Labour from 1892 and the American Federation of Labour from 1897. They also go far to explain why the creation of powerful unions of unskilled and semi-skilled workers took place in America only in the 1930s, whilst in Britain, where despite the Irish, immigration was not a problem, some successes in organizing the unskilled were achieved over forty years earlier.

Immigration affected the attitude of employers as well as of labour. In the more 'open' society of America immigrants who became employers felt more socially isolated because of their alien origin, and had less compunction about brushing aside obstacles to their success in business. Hence the strong-arm methods used on behalf of Carnegie by H. C. Frick at Homestead in 1892.

Trade unions require a secure legal status before they can undertake the task of organizing the labour force with any prospect of success. The existence of well-entrenched states, rights, a national tradition of hostility to 'monopoly' in any shape or form, and a

Supreme Court, which at least until the 1930s, interpreted the
United States Constitution in a manner inimical to the trade unions,
all made the legal position of the American unions less secure than
that of their British contemporaries. In Loewe *v.* Lawlor (1902-8)—
the 'Danbury Hatters' case—the Supreme Court declared illegal an
attempt to boycott a non-union shop. In Hitchman Coal and Coke
Company *v.* Mitchell in 1917 it upheld 'yellow dog' contracts, and
in Duplex Printing Press *v.* Deering it further limited the powers
of unions to exercise the boycott. In addition, there was the widespread use of the injunction by Government and employers to crush
strikes over a period of five decades. By contrast, in Great Britain the
trade union movement was sufficiently strong to make the adverse
judgements of the House of Lords in the Taff Vale (1901) and
Osborne (1909) cases but temporary obstacles to the progress of
organization, the damaging effects of the judgements being more
than offset by the Trade Disputes Act (1906) and the Trade Union
(Amendment) Act (1913).

In both countries the solid foundations of trade unionism were
laid by the better-paid, skilled craftsmen or 'labour aristocracy' rather
than by the poorly-paid unskilled workers whose condition was most
in need of improvement. The 'new model' of the British trade union
movement—William Allan's Amalgamated Society of Engineers—
was to some extent paralleled in America by Samuel Gompers'
Cigar Makers' International Union. The organization of the larger
and less fortunate part of the labour force was delayed until political
conditions became more favourable. In Britain the extension of the
franchise in 1884 and the gains achieved by the dockers and others
in 1889-90 helped to make unskilled workers more aware of their
power to better their condition. In America, Roosevelt's electoral
triumphs of 1932 and 1936, the legislation of the New Deal, and the
formation of the C.I.O. in 1935, were of decisive importance.

Throughout the twentieth century the British trade union movement has had close ties with the Labour Party; in America, because
of different social, political, and constitutional conditions the trade
union movement has not created any permanent link with a political
party. One important consequence of these differences has been that
the policies of the American unions more closely resemble Gompers'
'pure and simple' trade unionism—confining activities to economic
demands—while British unions, though naturally interested in

bread-and-butter issues, are to a greater extent concerned also with political aims.

Notes

1 Quoted in PELLING, H. M., *America and the British Left from Bright to Bevan* (1956), p. 18.

2 COLE, G. D. H., *A Short History of the British Working Class Movement 1789-1947* (1948), p. 427.

3 THISTLETHWAITE, F., *The Great Experiment* (Cambridge U.P., 1955), p. 86.

4 *R.C. Trade Unions*, BPP, XXXII, Minutes of Evidence Q. 3735.

5 U.S. Congress, Senate Subcommittee of the Committee on Education and Labour, Hearings. *Violations of Free Speech and Rights of Labour*, 74th Congress, 2nd Session, 1936, pt. I: Labour Espionage and Strike Breaking.

6 GOMPERS, S., *Seventy Years of Life and Labour* (New York, 1925), I p. 166.

7 RAYBACK, JOSEPH G., *A History of American Labour* (New York, 1959).

8 JONES, M. A., *American Immigration* (1960), p. 221.

Suggestions for further reading

Texts

COLE, G. D. H., *A Short History of the British Working Class Movement 1789-1947* (revised ed. 1948).

PELLING, H., *A History of British Trade Unionism* (1963). *American Labour* (Chicago, 1964).

RAYBACK, JOSEPH G., *History of American Labour* (New York, 1959).

ULMAN, L., *American Trade Unionism, Past and Present* (reprinted from S. E. Harris (ed.), *American Economic History*, Berkeley, Calif., 1961).

Specialized works

CLEGG, H. A., FOX, A., and THOMPSON, A. F., *A History of British Trade Unions since 1889* (Oxford, 1964).

COLE, G. D. H. and FILSON, A. W., *British Working Class Movements. Select Documents, 1789-1875* (1965), ch. 17-21.

HOBSBAWM, E. J. (ed.), *Labour's Turning Point 1880-1900* (1948).

LITWACK, L., *The American Labour Movement* [Documents] (Englewood Cliffs, N. J., 1962).

PELLING, H., *America and the British Left from Bright to Bevan* (1956).

TURNER, H. A., *Trade Union Growth, Structure and Policy: a Comparative Study of the Cotton Unions in England* (1962).

1 The background

In social matters as in economic, America and Britain were closely inter-linked in the nineteenth century. There was a fertile exchange of ideas, and reformers found in the other country inspiration and evidence to support their particular views.[1] American democracy was held up as a model to the unenfranchised mass of Britons, while social reforms in Britain had, and still have, some impact in America. It was of course on the sparsely populated and undeveloped western border of Indiana that Robert Owen experimented with his famous settlement of New Harmony, and it was London with its splendour and squalor, its striking contrasts between the dignified and spacious West End and the overcrowded slums of the East End, that provided American observers with so much to criticize and condemn.[2]

The social problems and progress of the two countries were bound to be influenced, of course, by the characteristics of the respective societies. In Britain class consciousness, based on differences in wealth, education, and occupation, permeated society and even existed as a divisive force within the working classes themselves. Class barriers very slowly yielded ground before the onslaught of equalitarian ideas, reforms in the franchise and in education, and the gradual creation of the 'national minimum'; but it would not be too much to say that even as late as the 1930s the country's social institutions still reflected the class structure and were still largely geared to the maintenance of class distinctions.

In America class consciousness was not absent, but it assumed a different form. In the early stages of American development the generous abundance of natural resources, the ease of changing occupations and of acquiring property, encouraged a considerable degree of equality. But as occupations became more specialized, and as industry, agriculture, and commerce became more capitalistic, so class divisions became more marked, especially the essential American distinction between the man who made good and became rich, and the failure who remained poor. Such a distinction existed even in colonial times between the wealthy merchant or professional man and the poverty-stricken backwoodsman and farmer, and the process by which this class structure developed in nineteenth-century frontier conditions has been studied in detail by Merle Curti in his analysis of a pioneer Wisconsin settlement.[3]

The open character of American society, and the enormous opportunities the country afforded for the ambitious, energetic, able, and unscrupulous, encouraged the rise of the self-made millionaire land speculator, lumber baron, railroad financier, investment banker, and business tycoon. Conditions of natural abundance, together with the constant influx of immigrants anxious to make good and possessing some degree of skill and powers of innovation, helped to give to Americans the bustling, industrious, restless, and ambitious character commented upon by so many foreign visitors. The American, wrote Michael Chevalier,

is brought up with the idea that he will have some particular occupation, that he is to be a farmer, artisan, manufacturer, merchant, speculator, lawyer, physician or minister, perhaps all in succession, and that if he is active and intelligent he will make his fortune. . . . No one else can conform so easily to new situations and circumstances. . . . In Massachusetts and Connecticut, there is not a labourer who has not invented a machine or a tool. There is not a man of any importance who has not his scheme for a railroad, a project for a village or a town, or who has not some grand speculation in the drowned lands of the Red River, in the cotton lands of the Yazoo, or in the cornfields of Illinois.[4]

The geographical and occupational mobility of Americans, their flexibility and adaptability, and their unlimited belief in progress created that prejudice in favour of self-reliance, better known, perhaps, as 'rugged individualism', that still forms an important characteristic of American society. This is not to say that American society was atomistic; on the contrary, neighbourliness (as instanced by the communal raising of log cabins in areas of new settlement), and conformity to the behaviour and manners of the community, were very much part of the American tradition. Furthermore, American government at all levels played an important part in the development of transport, the extension of settlement, improvement of farming techniques, conservation of resources, protection of industry, and provision of education. In nineteenth-century Britain, too, government intervention in railways, industry, and commerce, and in the fields of working conditions, education, housing, and health, became more widespread and effective, especially in the fifty years before 1914. Nevertheless, 'self-help' and self-reliance were widely-praised virtues, and the children's school books, as in America, spread the gospel of hard work, thrift, and sobriety. The post-1834 Poor Law was designed to force the able-bodied labourer to stand on his own feet, the Charity Organisation Society taught the need to distinguish between the deserving and the undeserving, and even at the end of the century social reform, it was urged by liberal philosophers, should go no further than 'hindering the hindrances' which prevented people from enjoying the good life.

The working classes' interpretation of 'self-help', however, was rather one of improvement through combination and co-operation. Trade unions began their long struggle for recognition and power over wages and working conditions; friendly societies, like the unions, provided a degree of protection against the common misfortunes of life; co-operative societies of consumers procured supplies of cheap and unadulterated food (producers' co-operatives, however, enjoyed little success); working men's clubs and mechanics' institutes provided wholesome entertainment and education; temporary co-operative building societies helped to house the poor, while savings banks encouraged a remarkable growth of working-class thrift. There were many too poor or too indifferent to benefit from these movements, but for a large number the rigours of daily life in Victorian England were greatly eased. It is often forgotten that the welfare state, when its modest beginnings appeared in the early twentieth century, was a logical outgrowth of these movements, and was in fact grafted on to the collective self-help which had developed during the previous hundred years.

2 National wealth and the standard of living

Social progress accompanied, and was made possible by, the rise in national wealth and living standards. During the nineteenth century and the first four decades of the twentieth century, the workers' share of the growing national income of Britain remained broadly stable at a little over 40 per cent. It was only after 1939 that this share increased substantially. Real wages, however, rose markedly in the last forty years of the nineteenth century, and the increase between 1860 and 1891 may have been of the order of 60 per cent. Thereafter there was a slight decline until the First World War. Then between the wars the basic factors of rising productivity and cheaper food re-asserted themselves, and there was an improvement of some 15 per cent between the later 1920s and 1938.

The long-term rise in real wages was supplemented of course by improvements in the environment in which people lived—in housing, education, health, security, a shorter working day, and in facilities such as libraries, workhouses, parks, swimming pools, paid holidays, and a widening range of cheap entertainment and leisure activities. Nevertheless, all this should not obscure the fact that there existed a substantial proportion of poverty-stricken slum dwellers, some of whom existed at barely subsistence level. Investigations by Charles Booth in London from 1886 showed that 22 per cent of the population of the metropolis could obtain the necessities of life only by constant struggle, and over 8 per cent could not even achieve this. In York, Seebohm Rowntree, chocolate manufacturer of that city, found in 1899-1900 very similar results; and in subsequent years surveys of other industrial towns confirmed these revelations. Between the wars a further spate of social investigations found that in widely different towns like Bristol, Liverpool, and York there was still widespread evidence of the effects of low wages and unemployment—slum housing, inadequate diet, squalor, and disease. The hard core of extreme poverty had been reduced, but there was still a large class of extreme poor whom the benefits of industrialization had largely passed by.

In America, as in Britain, the period of falling prices in the later nineteenth century was one of rapidly growing real incomes. Wage rates (at $1.25 or $1.50 a day for an unskilled man) remained nearly stationary, while prices fell considerably between 1865 and 1898. Recently published estimates of the rise in real incomes show a more favourable situation than was once thought to have been the case. Real wages in manufacturing increased by about 50 per cent in the period 1860-90, and by about a third between 1890 and 1913.[5] Real wages continued to rise in the 1920s, although by the end of that prosperous decade there existed a great inequality in the distribution of income. In 1929 the wealthiest 5 per cent of the population received a third of all disposable income. There was a slow decline

from this level in the slump years of the 1930s, but a major fall
occurred only with the high taxes and return to full employment of
the war years. In 1940 the top 5 per cent still had a quarter of disposable income, but in the war years the proportion dropped to 16
per cent, from which level it has since risen again.

As in Britain, the rise in real wages in nineteenth-century America
was accompanied by improvements in the environment. There was a
marked increase in the proportion of expenditure going to consumer
durables, stretching from stoves and food grinders to the reed organ
and treadle sewing machines, the washing machine, clothes presser,
and icebox; while in due course the introduction of electricity and
the motor-car reduced rural isolation and created new types of labour-
saving machinery and sources of entertainment. Although real wages
were rising, it is probable that already in the nineteenth century the
distribution of wealth was becoming more uneven. By 1892 there
were over 4,000 millionaires, and at the end of the century 10 per
cent of the families owned some three-quarters of the national
wealth.

The great wealth of a minority, and the comfortable circumstances
of many, proved the point that America was the land of opportunity
for the European immigrant. But of course many of the immigrants
merely added to the mass of poverty and unemployment. In 1890, it
has been estimated, 11m. of the 12½m. families in the United States
had an average annual income of only $380, and at least a quarter
of urban workers were unemployed for a part of each year owing to
seasonal variations in production and other factors. Severe slumps
affected many workers following the three great financial crashes of
1873 (originating in the collapse of Jay Cooke, the great Civil War
and railroad financier), 1893 (when nearly 600 banks failed and
some 3m. workers lost their jobs), and 1907 (when J. Pierpont
Morgan and the Federal government between them restored confidence after the collapse of the Knickerbocker Trust).

There was also a great deal of rural distress in the era of falling
prices from the end of the Civil War to the later 1890s and again
between the wars. Low prices for produce, periodical crop failures,
and heavy indebtedness and high interest rates, meant that many
farmers experienced hardship and some were forced into bankruptcy.
Farming conditions varied greatly, of course, according to region, soil,
products, and communications. The worst conditions were found

then, as now, among the sharecroppers of the cotton belt and the hill farmers of the Appalachians, and in the semi-arid regions of the high plains.

The growth of large industrial cities spelled poverty of a different kind for many thousands of unskilled workers. Overcrowding in slum tenements, without ready access to fresh air and healthy relaxation, produced squalor and disease, care-worn adults and stunted children. In working-class sections of New York City in the 1890s people were crammed into tenement blocks at nearly 1,000 persons to the acre, and similar examples of gross overcrowding could readily be found in the other large industrial centres. Inadequate housing, diet, and sanitation spread epidemic disease, like that which killed off a tenth of the population of Memphis in 1873. For how many poor immigrants, swallowed up in squalid slums in a harsh and extreme climate, did America provide a premature grave rather than a golden future?

3 The problems and the remedies

The growth of industrialized society in Britain and America in the nineteenth century created many social problems, but the three greatest evils were poverty, ignorance, and bad health and housing. These three core problems were of course interlinked, since inadequate education was a major cause of poverty, and it was the worst-paid who were the worst-housed and the most liable to ill-health and premature death, which again led in turn to poverty.

a **Britain**   The problem of poverty was not capable of solution in the conditions of nineteenth-century Britain. Poverty was widespread (affecting some third of the population, if the figures of Booth and Rowntree were typical), and its roots lay in the low and irregular earnings of the poorly educated unskilled labourer, the illness and early death of the breadwinner, and the high proportion of income spent on drink and gambling. The long-term remedies thus lay in the diminishing numbers and higher productivity of the unskilled, better public health and personal health services, and education. The nineteenth-century Poor Law rested on the Act of 1834, the main purpose of which was to discourage the able-bodied from seeking relief, so keeping down the poor rates. The post-1834 workhouse, with its punitive rules and harsh discipline, discouraged all but the desperate from seeking its shelter. However, as time went by conditions in the workhouse were slowly moderated, and large numbers of widows, sick, and aged were relieved in their own homes by weekly doles of money, as they had been for long before 1834.

The evidence of Booth, Rowntree, and others showed quite clearly, however, that there existed a whole mass of poverty completely untouched by either the Poor Law or the numerous charitable organizations of the time. In line with the arguments of the Fabians, a society of middle-class intellectual Socialist reformers founded in 1884, state action was increasingly urged to tackle the problem. It so happened that the time was becoming ripe for effective state intervention in the social sphere. Innovations in social policy abroad, particularly in Bismarck's Germany, showed what could be done to provide insurance against unemployment and sickness, create health facilities such as maternity clinics and home visiting by trained nurses, and advance the cause of education. Political and administrative changes in Britain paved the way: the widening franchise gave to social matters a heightened political importance and urgency, a development which was encouraged by the rise of various Socialist movements in the 1880s and the formation of the Labour Party in 1906; while administrative reforms—especially the gradual modernization of the Civil Service and the reorganization of local government (following the landmark of 1888, when the County Councils were created)—provided the necessary machinery, and a corps of professional experts such as Medical Officers of Health and Schools Inspectors. Already the more progressive cities had shown what could be done to overcome the worst slums and inadequacies: in the 1870s Joseph Chamberlain, the Radical Mayor of Birmingham, endeavoured to make his corporation into a model municipality, providing parks, museums, art galleries, sewage farms, slaughter houses, artisans' dwellings, and even a municipal bank.

Money—the essential ingredient—was also forthcoming. In 1894, and again in 1907, death duties were stiffened, and in 1909 Lloyd George raised the income tax to 1s. 2d. in the pound—an unprecedented level in peacetime. 'This is a war budget', said Lloyd George, 'it is for raising money to wage implacable warfare against poverty and squalidness.' Lloyd George's 'war budget' also introduced a new super-tax of 6d. in the pound on incomes of over £5,000, a steeper scale of death duties, and a new tax on increases in land values. This last was suggested by Henry George, the American writer, in his *Progress and Poverty*, but as a tax it posed too many practical problems and was eventually dropped. The budget brought to a head the antagonism between the Liberal-dominated Commons and the Conservative-dominated Lords, and the subsequent constitutional struggle resulted in the Parliament Act of 1911, which greatly reduced the Lords' power over legislation and removed any power to delay a money Bill. The principle of using taxation as a means of redistributing income and of providing social services was thus established. Within a very few years the First World War was to raise greatly the levels of taxation, and they never fell back to their pre-war levels: an enormous rise in the permanently acceptable level of taxation was a vital pre-requisite of the welfare state.

The foundations of the modern British system of social security were laid by the Liberal Government of 1906 in legislative measures as well as fiscal reforms. While the Royal Commission on the Poor Law, which had begun work in 1905, was still deliberating, new policies designed to relieve unemployment and poverty were already emerging. In 1908 old-age pensions—7s. 6d. a week for old couples of limited means—were introduced, and in 1909 employment exchanges, meant to reduce frictional unemployment which arose through lack of contact between master and man, were established. Then in 1911 came the National Insurance Act. This was based upon German models and was grafted on to the existing voluntary schemes of insurance provided for members by friendly societies and trade unions, under which many workers already enjoyed some degree of protection against unemployment and sickness. The Act made use of the voluntary organizations for administering the national scheme, a plan which had the merit of economy, and emphasized the insurance aspect while gaining support for the Act of the friendly societies and trade unions. The workers, the employer, and the state each contributed $2\frac{1}{2}d$. per week, and the worker was guaranteed 7s. a week during unemployment up to a maximum of 15 weeks in any year. (When the Act was introduced weekly wages of the unskilled were about 20s. a week, and skilled men's wages were some 30s. or more.)

The unemployment provisions of the Act (Part II) at first applied to only $2\frac{1}{4}$m. workers in certain trades subject to severe fluctuations in employment: building, shipbuilding, mechanical engineering, ironfounding, vehicle construction, and saw-milling. (Part I of the Act, which dealt with insurance against sickness, covered far more people—all those wage earners with income below £160 per annum, and aged between 16 and 70.) Between 1916 and 1920, however, Part II of the Act was extended to cover all workers, except those in agriculture, domestic service, and certain occupations with low levels of unemployment. By 1927 14m. workers were covered. Between the wars, of course, the persistently high unemployment in the staple industries and elsewhere meant that many workers ran out of insurance benefit. In the depressed areas the strain on the Poor Law and local rates became intense, and in 1934 a new central authority, the Unemployment Assistance Board, administered the funds (originating mainly from the central government) which since 1931 had supplemented the relief provided by the Poor Law. The position then was that a person who became unemployed relied first on insurance benefit, and when that was exhausted, on unemployment assistance, subject to a means test—'the dole'.

Unemployment reached its peak of nearly three millions in the winter of 1932-3, and some 800,000 depended on the dole, regulated in 1934 by the Unemployment Assistance Board. Meanwhile, in 1929, the Local Government Act had abolished the Boards of Guardians instituted by the Poor Law of 1834, and placed responsibility for poor relief (now renamed 'Public Assistance') on the County Councils and County Boroughs for those in poverty who were too young or too old or sick to work. This measure thus created larger areas of administration allowing greater efficiency and economy, and followed the line of the 'break-up' of the Poor Law into specialized services as recommended by the Minority Report of the Poor Law Commission of 1905-9. As a reform it delighted the Webbs, the moving Fabian spirits behind the Minority Report—and incidentally it would have delighted Chadwick, the main author of the Act of 1834, who firmly believed in the advantages offered by large units of administration.

Poverty, although relieved, did not disappear, as new social surveys of the 1930s showed. At the current wages for the unskilled of £2 to £2 10s. a week, an employed family man might be worse off than one receiving unemployment assistance. Rowntree's second survey of York, *Poverty and Progress*, showed that while extreme poverty was only half as common as in 1899, nearly a third of the working class of York had too little in wages (or in relief) for the minimum income necessary to sustain a healthy life: this, he calculated, was 53*s*. for families with three dependent children. Progress there had been, but poverty remained.

Bad housing and bad public health—intertwined evils—had early received attention in nineteenth-century Britain. Chadwick's great Report of 1842, *The Sanitary Condition of the Labouring Population*,[6] drew together the existing evidence of overcrowding, disease, inadequate water supplies, and lack of sanitation, and began a public debate which has gone on to the present day. The Public Health Act of 1848 was a first modest attempt at reform, but the problem was a complex and enduring one beyond the resources of a society that had still to make fundamental discoveries in the causes and prevention of disease.

Inadequate housing and deplorable sanitary conditions sprang basically from the rapid flow of labour into large industrial towns, creating hasty development and overcrowding. It was not until late in the century that the town authorities had the powers or were sufficiently aroused to undertake slum clearance, make building regulations, and introduce adequate systems of sewage disposal and water supply. The large average size of the Victorian family put pressure on housing and gave rise to overcrowding. Further, a large part of the working population had incomes too low to be able to afford a decent standard of housing. It simply did not pay to build houses for families with low and irregular incomes, whose honesty and habits of temperance and cleanliness were doubtful. Thus there was always at the bottom of Victorian society a large group of people who were badly housed, or indeed not housed at all.

Much of the legislation, such as the Torrens Act of 1869 and the Cross Act of 1875, was merely permissive and had little effect. Only in 1890 did slum clearance and rebuilding become mandatory on local authorities. While private reformers experimented with model industrial estates, garden cities, and cheap tenements for the poor, building and sanitary by-laws made the mass of English housing conform to minimum standards of space, water supply, and sanitation. The Public Health Act of 1875 brought every area of the country under the charge of a Medical Officer of Health, and hospital and general medical practice moved on to modern lines following the

work of Pasteur, Simon Koch, and others. By the late nineteenth
century British towns were in general safe to live in, and violent
uncontrollable epidemics were a thing of the past. Nonetheless, the
towns still contained vast slum areas, and too often were unhealthily
dirty and smoky, and depressingly monotonous and ugly.

The First World War had a great impact on attitudes toward
housing and led to the introduction of new policies. Rent controls
were introduced during the war to check the inflationary effects of
the cessation of house building and the control of rents of smaller
houses persisted after the war and down to the present. Subsidies to
lower the cost of housing provided for rent by local authorities were
introduced in 1919, and were supplemented by subsequent legislation in 1923, 1924, 1930, and since the Second World War. For the
most part, however, this legislation failed to help the very poorest
classes who, as in Victorian times, continued to be extremely ill-
housed. In 1939, despite large-scale slum clearance and rapid building of private housing estates in the 1930s (aided by low interest
rates and cheaper methods of construction), large areas of old, sub-
standard housing still existed, although the general situation was
better than it had been for perhaps two centuries.

English education developed along class lines. The state system, as
it grew after 1870, provided a basic elementary education for the
working classes; for the children of the middle classes there existed
a variety of private schools from the little Dame schools and local
grammar schools to the great public schools of national reputation,
whose fortunes were revived in the nineteenth century by head-
masters such as Arnold of Rugby and Thring of Uppingham.

The building of schools by the government itself came only late
in the nineteenth century partly because of the activities of the
voluntary societies—the National and British Societies, aided after
1833 by government grants—and partly through the existence of
religious and political objections to the principle of state-provided
education. In the later nineteenth century there was a growing sense
of the inadequacy of the English system. The extension of the franchise and the consequence that 'we must now educate our masters',
the pressure of trade unions, the growing needs of industry, commerce, professions, and public administration for personnel with a
certain minimum of education, the belief that mounting foreign
competition, especially that from Germany, was based upon superior

education—all contributed to a feeling that reform and expansion were needed.

Thus, from the Act of 1870, a series of measures raised the minimum school-leaving age, and in 1891 abolished fees in state schools. The 1890s saw a rapid growth of technical colleges, and in 1902 the principle of direct state support was formally extended to secondary education, while administrative reorganization placed the responsibility for secondary and higher education upon the county councils created in 1888. The Fisher Act of 1918 marked a further advance by raising the school-leaving age to 14, and abolished the part-time system under which children over 11 had been allowed to spend half the day in school and the other half at work.

Between the wars, the agitation of the Labour Party for 'secondary education for all' was widely heard. In 1926 the Hadow Committee supported the view that the inadequacy of secondary education was resulting in human wastage and loss to the nation of unexploited talent among the working classes. The government followed up this lead and encouraged local authorities to go further in providing separate secondary schools or classes for children over 11 who had not won places through the 'scholarship' system in grammar and technical schools. By 1938 this 'Hadow reorganization' encompassed some 60 per cent of children of secondary age, and secondary education for all finally became a reality with the great Butler Act of 1944.

b **America** Despite the abundance of natural resources and rapid industrialization, serious social deficiencies, including widespread poverty, existed both in the countryside and in the towns of America. It has been estimated that in 1890 some 11m. of the total of 12½m. families received an average annual income of only $380. The enormous material progress made in industry and agriculture, the rise of great industrial and commercial centres, and the march to success and vast personal wealth of such figures as Carnegie and Rockefeller, created a sense of complacency which obscured the true social facts. Carnegie even denied the very existence of pauperism in America (despite the existence of such a classification in the Federal census), and academic exponents of *laissez-faire* philosophies claimed that no evidence of distress or misery had been produced by the pessimists.

Just as these opinions appeared, radical thought and literature, concerned since the Civil War with such varied questions as feminism, temperance, Negro rights, labour claims, land reform, currency, and civil service and city government reform, burst forth into its great period of 'Progressivism' (*c.* 1890-1917). The dominant theme of this period was hatred of corporate wealth and power, and it was marked by 'muckraking' attacks on the great corporations such as Standard Oil, the meat-packing industry, and wheat speculation.[7] But a good deal of attention was directed also towards poverty and social conditions.

The first attempt to survey the problem of poverty comprehensively and systematically was made by Robert Hunter in 1904. He deplored the lack of reliable statistics for the problem in the United States, and referred to the pioneer work of Booth and Rowntree in England. However, he was able to draw on a variety of sources to produce the following broad survey of the problem:

There are probably in fairly prosperous years no less than 10,000,000 persons in poverty; that is to say, underfed, underclothed, and poorly housed. Of these about 4,000,000 persons are public paupers. Over 2,000,000 working-men are unemployed for four to six months in the year. About 500,000 male immigrants arrive yearly and seek work in the very districts where unemployment is greatest. Nearly half of the families in the country are propertyless. Over 1,700,000 little children are forced to become wage-earners when they should still be in school. About 5,000,000 women find it necessary to work and about 2,000,000 are employed in factories, mills, etc. Probably no less than 1,000,000 workers are injured or killed each year while doing their work, and about 10,000,000 of the persons now living will, if the present ratio is kept up, die of the preventible disease, tuberculosis.

The causes of poverty were much the same as Booth and Rowntree found in England: lowness of wages, unemployment and irregularity of earnings, death, injury or sickness of the wage-earner, and misspending of income on drink and other non-essentials. As in England, poverty was concentrated among the mass of unskilled workers, most of whom earned, Hunter believed, less than the $460 a year (or $300 in the South) estimated as the minimum necessary to support a family of two adults and three children.[8]

The central problem of reform, as pinpointed by Hunter and many others, was that of getting effective legislation passed and enforced against the apathy of the majority, with their predilection for state rights, and against also the active opposition of the influential minority of property owners and business men. The railroads each year might kill over 2,500 employees and maim nearly 40,000 more (the figures for 1900), the anthracite mines of Pennsylvania might employ children of eight or nine upwards to work 10 hours a day picking slate out of coal in the 'breakers', slum tenements in New York City might kill off whole families with tuberculosis—but property rights and profits must be respected. Existing legislation was difficult to enforce, and in any case touched only the fringe of the problem. Hunter estimated that the official poor—the public paupers in receipt of institutional care (often provided as in England, in an old mixed poorhouse), or receiving outdoor relief of meagre doles of money or goods—represented only two-fifths or less of the total in poverty. In New York City the newly created Board of Health passed a series of laws on tenement houses from 1867. But these laws applied only to new buildings, and so ensured that the old buildings, with their lower rents, remained grossly overcrowded and insanitary while making for their owners an annual profit of 40 per cent.[9]

Misgovernment of the cities sprang from the view that politics, as also social institutions, should be subservient to business; that politics and administration were fields for those men with insufficient talent to succeed in business; and that, as Lincoln Steffens said, it was thought 'natural, inevitable, and—possibly—right that business should be—by bribery, corruption, or—somehow get and be the government'.[10] The city 'boss' controlled the slum districts where he had large property interests. In return for votes he dispensed patronage, city jobs, reduced court sentences, railroad passes, admission to hospitals. In some cities the policeman did not dare to enter places which he knew violated the law; his superior took orders from the boss, as did the mayor also. The practice of electing important city officials, and the division of powers among mayor, department heads, aldermen, councillors, and magistrates created confusion, irresponsibility, and administrative incompetence. The low salaries paid to municipal officials and civil servants attracted an inferior class of worker and encouraged corruption and the taking of bribes. In this situation the voting power of the mass of poor was nullified, and reformers were seldom elected; or if elected, they found it almost impossible to achieve progress or to maintain it when achieved.

By the constitution the reform of social conditions was the province of the states and cities, and this necessarily meant that the growth of effective legislation was gradual and piecemeal, while evasion was made easy. Children could be sent across state boundaries to work (as from New York to New Jersey) and thus escape control in either state, putting-out work could be sent to states which lacked restrictions on home employment, and the greatest field of child employment—farming—was almost entirely unregulated. Lack of Federal control meant also that businessmen could threaten to transfer their concerns to other cities or states if labour legislation was passed, while reformers had to meet the power of the city bosses and overcome the apathy of the state legislatures, in which the rural areas were over-represented.

The progressives were drawn principally from the middle class; as in England, it was mainly the educated and intelligent man and woman of professional status or independent means who developed a strong social conscience. Uncommitted to business or politics, and free of the dogma that nothing should stand in the way of profits and property rights, this group of writers, university professors, teachers, ministers, and leisured women had the time and resources to become amateur social investigators, reformers, and propagandists. 'Between 1897 and 1914 Progressive societies multiplied rapidly in number and membership. Child Labour Committees, Consumer's Leagues, Charities Aid societies, church organizations and women's clubs appeared in all our industrial cities and states and formed national associations with branches everywhere. They employed professional social workers, secretaries, treasurers and sent trained lobbies to state capitals and to Washington. They sent practical lecturers to address groups all over the country, published their own periodicals, and competed successfully for space in popular journals.[11]

The principal concern of these Progressive societies was the plight of the 2m. children revealed by the census of 1900 as employed in wage-earning occupations. A typical Progressive publication of 1914 castigated the human cost in terms of physical suffering, mental stunting, early deaths and deformity, that this figure implied. It stated that one in every seven children between the ages of 10 and 14 was not at school, and pointed to child employment as a major factor in the existence in America of 6m. illiterates.[12]

In England the history of effective factory legislation had begun with the Act of 1833 which appointed inspectors to enforce the law that no children under 9 should be employed in textile mills, and that children under 13 should work no more than 9 hours a day. Subsequent acts in 1844 and 1847 extended the law to women and also governed the use of dangerous machinery, and after 1842 no women or children could be employed underground in coal mines. In 1867 all factories were brought within the pale, and subsequent legislation further widened the scope of the law, provided for workmen's compensation for accidents (ineffectively in 1880, and effectively in the Acts of 1896 and 1906), and eventually brought control to the workshops of the sweated trades—the surviving domestic industries—in the Trade Boards Act of 1909. Even more important than the Factory Acts in restricting child employment were the provisions for compulsory school education in the Education Acts from 1870 onwards.

In America the introduction of effective factory legislation came much later, partly because the factory system itself developed rather later than in England (and in the South very much later), and partly because the size and nature of the problem was not realized until about the beginning of the twentieth century. By then twenty-eight northern states had some kind of child labour laws, but none of these laws was adequate in scope or was fully enforceable. In the early years of the new century, however, Progressive Child Labour Committees made rapid progress. New laws, or amendments to old ones, extended regulations to children employed in non-factory occupations such as newsboys, bootblacks, pedlars, and messengers, and included such measures as compulsory education, a maximum 8-hour day, prohibition of night work. By the time of the First World War, legislation in many states had extended also to women, and covered public health, workmen's compensation, minimum wages, and tenements—and in some states there were special provisions for enforcement.

In the years between the opening of the new century and the First World War the Progressives also made some important gains in the sphere of national legislation. True, much of the legislation was merely nominal and was largely ineffective, such as the first Pure Food and Drug Act of 1906. Under Theodore Roosevelt and Taft, Republican administrations learned to make concessions that kept the Progressives at bay and removed some of their impetus while maintaining intact the privileged position of the large corporations.

Some of the concessions, however, were of enormous importance for the future—the 8-hour day for Federal employees, establishment of the Bureau of Mines to supervise safety and working conditions, the Children's Bureau, the Labour Department, and last but perhaps most important the Income Tax, submitted to the voters in 1909 and finally achieved in 1913. Between 1902 and 1913 total Federal, State, and Local Government expenditure on education more than doubled, and education and public welfare together accounted for a fifth of total government spending in 1913.

Some progress thus was made, but much remained to be done. New laws were one thing, enforcement was another. The main causes of poverty—low wages, unemployment, industrial accidents, unhealthy living and working conditions—remained largely untouched. Further, the opposition of business men was growing and was becoming organized. Some Progressives gave up the struggle, others turned to socialism or regulation of the trusts. Then the First World War took priority of interests and energies. After the war the movement took another form. Instead of trying to enforce increasingly detailed legislation, the leading states developed new agencies, industrial commissions, whose function was to set up and maintain general standards, originally in the fields of health and safety but in time extending to the whole gamut of factory regulation. Progress was very uneven, however: in 1925 twelve states still allowed children under 16 to work for over 48 hours and up to 60 hours a week, and thirteen states allowed boys of 14 to work in mines; child labour in agriculture was still largely unregulated. Over the whole country nearly 400,000 children aged 10 to 13—probably an underestimate—were at work in 1920.[13]

It was the great slump of the 1930s, and the New Deal programme arising out of those years, that gave social reform a new impetus and a changed direction. The sense of economic crisis that followed the Stock Exchange Crash of 1929, the appearance of mass unemployment, the bank failures that destroyed the savings of years, the street beggars and the soup-kitchen lines convinced many Americans that 'rugged individualism' was a myth and that the individual workman and his family were helpless in the face of this economic blizzard of unprecedented severity. Hoover's view, echoed by many conservatives, that poverty was due to individual failing, and that 'some folk won't work', was no longer tenable. Only massive intervention by the Federal Government could provide the security that the economic system had so signally failed to provide.

For political and practical reasons the Federal intervention was necessarily piecemeal and mainly directed along already established lines. The Fair Labour Standards Act of 1938 set minimum standards for all labour engaged in inter-state commerce or in the production of goods for such commerce, and eventually covered some 13m. workers. The Act authorized the introduction of a maximum working week of 40 hours and a minimum wage of 40 cents an hour, and it also prohibited the employment of children. The measure represented the logical Federal capping of earlier measures in the individual states, and followed on the creation of employment exchanges (1933), the regulation of railroad workers' pensions (1934), and control of working conditions of labour engaged on public contracts (1936). Similarly, the Social Security Act of 1935 represented a Federal generalization of the limited measures introduced in some states to provide old-age pensions, and the solitary example of unemployment insurance (Wisconsin).

The Federal intervention of 1935 was designed to *encourage* state provision of social security, not to enforce it. There were in fact two schemes for providing help for the old. Where the state participated, the Federal Government met half the cost of paying pensions to needy persons over 65, and enabled workers, through graduated contributions paid partly by themselves and partly by the employers, to participate in pension schemes; under the second scheme, however, all workers earning less than $3,000 a year in 1935 (with the important exception of those in certain large occupations such as agriculture and domestic service), were compelled to join a Federally-financed programme under which pensions proportionate to earnings at retirement were paid from 1942 onwards. For security against unemployment, where the individual states had adequate unemployment insurance schemes 90 per cent of a Federal payroll tax on employers was handed over to the state to support them. Finally, the states were given annual appropriations to provide relief for dependent children, support maternity and child welfare schemes, and give aid for crippled children, the blind, and for vocational retraining. Further, under the New Deal's work-providing programmes, thousands of miles of roads were built, together with bridges and sewers, many airports, and thousands of public buildings, parks.

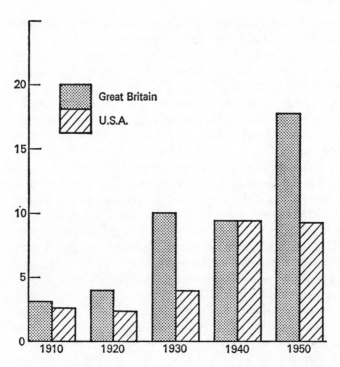

Figure 31. Social welfare expenditure as a percentage of gross national product 1910-50

playgrounds, reservoirs, and power plants. Low-cost housing and slum clearance under the U.S. Housing Authority of 1937 was another offshoot of the attempts to provide jobs, but in this case the opposition of private real-estate interests restricted the new housing to very small proportions.

In contrast to Britain, the development of social reform and welfare legislation came late and piecemeal. In 1939 the measures in force and the actual achievement still varied widely from state to state. In part this diversity sprang from the size and diversity of the economy itself; in part it sprang from the existence of the Federal system and the predominant belief in the sanctity of state rights—a sentiment which often provided an excuse and cloak for the maintenance undisturbed of vested interests concerned to preserve private enterprise, low taxes, and a provincial obscurantism on social matters. The rapid growth in the United States of agriculture, industry, and commerce had made the country populous and wealthy, but the dominance in politics and the national consciousness of business and its interests often proved a great obstacle to progress in providing social security and justice.

In the development of education, for example, the influence of business and practical needs were particularly marked. 'Scientific Schools' or technical institutions were established in connection with Yale, Harvard, and other colleges as early as the 1840s, while from the 1820s Mechanics Institutes were opened in the major cities. Elementary education before the Civil War, however, was often weak or non-existent in parts of the country, particularly in the South, although the New England states required young workers under 14 or 15 to spend some three months a year at school. From 1862 the Morrill Land-Grant Act provided the newly-established western states with means to found agricultural colleges, following the lead set by Michigan in 1857. And in 1890, the second Morrill Act provided Federal grants to enable the new colleges to expand in size and raise their standards. A number of these land-grant agricultural colleges grew into great state universities of international reputation. But the importance attached to agricultural education remained strong, and was seen in Acts of 1914 and 1917 which provided Federal Aid for farm demonstration work and agricultural education.

After the Civil War elementary education still suffered, as in England, from poor school attendance, an inadequate supply of school places and of teachers in some areas, and a restricted view on the part of parents and school authorities of the scope and value of education. As the school system developed there was a marked tendency for teaching and curricula to reflect the ideals and interests of the business community.

New Englanders sought almost from the start to impose the ideals of eastern cities upon the merchants and farmers of the West. After the Civil War similar intentions dominated urban educators in relation not only to farmers but also to city workers. Standard textbooks, written to a large extent by people associated with city schools and distributed by publishing houses in New York, Boston, and Philadelphia were bound to convey urban mores and business ideas, and it early became a matter of policy for educational agencies to see that contrary ideas were shut out. . . . Business led the drive in the late nineteenth century for the training of skilled artisans and mechanics in the public schools and at the public expense. The objective was education for industrial efficiency.[14]

The trend continued between the wars when the business leaders, supported by the middle classes, sought to eliminate radical ideas and make 'socialism' and 'communism' dirty words. 'Community pressure, and direct intimidation, were employed to make recalcitrant teachers toe the conventional mark. But more important, textbooks were written in accordance with business ideas, or corrected to get these ideas across. Whole courses, especially in government and civics were introduced to preach the business gospel, while business publications themselves were used in many schools.[15]

Meanwhile, the numbers in school and college rose, although the levels of attainment were still often unsatisfactory. While by 1920 the majority of northern states required children leaving school to have reached at least the sixth grade (nine states specified the eighth grade). in the South a definite leaving standard (usually the fifth grade or 'proficiency in specified subjects') was laid down in only seven states. In all, thirty-five states allowed children to go to work without a common school education, and eleven states discounted the opportunity of further education by permitting children under 16 to work from nine to eleven hours a day. School attendance remained poor: in 1920 the average number of days attended by each pupil under 18 years of age was less than 100 in twenty-five states, and the annual expenditure per pupil attending school was below $50 in fourteen states, all in the South. In twenty-two states with large rural, Negro or immigrant populations (fifteen of them in the South), the proportion of illiterates among persons of 10 years and over was more than 5 per cent. The proportion of total government spending devoted to education was about 18 per cent in 1913 and in the 1920s, but fell below this level in the 1930s.

Many Americans believed they were right in placing the creation of wealth before the security and welfare of the under-privileged, and the high living standards of the middle classes seemed to some to justify this view. But there remained, and remains, at the base of American society a large body of people badly educated, very poor by the standards of the affluent part of the nation, and basically insecure—lacking the certainty of adequate relief in time of unemployment, ill-health, accident, and old age. Nevertheless, the New

Deal measures did provide the foundation for future progress. And the wealth of the country, and the income and special security taxes, as in England, provide the financial means for the more just society which both countries are still in the process of creating.

4 Conclusion

Social reform and the development of a 'welfare state' in Britain came gradually: severely limited early reforms paved the way to the broader measures of later years. There was little or no conscious planning, but rather the adoption of *ad hoc* measures to meet particular problems as they became urgent. The impetus to reform came from a variety of directions—the stirring of the social conscience by middle-class investigators and propagandists like Booth, Rowntree, and the Fabians; the socialist and labour movements, made politically powerful by extension of the franchise and the organization of unskilled workers; the example provided by reform overseas, particularly in Germany; and the appreciation of social inadequacy revealed by the Boer War and the First World War. Progress in reform depended ultimately on the growth of a favourable public opinion, the acceptance of higher levels of taxation (here the First World War had an important influence), rising national wealth, and administrative reforms in the Civil Service and local government.

The American experience showed many of the same factors, but there were important differences. The stimulus again came from middle-class progressives and overseas example, in this case the example of Europe, particularly Britain; administrative reform and the income tax were also significant. On the other hand, the movement began later, and without the assistance of an American Booth, Rowntree, or even a Chadwick; the socialist and labour movements were smaller and relatively without influence; wars had a more limited effect. A favourable public opinion was much slower to develop, partly because of the primacy of business interests in American education and politics, and the cherished belief in 'rugged individualism'. Great and persistent obstacles were placed in the path of reform by corruption in the cities and by the constitutional entrenchment and public reverence for state rights; this meant in effect the preservation of large areas of low standards, and limited and ineffective measures. While progressive states, such as Wisconsin, led the reform movement, Federal intervention, begun in the progressive era before the First World War, and greatly extended by the New Deal of the 1930s, proved necessary to bring in the laggards, and so meet the problems of the poor and neglected in the wealthiest country in the world.

Notes

1 Particularly was this so among nonconformist groups in the movement for the emancipation of women, and in educational reform. See F. THISTLE-THWAITE, *America and the Atlantic Community* (New York, 1963), ch. 3-5.

2 See for example *Palace and Hovel* by DANIEL J. KIRWAN (ed. A. Allan, 1963), esp. ch. 21-5.

3 CURTI, MERLE, *The Making of an American Community: a case study of democracy in a frontier setting* (Stanford, 1959).

4 CHEVALIER, M., *Society, Manners, and Politics in the United States* (1839; New York, Anchor Books ed. 1961), pp. 267-70.

5 See LONG, CLARENCE D., *Wages and Earnings in the United States* 1860-1890 (Princeton, 1960), p. 61, and REES, ALBERT, *Real Wages in Manufacturing* 1890-1914 (Princeton, 1961), p. 120.

6 Recently re-issued with an Introduction by M. W. Flinn (Edinburgh U.P., 1965).

7 See for example TARBELL, IDA M., *History of the Standard Oil Company* (New York, 1904), SINCLAIR, UPTON, *The Jungle* (1906), NORRIS, FRANK, *The Octopus* (1901), and *The Pit* (1903).

8 HUNTER, ROBERT, *Poverty* (1904), pp. 52-3, 327.

9 FORD, JAMES, *Slums and Housing* (Harvard, 1936) I, p. 166.

10 STEFFENS, LINCOLN, *The Autobiography of Lincoln Steffens* (1931), II, p. 606.

11 COCHRAN, THOMAS C. and MILLER, WILLIAM, *The Age of Enterprise* (New York, 1961), pp. 276-7.

12 MARKHAM, E., LINDSEY, B. B. ,and CREEL, G., *Children in Bondage* (New York, 1914), p. 306.

13 National Industrial Conference Board, *The Employment of Young Persons in the United States* (New York, 1925), pp. viii, 6, 64.

14 COCHRAN and MILLER, *op. cit.*, pp. 270-1.

15 *Ibid.*, pp. 332, 338.

Suggestions for further reading

Texts

BRUCE, M., *The Coming of the Welfare State* (1961).

COCHRAN, THOMAS C. and MILLER, WILLIAM, *The Age of Enterprise* (Harper Torchbooks, New York, 1961).

MOWAT, C. L., *Britain between the Wars* (1955), esp. ch. 4, 8-9.

Specialized works

BOWLEY, M., *Housing and the State* (1945).

BRIGGS, ASA, *Seebohm Rowntree* (1961).

DOUGLAS, P. H., *Real Wages in the United States 1899-1926* (New York, 1930).

EAGLESHAM, ERIC, *From School Board to Local Authority* (1956).

FORD, JAMES, *Slums and Housing* (Harvard, 1936).

HUNTER, ROBERT, *Poverty* (1904).

LEWIS, SINCLAIR, *Main Street* (1920).

ROWNTREE, SEEBOHM, *Poverty: a Study of Town Life* (1901).

SIMEY, T. and M. B., *Charles Booth, Social Scientist* (Oxford, 1960).

SINCLAIR, UPTON, *The Jungle* (1906).

STEFFENS, LINCOLN, *Shame of the Cities* (1904).

THISTLETHWAITE, F., *America and the Atlantic Community; Anglo-American Aspects*, 1790-1850 (New York, 1959).

WEBB, BEATRICE, *My Apprenticeship* (1926).

1 The impact of war on the Atlantic economy

The First World War marked a watershed in the economic relations between Britain and America. In the world's capital market London had been 'leader of the international orchestra' before August 1914. After the armistice it was apparent that it had lost its pre-eminence and that, at least in terms of international loans outstanding, New York had taken the lead. In 1914 the aggregate of British funds invested in the U.S.A. was some £800m. whilst American investment in Britain was equivalent to a mere £55m. By March 1919 British investment in the U.S.A. had shrunk to £600m. whilst outstanding American loans to Britain had risen to £1,027m. This transformation had come about as a result of the rapid growth of the positive balance of American foreign trade from $56m. in 1914 to $3,475m. in 1917.[1] This huge surplus provided the basis for the dramatic increase in overseas lending. In the short space of four years the roles of the two countries had been reversed. Britain was creditor on a large scale in 1914 and America the debtor; by the time of the armistice America was creditor and Britain debtor. Thus began a long period of British financial dependence on the U.S.A.

During the war-time emergency America supplied a much larger proportion of total British imports than she had done in peace time. To economize in shipping and deal more effectively with the German submarine menace, Britain obtained her food and raw material imports from the nearer rather than the more distant sources of supply. Thus imports from America, which had formed 18 per cent of the total value of British imports in 1913, rose to 39 per cent of the total by 1918. But this was only a temporary increase. After the war Britain reverted to her traditional sources of supply, and by 1923 the American share, at 19 per cent, had dropped back almost to the pre-war level. The proportion of British exports going to the U.S.A.— 6·6 per cent—was virtually unchanged by the war.

In both countries there was a rapid expansion of those industries which contributed most directly to the war effort whilst those which were less vital to national survival experienced a relative decline. In Britain the engineering industry experienced the biggest expansion of output and the most far-reaching changes in organization. Because of the necessity of large-scale production of standardized munitions, the importance of specialized machinery as compared with manual skill greatly increased. British steel production rose by 50 per cent, with the basic open hearth furnaces providing a substantial contribution to production for the first time. Shipyards were very busy throughout the war. After two years of comparative neglect by Government, from the end of 1916 British farmers were encouraged to plough up pasture land, and some three million additional acres were cultivated by December 1918, with the result that the production of wheat was raised by 60 per cent, oats by 68 per cent, and potatoes by 71 per cent, compared with the immediate pre-war years. On the other hand, the consumption of raw cotton by the Lancashire factories declined by a quarter in the four years of war. Domestic house building was virtually at a standstill.

Since the American Government did not declare war against Germany until April 1917 the direct impact of the war on the American economy was of briefer duration. The biggest contribution of American industry to the allied war economy was in the production of ships. In the summer of 1914 the registered tonnage of American shipping was 5m., compared with a British tonnage of over 19m. In 1916 launchings from American yards amounted to only 384,899 tons. By 1918, however, American launchings at 2,602,153 tons were over double those of the United Kingdom, largely through the production of standardized 'Liberty' ships. The performance of the American railroad industry, under Government supervision from the end of 1917, was second only to that of shipbuilding. At the end of 1918 productivity was 42 per cent above the level of 1914. To feed the railroads, the shipyards, and the rapidly expanding iron and steel industry, the output of coal rose by a third in the war years. Although the index of physical production in agriculture remained virtually unchanged, this apparent stability masked big shifts of emphasis within the industry. Production of wheat for export to Europe took precedence. The acreage of this crop planted rose by nearly a half in four years, and in 1915 the first billion bushel wheat harvest was gathered. On the other hand, the acreage under corn remained practically stationary. Changes in the American engineering industry were less far-reaching than they were in Britain. The organization of the industry was, in any case, less in need of modernization and it had less time in which to become dominated by war demand. The differing situations of the two industries are illustrated by the trend of motor-car production. In America the output of cars rose from 440,000 in 1913 to 1,750,000 in 1917, fell to 943,436 in 1918, but quickly recovered to 1,651,625 in 1919. In Britain, deeper and more prolonged involvement in the European war led to the adaptation of many of the car factories to the production of tanks. The result was that at the time of the armistice there were only three private cars in use for every four being driven before the war.

In both Britain and America leading statesmen at first believed that it would be possible to prosecute the war with the minimum of state interference in economic life. In Britain, Winston Churchill coined the slogan 'business as usual' to reassure the public that the war would be of brief duration and that the mechanism of the market would secure adequate supplies for the equipment of the armed forces. The result of following these maxims was rapidly rising prices and profiteering in scarce commodities. Serious bottle-necks in the supply of shells and other vital materials of war re-mained. By means of a series of 'nightmarish improvizations'[2] the government stumbled into a policy of much greater state involve-ment in the economy. In America Congress could at least profit from British experience, but there was by no means an orderly transition to a war-time economy. After April 1917 'agencies of control were created in confusing array, altered, brought into conflict with one another, co-ordinated and reco-ordinated, until finally, when the war was over, something like order had emerged.[3]

By the end of the war the state in Britain was employing 5,700,000 men in the armed forces, besides some 3,400,000 men and women in the manufacture of munitions. State control over industry and agriculture was virtually 'all pervasive',[4] with government agencies managing all principal forms of transport and purchasing 90 per cent of the imports, controlling prices, and marketing some 80 per cent of the food consumed at home. In America 4,744,000 men were en-listed into the armed forces and some 9m. persons employed in the war industries. Through the War Industries Board, the Railroad Administration, the Food Administration and their agencies, the Federal Government controlled the most important sectors of the economy. In Britain the standard rate of income tax was raised from 1*s*. 2*d*. in the £1 in the last peace-time budget to 6*s*. in 1918-19. Surtax was raised in proportion, and an Excess Profits Duty siphoned off about a third of the additional profits directly attributable to the war. In America the standard rate of income tax was raised from 2 to 4 per cent during the war, and the exemption limit for single persons was lowered from $3,000 to $1,000, and for married couples from $4,000 to $2,000. Surtax was increased far more steeply, rising from a maximum of 13 per cent in 1913 to 63 per cent in 1919.

Standardization and mass production in industry were greatly encouraged by the unprecedented demands for uniforms, rifles, and all the other requirements for clothing, feeding, and equipping the vast armies of the allies. Administratively, it was simpler to place huge orders for supplies with the large-scale producers rather than to spread them amongst a much larger number of smaller producers with the attendant risk of variation in the quality of the product.

Among the more important indirect effects of the war were the growth of nationalism and protectionism in Europe and the Middle East. Encouraged by President Wilson's 'Fourteen Points' speech of January 1918, many hitherto subject peoples achieved their political independence after the war. Small states such as Finland, Czecho-slovakia, and Syria seized the opportunity of their newly-won free-dom to erect tariff barriers in an endeavour to achieve as great a degree as possible of economic independence. The dislocations of war also led to an upsurge of protectionism in Britain and America, though in the former case the McKenna duties of 1915 (on motor cars and cycles, watches, clocks, and film), were a new departure from long-established policies of freedom of trade, whilst in the latter the Emergency Tariff of 1920 and the Fordney-McCumber Act of 1922 represented, rather, the raising of rates of duty on a tariff, which was largely protectionist even in 1913. These develop-ments impeded the recovery of the British economy in the post-war world far more than they did the American, for foreign trade was (and is) the life-blood of the British people. It was of far less signi-ficance to the prosperity of America.

2 The reversion to a peace-time economy

The desire of business interests on both sides of the Atlantic immediately the armistice was signed was to return to 'normal' trading
conditions, free of government controls, at the earliest possible
opportunity. In London *The Economist* voiced the general demand
that the nation should 'cease to pay people for putting difficulties in
the way of private enterprise'.[5] Following that 'khaki' election of
14 December 1918 Parliament yielded to these demands. The immediate post-war atmosphere was vividly recaptured by the leading
economic historian of the inter-war period:

'From the first day after the armistice, when the Government was
told that "every trade and industry they have touched they have
hampered and injured", a roar of protest arose in the House of
Commons against the continuance of war-time restrictions, and the
denunciations of the "vague megalomania" which perpetuated
"huge and acquisitive departments" were echoed in the press.
The cabinet scanned the sky, trimmed its sails and ran before the
storm.'[6]

Since the war-time period was regarded as 'abnormal', the enhanced powers conferred on the Government for mobilizing the
resources of the nation were granted for a strictly limited period only.
Administratively, the line of least resistance was to allow these
abnormal powers to lapse as quickly as possible. Positive belief in the
advantages of the continuance of controls in peacetime and a willingness to sponsor new and more permanent legislation were needed if
government was to play a larger part in economic affairs after 1918
than had been the case in 1913. Lloyd George's coalition government (1919-22) lacked both. Before the armistice, the Ministry of
Reconstruction had appointed dozens of committees to make recommendations for the reorganization of Britain's post-war economy. But
their recommendations were largely ignored, the Government using
the committees 'as a drunken man uses lamp posts—for support
rather than for illumination.'[7] By the close of 1919 demobilization
had been completed and the majority of war-time emergency controls
over industry had been lifted. In three major industries—agriculture, coal mining, and the railways—decontrol was delayed for
exceptional reasons until 1921. The devastation caused by the war
to the French coal industry led to abnormally high prices obtained

for British coal exports in 1919 and 1920. The Inland Revenue gained a windfall of £170m. for the financial year 1918-19 alone, since taxation took 80 per cent of the excess profits of the industry. With such a godsend the Government was in no hurry to abandon its interest. By January 1921 it was a very different story. With the recovery of production on the European continent the price of coal collapsed, and the Treasury faced a prospect of heavy losses at a time when revenues were already falling because of the trade recession. In February 1921 it was announced that decontrol would take effect from 31 March of that year instead of on 31 August, as previously notified. The consequences of this panic decision for the morale of the industry, and particularly for its labour relations, were catastrophic. Decontrol of agriculture came about in much the same fashion. Farm price support, instituted in the Corn Production Act of 1917, was continued under the Agriculture Act of 1920, but quickly abandoned under the Corn Production (Repeal) Act, 1921, when world food prices tumbled. Decontrol of the railways was carried out in a more orderly fashion. A consolidation of railway management would have come about early in the twentieth century even without the stimulus of war. Under the Railways Act of 1921 control was passed from the Railway Executive Committee, which had managed the lines since 1914, to four main-line companies formed from the grouping of the more than 120 companies providing rail services before August 1914. When the new groups took over operations under the act the last important relic of war-time government control disappeared.

The fundamental objective of the American Government after the war was the same as that pursued in Britain—the restoration of freedom for business interests. On 28 January 1920 the Secretary of the Treasury wrote to the President of the U.S. Chamber of Commerce as follows:

'From the moment of the cessation of hostilities the Treasury of the U.S. has pursued a policy of looking toward the restoration as promptly as possible of normal economic conditions, the removal of governmental controls and interference and the restoration of individual initiative and free competition in business.'[8]

The change to a peace-time economy was made with even greater speed and thoroughness than was the case in Britain. Demobilization of the armed forces was practically complete by October 1919.

The War Industries Board began to end price controls within two days of the armistice, and some government housing schemes, more than half completed, were abandoned with unseemly haste. Only in the case of agriculture, shipbuilding, and transport, was the abandonment of controls to any extent delayed. Nevertheless, the Government dropped price support for wheat in June 1920, a year earlier than was the case in free trade England. A similar concern to that felt in Westminster to consolidate private management, prompted the maintenance of the Railroad Administration until after the passing of the Transportation Act in February 1920. The Emergency Fleet Corporation continued to build ships into the first half of 1920, but under the Merchant Marine (Jones) Act of 5 June 1920 there was a large-scale selling of government-built ships to private owners, $25m. of the proceeds being earmarked as loans to private shipbuilders. This policy was adopted with the object of retaining for the United States a larger proportion of its trans-oceanic carrying business than it had enjoyed in 1913.

3 The British economy in the 1920s

The achievements of British and American industry between the wars may be summarized by stating that the increase in industrial production was greater in America than it was in Britain in the 1920s, while in the 1930s the British performance was much the better of the two.

Between 1920 and 1929 real income per head in Britain rose by an average of only 0·93 per cent per annum, with nearly all the increase coming after 1924. In America, by contrast, real wages in manufacturing industry rose at an annual rate of 3·1 per cent between 1921 and 1929. (The percentage growth would be somewhat lower if it were possible to include reliable statistics of agricultural earnings.) In Britain in the 1930s real income per head grew at a rate of 1·99 per cent a year, whilst at the same time in America *per capita* income fell between 1930 and 1933 inclusive, and did not reach the 1930 level again until 1936. It was still slightly below the 1929 figure in 1939.[9]

Although some of Britain's economic difficulties were a direct consequence of the war, it would be wrong to claim that the after-effects of war were a principal cause for the slow economic recovery of these years. The dangers of this kind of escapist interpretation have been clearly shown by a leading economic historian:

The war was a social cataclysm, the like of which had never been known before, an event of such magnitude that it was plausible to attribute to its power all the changes observable after it. But the war was also a strictly temporary phenomenon, whose effects also should be temporary, especially if special steps were taken to speed up their removal. Seen in this way the economic problem of the nineteen-twenties was to undo the damage wrought by the war, and in practice that came to the same thing as seeking happiness in the restoration of something very like the *status quo ante*. On such lines the judgement of most informed and thinking men ran. And in so judging they were wrong. Had there been no war the United States would still have become the world's great creditor; industrialization would still have spread in new areas, to the destruction of some British markets; substitutes for coal would still have grown in importance; the sources and costs of primary commodities would still have changed.[10]

An outstanding preoccupation of both the Government and the banking community in the early 1920s was to restore the value of the pound to its pre-war parity with the dollar and to re-establish the international gold standard. The determination with which these objectives were pursued was partly the result of a natural desire to return to the familiar pattern of trading of 1913, when London was the unchallenged money market centre of the world. This longing found early expression in the Interim Report of the Cunliffe Committee, presented just three months before the armistice:

In our opinion it is imperative that, after the war, the conditions necessary to the maintenance of an effective gold standard should be restored without delay. Unless the machinery which long experience has shown to be the only effective remedy for an adverse balance of trade and an undue growth of credit is once more brought into play, there will be grave danger of a progressive credit expansion which will result in a foreign drain of gold menacing the convertibility of our note issue and so jeopardizing the international trade position of this country.[11]

That this view was widely held is revealed in the statement made by a leading banker, Sir Felix Schuster, to a meeting of the Institute of Bankers in 1921: 'Let us have done with short cuts and by paths and return to the old standard. The road may be long and painful but our fathers trod it before us and we know the way.'

Runaway inflation in central Europe in the early 1920s only re-inforced these beliefs. In December 1923 wholesale prices in Germany were 1,300,000,000,000 times those of 1913. Financial experts were concerned that unless Britain's floating debt was reduced and the issue of Treasury notes (which first appeared in August 1914) drastically curbed, the cost of necessary imports would be prohibitively high and Britain would be priced out of her export markets.

By a Treasury minute of 15 December 1919 the Government accepted the recommendations of the Cunliffe Committee and drastic deflationary measures were introduced in the following year. Bank rate was raised to 7 per cent in April 1920, and kept at that level for a year. The volume of floating debt was greatly reduced, the budget was balanced, and bank deposits and the note issue cut back. The price paid in human terms was a high one. The level of unemployment soared from 2 per cent of the insured population in the spring of 1920 to 18 per cent a year later. But the external value of the pound was raised nearer to its pre-war level.

An important side-effect of the post-war deflation and rapidly falling prices of 1920-2 was an increase in the real cost of servicing the national debt. American deflation, starting in mid-1920, enhanced the value of gold and thus made the British deflationary process still more painful. In the inter-war period an impression was created that the German Government bore the heaviest burden of debt because of the obligation to make reparation payments. In 1929-30, however, the British Government spent 46 per cent of its budget on debt redemption and servicing whereas the German Government spent 23 per cent.[12] The consequence for Britain was an income tax never below 4s. in the £1, compared with 1s. 2d. in 1913. It was widely believed that the continuance of such a 'high' rate of tax depressed the volume of private investment.

Much controversy has raged over the wisdom, or otherwise, of returning to gold in April 1925 at the pre-war parity of 4·86 dollars to the pound.[13] In his famous pamphlet *The Economic Consequences of Mr. Churchill*, J. M. Keynes argued that the pound was over-valued to the extent of 10 per cent and that, in consequence, the price of British exports, particularly coal, was raised in proportion. On the other hand, undue emphasis should not be given to the international monetary reasons for the slow recovery of the British economy lest the more fundamental weaknesses in industrial organization be overlooked. What is not disputed is that Montagu Norman, who was Governor of the Bank of England from 1920 to 1944, had received his early training before 1914 with Brown and Shipley, a firm that specialized in international lending between Britain and America, and that international finance rather than domestic industrial growth was the dominant interest throughout his career. Captains of industry were rare visitors to Threadneedle Street in the 1920s. Norman's diaries show that, even after 1926, in an average week there were over thirty appointments with international businessmen and bankers, financial specialists, politicians, and diplomatists for every stray visit by an industrialist in trouble.[14] Since in Norman's view industrial investment and employment in Britain were not his responsibility, it is not surprising that industry sometimes lacked the positive encouragement to modernize its capital equipment that it so badly needed.

One clear indication that all was not well with the British economy in the 1920s was the persistence of a high level of unemployment:

TABLE 26

Unemployment in Great Britain 1922-9

Year	Total unemployed (in thousands)	Percentage of insured population unemployed
1922	1,543	16·0
1923	1,275	11·6
1924	1,130	10·9
1925	1,226	11·2
1926	1,385	12·7
1927	1,088	10·6
1928	1,217	11·2
1929	1,216	11·0

Source: Mitchell and Deane: *Abstract of British Historical Statistics*, p. 66, *Ministry of Labour Gazette*. Owing to the exclusion of agricultural workers and other categories the figures are incomplete.

Throughout the 1920s more than three-quarters of the total number of unemployed came from those industries which had flourished before 1914—coal mining, cotton textiles, shipbuilding, and iron and steel. Viewed from one standpoint an important reason for the continuance of an unemployment level of over 10 per cent

throughout the inter-war period was the failure of the newer industries, which included motor-car manufacture, electrical engineering,
chemicals, and artificial fibres, to grow sufficiently rapidly to absorb
those thrown out of work through the depression in the older basic
industries.

The difficulties of the basic industries were of pre-war origin.
Britain had over-committed herself to the prosperity of these trades
before 1914.[15] The remarkable concentration on overseas investment in the decade before 1914 may have had the effect of starving
the older industries of the necessary capital for their modernization,
and denying the newer industries the opportunity for healthy
growth, but technological factors, the attitudes of businessmen, and
the situation in the home and overseas markets also influenced the
pattern of industrial development. America was readier to turn to
newer industries in the 1920s than was Britain because a smaller
proportion of its total resources was concentrated in the basic
industries, and there was, therefore, less call for 'defensive' investments for their preservation.

After 1924 one problem of the coal industry was a world glut of
supplies in relation to an almost stagnant demand.[16] But even if
demand had expanded at the remarkably rapid rate of the pre-war
years, Britain would have experienced difficulties in maintaining
the level of her exports because of the cramping effects of the return
to gold in 1925 and the faster rise in productivity in the mines of the
European continent. Before 1914 coal mining in Britain was largely
pick-and-shovel work. Only 8 per cent of the record output of 287m.
tons of coal raised in 1913 was mechanically cut. By 1921 the proportion had risen to 14 per cent and by 1930 to 31 per cent, but in the
meantime the proportion of American coal mechanically cut had
risen from 60·7 per cent in 1920 to 78·4 per cent in 1929. There were
far too many small mining concerns in Britain. The Samuel Commission, which examined conditions in the industry in 1925, reported that there was a total of 2,481 mines run by 1,400 separate
business concerns, but that 84 per cent of the total output came from
but 323 of the firms. In the light of these facts it is scarcely surprising that the output of the industry, after climbing from a total
of 229m. tons in 1920 to a post-war peak of 276m. tons in 1923,
fell back to 237m. tons in 1928. Employment, which stood at
1,248,000 in 1920 shrank to 939,000 in 1928, at which time 23·6

per cent of the industry's labour force was unemployed. Although a majority of the members of the Sankey Commission in 1919 had recommended some form of national ownership of the industry, and the Samuel Commission, six years later, urged nationalization of mining royalties, the Government was slow to act. Not until 1930 was cartelization encouraged under the Coal Mines Act of that year. As late as 1945 the Technical Advisory Committee (Reid Committee) reported that the individualism of a large number of self-contained units was unlikely to encourage major developments in the science of mining.

The plight of British shipbuilding was also in large measure due to a change in the conditions of world demand and supply. Immediately after the war order books were full, the prices of ships soared, and there was 'a particularly wild orgy of speculation' during which thirty companies with a capital of £4m. were formed in the space of one month.[17] In 1920 a record total of 2m. tons of shipping was launched. But by 1921 there was over-supply and ships bought at £24 10s. a ton were selling at £5 10s. a ton. Shipping freights fell in sympathy. Faced with a decline in their revenues, shipowners made do with older ships for a longer period of time than they had done previously. Before the war orders for new ships had been sustained because of a brisk second-hand market. With the decline of such sales after 1921, the depression of the industry was aggravated. Throughout the 1920s the annual shipbuilding capacity of British yards remained at about 3m. tons, which was equal to the entire world's need for new ships. Under-capacity working and heavy unemployment were the inevitable results.

The iron and steel industry experienced a speculative boom in the years 1919-20, when nominal capital grew from £20m. to £67m., an increase quite out of relation to the real value and prospects of the industry, which was financially embarrassed in the 1920s in consequence. In the years following the immediate post-war boom, the industry suffered both because of the disappointing performance of the economy as a whole, and because of its own competitive weaknesses. Pig-iron production, which exceeded 8m. tons in 1920, failed to reach this figure again until 1937, though this failure is partly explained by a greater utilization of scrap iron in the industry. Although production of steel, which had reached 9,067,000 tons in 1920, rose to 9,636,000 in 1929 (after an earlier decline), world output increased by 63 per cent between 1913 and 1929, whilst British output rose by only 8 per cent. Throughout the 1920s there was much redundant capacity and a fifth of the labour force was unemployed. In the later years of the decade there were some impressive improvements in productivity, but the industry was 'inferior by the nature of the labour supply, character of the home market, lack of sufficient scientific training, oldness of plant, changing conditions of ore supply, dearness of transport, unsuitable sites for older works and inflexibility in face of new circumstances'.[18]

A wholly unjustified speculative mania also swept through the cotton industry after the war: 238 mills with 42 per cent of the cotton spinning capacity and a value of £10,815,000 changed hands for £71,875,000 within a few months of 1919-20, leaving the industry in a financial strait-jacket which hampered necessary modernization. With the shrinkage of markets, particularly in India and the Far East, production of yarn shrank from 1,963m. yards, annual average, in 1911-13, to 1,395m. yards in 1927-9, whilst export of yarn fell from 210m. yards in 1913 to 167m. in 1929. Piece goods production fell by a quarter over the same period, while exports slumped from 7,075m. yards in 1913 to 3,765m. in 1929. Although the decline in output was wholly due to falling exports, domestic demand meanwhile increasing, a greater foothold in overseas markets could have been secured if the industry had not possessed so many small firms with antiquated equipment. The necessary reorganization of management was largely delayed until the 1930s.

An old-established industry which could have contributed more decisively to economic recovery—as it did in America—was building construction. There was no doubt about the severe housing shortage in Britain after the war, but there was no building boom in the 1920s because the industry lacked profitability. Whereas rents were kept down under Rent Restriction Acts from 1915 (in 1930 only one in ten houses was decontrolled), there was no control over building cost and interest rates, both of which remained at a high level. In the event, the government helped employment through loans under the Housing Acts of 1919, 1923, and 1924, and by these means two-thirds of the million and a half new houses completed in the 1920s were financed. The proportion would have been larger but for economy cuts in government expenditure in 1921, which reduced the number of houses built under the Act of 1919 from a planned 500,000 to 216,000.[19]

It is only when one looks at the performance of the newer industries that a more cheerful picture is obtained of post-war Britain. Between 1924 and 1930 workers employed in these industries rose from 10·2 per cent of the total to 12·7 per cent. Whilst it is not possible to agree with a recent writer that this steady shift of men and resources 'more than counteracted the adverse effects of the decline in the basic sector',[20] the trend helped to lay the foundations for the more impressive achievements of the economy in the later 1930s.

One of the success stories of the inter-war period was the growth of electricity supply. The industry had got off to a late start due to faulty legislation in 1882 and 1888 which limited the operations of electricity undertakings within municipal boundaries. Not until 1900 did Parliament allow companies to supply power to wider areas limited by county rather than municipal boundaries.[21] In the early 1920s, therefore, there were no less than 438 companies supplying electric power, more than three-quarters of them very small concerns. A bewildering variety of voltages was supplied. After a fruitless effort by means of the Electricity Supply Act of 1919 to persuade the small companies to amalgamate, they were compelled to hand over to a Central Electricity Board, which monopolized all electricity wholesaling, under the Electricity Supply Act of 1926. Between 1927 and 1933 the board distributed power through 4,000 miles of grid, making possible an increase in the number of consumers from 730,000 in 1920 to 8,920,000 in 1938. In many respects this impressive progress was decisive for the improved growth rate of the economy in the 1930s. It made possible the shift from the old coal, steam and iron development block to the new electric power, light industry complexes. Between 1912 and 1930 the proportion of power supplied electrically to industrial undertakings increased from 25 per cent to 66·2 per cent.

The motor industry offered valuable potentialities for the growth of other 'feeder' industries such as rubber, electrical goods, paint, and steel alloys, and thus its expansion was of key importance to the whole economy. At the beginning of this period there were far too many producers in the business for efficient large-scale production. Manufacture was more a case of skilled craftsmanship than mass assembly. But improvement was rapid. From the remarkably low level of 73,000 cars and commercial vehicles produced in 1922, the number rose to 239,000 in 1929—an output still little more than a tenth of that achieved by the 1960s. Even this level of advance would not have been possible but for the reduction in the number of producers from eighty-eight in 1922 to thirty-one in 1929, when three firms produced three-quarters of the output. Export performance in the 1920s was disappointing partly because the method of taxation of vehicles—on the basis of horse-power—encouraged the production of low horse-power vehicles such as the famous Austin Seven, whilst customers abroad, whose roads were often not up to British standards, were looking for more powerful vehicles. At the end of the decade only one car in eight was exported.

One of the largest industrial combinations to emerge in the 1920s was Imperial Chemical Industries, formed in 1926 from a merger of four already large concerns. This £65m. undertaking possessed the resources both to undertake the fundamental research so vital to the progress of the industry and to organize large-scale production of its very wide range of products. One branch of the chemical industry which expanded with great rapidity in the 1920s was the production of rayon and other artificial fibres. British production of rayon in 1929 was three times that of 1922; but although these advances were impressive they fell behind the performance of rival producers.

The progress of the new industries was not adequate to transform the overall picture of the economy for a number of reasons. The newer industries were capital-intensive rather than labour-intensive. For a comparable value of output they employed a smaller labour force than did the old-established industries, especially coal mining. The firms which encouraged research were exceptional. The Balfour Committee on Industry and Trade made the sad comment in 1929: 'Before British industries taken as a whole can hope to reap from scientific research the full advantage which it appears to yield to some of their more formidable trade rivals, nothing less than a revolution is needed in their general outlook on science. . . . In our opinion it is the imperfect reception towards scientific ideas on the part of British industry which is at the moment the main obstacle to advance, and a change in this attitude would open up prospects of development which are at present beyond the range of possibility.'[22] Home sales of the new products increased far more rapidly than did exports, so that their contribution to the country's balance of payments remained relatively small. The largest category of British exports remained those expanding least in world trade:

TABLE 27

Export of manufactures from Britain and U.S.A. in 1929

Percentage of groups expanding, 1913-1929 in world trade by

	Less than 75%	75-150%	More than 150%	No data
Great Britain	42·1	33·5	4·3	20·1
U.S.A.	17·1	38·8	28·6	15·5

Source: W. A. Lewis, *Economic Survey* 1919-39 (1949), p. 78.

That Britain's balance of payments remained favourable in the 1920s was due only to the very favourable terms of trade of those years and the high earnings from invisible exports.

A feature of the decade was the disbelief amongst economists and statesmen that positive action could do much to relieve unemployment and hasten the transition from the older to the newer industries. The view of Pigou, the leading Cambridge economist was that there would 'always be at work a strong tendency for wage rates to be so related to demand that everybody (would be) employed.'[23] In the opinion of R. G. Hawtrey, the leading authority on monetary economics, public works programmes were 'merely a piece of ritual, convenient to people who want to be able to say they are doing something, but otherwise irrelevant.'[24] The most commonly held belief was that wage rates were not sufficiently flexible for costs to be reduced and hence for export prices to be lowered. A prominent Liberal economist expressed the consensus when he wrote that 'a sufficient lowering of real wages over a wide range of occupations would undoubtedly have been a remedy' for much of the unemployment between 1922 and 1929.[25] Treasury hostility to public works expenditures was expressed in the 'Memorandum on the Finance of Development Loans prepared by the Treasury', and Conservative and Labour chancellors alike adhered to the objective of balanced budgets and held a common disbelief in the efficacy of increased government spending as a tonic for recovery, even though at the time there was much underemployment of men and resources.

In sum, therefore, there were important sectors of British industry which were expanding in the first post-war decade, but the overall achievement was less impressive than that of America, even though it could be argued that the foundations of British recovery were more soundly laid. The earlier over-commitment in the basic industries, mistakes in monetary policy, and the remoteness of much contemporary economic discussion from the realities of the industrial world were among the more important reasons why Britain did not do better.

4 The American economy in the 1920s

America returned to a *laissez-faire* economy with even fewer inhibitions than did Britain in the 1920s. Prevailing business opinion was clearly enough expressed in one of the best-known contemporary novels:

' "In my opinion, what the country needs, first and foremost, is a good sound, businesslike conduct of affairs. What we need is a business administration", said Littlefield. (Babbitt:) "I'm glad to hear you say that! I certainly am glad to hear you say that! . . . What the country needs—just at the present juncture—is neither a college president nor a lot of monkeying with foreign affairs, but a good, sound, economical business administration, that will give us a chance to have something like a decent turnover." '26

Under the Republican administrations of Harding, Coolidge, and Hoover between 1920 and 1932 the country obtained the kind of business government so stridently advocated after the war. It was taken as axiomatic that 'the welfare of business, especially big business . . . necessarily means the public welfare. The two are absolutely inseparable.'27 Trust in the efficacy of business leadership even permeated the churches as revealed in a notice on a New York church billboard: 'Come to Church. Christian worship increases your efficiency. Christian F. Reisner, Pastor.'28 Among the indications of the predominance of the interests of big business in American Government in the 1920s were the appointment of Andrew Mellon as Secretary of the Treasury (1921–8), pledged to a policy of reducing taxes on the highest income brackets; the reduction of government spending on public works and buildings, health, and welfare, but a substantial increase in the expenditure of the Department of Commerce on information services for businessmen; and the passage of the highly protectionist Fordney-McCumber Tariff (1922). During the decade the lenient attitude taken by the Supreme Court towards big business in cases brought before it under the anti-trust laws (notably in U.S. *v.* United States Steel Corporation 1920), may be contrasted with its hostility to trade unions shown in such decisions as Duplex Printing Press Company *v.* Deering (1920-1), which upheld the use of the injunction in industrial disputes. The Presidency played a largely passive role in this period. It was the conviction of Calvin Coolidge that 'the least government was the best government'.

Despite the one-sidedness of its government, America was booming through most of the years of the 1920s. The gross national product rose from a total of $73·3 billion (at 1929 prices) in 1920 to $104·4 billion in 1929, whilst income per head increased from $688 to $857 over the same period. The overall improvement disguised the uneven performance of the different sectors of the economy and the growth in the inequality of income distribution. Unemployment averaged below 5 per cent of the gainfully employed population—less than half that experienced in Britain:

TABLE 28

Unemployment in U.S.A. 1920-9
(In thousands of persons 14 years and over. Annual averages)

Year	Unemployed	Per cent of civil labour force
1920	1,670,000	4·0
1921	5,010,000	11·9
1922	3,220,000	7·6
1923	1,380,000	3·2
1924	2,440,000	5·5
1925	1,800,000	4·0
1926	880,000	1·9
1927	1,890,000	4·1
1928	2,080,000	4·4
1929	1,550,000	3·2

Source: *Historical Statistics of the U.S.*, Series D46-7, p. 73.

The industries which prospered through much of the decade were building construction and the manufacture of automobiles, petroleum, radios, chemicals, and electrical equipment. Depressed sectors of the economy included agriculture, coal mining, New England textiles, and leather.

One of the most remarkable features of the post-war economic expansion was the boom in real estate investment and building construction. The conditions in America were almost the exact opposite of those prevailing in Britain, for rents remained for some years at a high level, building costs were low, and credit was abundant. The index of the value of new building in current prices (1920-30 = 100) rose from 50·9 in 1920 to a peak of 137·7 in 1925, before tapering off to around double the 1920 figure in 1929 as rents fell and building costs rose.[29] Development in some of the states, such as California and Florida, had all the characteristics of a mania. The population of Miami soared from 30,000 in 1920 to 75,000 in 1925. Swollen advertisement columns enabled the *Miami Daily News* one day in the summer of 1925 to print an issue of 504 pages, the largest in newspaper history.[30] Older established cities like Chicago and New York acquired new skylines.

Of the newer industries automobile manufacture enjoyed great prosperity in the early 1920s. Over 1,905,000 passenger cars were sold in 1920. By 1923 output had reached 3,624,000. There was a levelling off of demand in 1924, but by 1929 there was an output of 4,455,000—a total not to be exceeded for another twenty years. The industry flourished because the prices of popular models of cars were reduced to bring them within the range of the lower incomes (the price of the Ford Model T. Runabout fell from $550 in 1920 to $260 in 1924), and because sales were stimulated by the spread of hire-purchase arrangements. Some measure of the importance of the industry can be gained from the fact that in 1929 it accounted for 12·7 per cent of the value of all manufactures, it used 15 per cent of the nation's steel production, and employed over 7 per cent of all the wage-earners employed in manufactures.

The building construction and automobile industries acted as a kind of flywheel for the continuing prosperity of industry as a whole since they created vast derived demands for timber, bricks, glass, furniture, upholstery, steel alloys, electrical fittings, etc. Further, the prosperity of building construction and automobiles reacted on

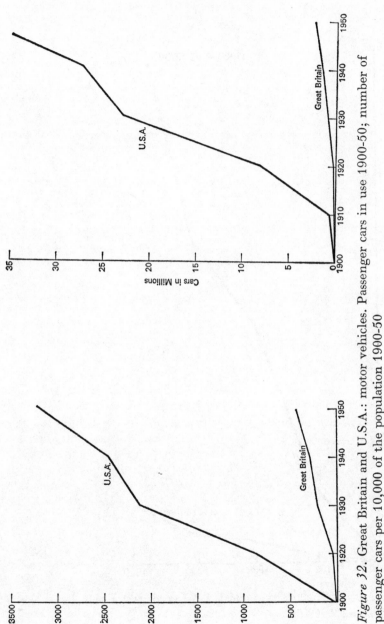

Figure 32. Great Britain and U.S.A.: motor vehicles. Passenger cars in use 1900-50; number of passenger cars per 10,000 of the population 1900-50

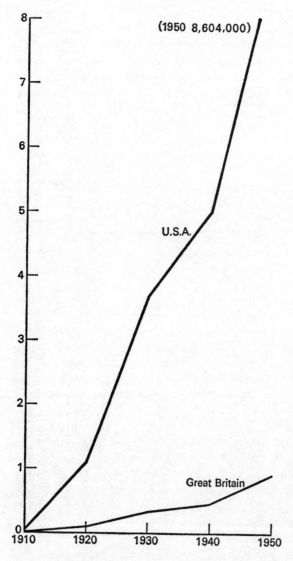

Figure 33. Great Britain and U.S.A.: goods motor vehicles
registered 1910-50

each other. The sale of passenger cars and commercial vehicles led to demands for better roads. The spread of a network of metalled roads released the country resident from dependence on a near-by railroad and increased the demand for more automobiles. In the early days of the motor-car local and state authorities had undertaken the building and maintenance of roads, but by 1916 it was evident that their resources were inadequate for these tasks. Under the Federal Highways Act of that year the principle of Federal matching grants was accepted, though the outbreak of war prevented its immediate application. In 1921 another Federal Highways Act was passed providing for Federal matching grants for 'such projects as (would) expedite the completion of an adequate and connected system of highways, interstate in character.' By 1923 the Bureau of Public Roads of the Department of Agriculture had completed a tentative map of roads reaching every city of 50,000 or more inhabitants.[31] The Federal Government was not reluctant to spend money for such an objective and the next few years saw the rapid execution of the plan. Construction programmes for highways and buildings together employed more men than any private industry in the 1920s.[32]

The prosperity of the petroleum industry was clearly dependent to a considerable extent on a flourishing automobile industry. The rapid spread of electric power and growth in motor-car registrations were responsible for the greater importance of gasoline as compared with kerosene in total production. Gasoline production multiplied four times within the decade. There was a shift of the main centres of production from the older oilfields of the east to new fields in states further west, especially Oklahoma, Texas, and California.

The question whether electric power generation should be left entirely in private hands or should be subject to a greater or lesser degree of public control was a matter of great controversy in the twenties. Whereas in Britain consolidation was carried through under the aegis of the state, in America eleven privately-owned holding corporations controlled 85 per cent of electricity supply by 1929. The year before this, the Federal Government had approved the Boulder Dam project to generate electric power from the Colorado River; but the scheme met great opposition during the Republican era, and a similar project at Muscle Shoals on the Tennessee was vetoed by both Coolidge and Hoover. The installed generating capacity of electric power stations rose from 19·4m. kilowatts in 1920 to 38·7m. in 1929. The widespread availability of this new form of power provided the opportunity for a great expansion in the supply of electric appliances for domestic use. The value of the output of electrical household appliances rose from $82·8m. in 1920 to $176·7m. in 1929. The sale of radios increased in even more spectacular fashion from $17m. in 1920 to $366m. in 1929.[33]

Despite these remarkable advances in material welfare, prosperity was unevenly spread throughout the American economy. Coal mining was an outstanding example of an industry which languished after the war. It employed more men than any other major occupation with the exception of agriculture and transport. But the industry suffered from excess capacity arising from the rapid opening of new mines in times of boom and war and a subsequent slump in demand which was the result of the emergence of new fuels. Nearly 700,000 men were on the books of the industry when there was permanent work for only 500,000.[34] Whereas in Britain the labour surplus was wholly unemployed, in America the typical miner was on short time, working only two or three days a week. Labour relations were even more embittered than they were in Britain. Twenty strike-breakers were killed in fighting with miners in Williamson County, Illinois during the national coal strike in the spring of 1922.[35] There was scant regard for life in the operation of the mines. The number of fatalities per thousand miners employed was over three times as great as in Britain, although the American mines were generally shallower. The United States Coal Commission made a thorough investigation into the conditions of the industry in 1922-3 and urged reforms in management and measures to stabilize demand, but its reports, like those of the Sankey (1919) and Samuel (1925) Commissions in England, were largely ignored by government.

The depression in the cotton and woollen textile industries was the result of fierce competition driving down prices to unremunerative levels rather than a lessened total demand. Nevertheless, the decline in total immigration from over 6,300,000 in the years 1910-19 to 4,347,000 in the years 1920-9, and the fashion for smaller families, did not help matters. In 1928, for the first time, the value of the products of Southern textile mills exceeded that of New England, and it was the competition of the cheap labour of the South that depressed profits and wage rates in the older-established centres of production. Silk and rayon manufacture, by contrast, enjoyed greater prosperity.

An important sector of the economy which did not share the general prosperity of the 1920s was agriculture. This was not because of any failure to increase the efficiency of the industry. Output per worker in farming rose by 26 per cent between 1920 and 1929, the result of the employment of more tractors, trucks, and combines, the improved feeding of livestock, and the increased use of fertilizers. The difficulty, rather, was that many farm prices were determined by world market conditions, and the demand for American farm produce in the European markets rapidly slumped below its inflated war-time level. Partly because of the higher American tariff after 1921, Britain found it easier to develop trade in foodstuffs with the Argentine and Australia than with America. British demand for American wheat fell sharply from its wartime peak:

TABLE 29

U.K. imports of wheat 1913-22 (millions of cwt.)

Origin	1913	1914	1915	1916	1917	1918	1919	1920	1921	1922
U.S.A.	43	42	51	72	65	50	46	54	47	43
Argentine	15	7	12	5	7	14	7	31	4	19
Australia	11	12	—	4	12	4	17	22	22	19

Source: League of Nations, *Economic Fluctuations in the U.S. and U.K.* 1918-22 (Geneva, 1948), p. 86.

While other entrepreneurs saw their profits mounting during the post-war years, most farmers had the opposite experience. Cash receipts from farming fell from $12,600m. in 1920 to $11,312m. in 1929. The arable farmer suffered more severely than the livestock farmer since the fall in meat prices was not so severe as that of grain crops. But the farmer found that he was having to sell more and more produce each year to buy a given quantity of clothing, domestic utensils, and farm machinery from the manufacturer. The ratio of prices received by farmers to prices paid, including interest, taxes and wages (1910-14 = 100), fell from 99 in 1920 to 92 in 1929, and to 83 in 1930.[36]

Although members of Congress were well aware of the plight of many farmers, all their attempts to rescue them from economic depression miscarried in the 1920s. The McNary-Haugen plan, which would have held the prices of cotton, wheat, corn, rice, and hogs above world prices, was vetoed by both Harding and Coolidge. W. S. Spillman's domestic allotment plan for restricting acreages planted stood no better chance of success in the face of opposition from economists and the administration.

Depressed farm incomes were bound to have an adverse effect on the general health of the economy, for even at the end of the decade, the farm population formed more than a quarter of the total population of the U.S.A. The contradiction between the greatly increased productivity of industry and the limited ability of the ordinary consumer to buy was aggravated by the reduced incomes of American farmers.

It was this contrast between the greatly enhanced ability to produce and the inability to distribute equitably what was produced that was the basic weakness of the American economy in the 1920s. Much of the responsibility for the eventual breakdown sprang from 'a foolhardy assumption that the special interests of business and the national interest were identical'.[37] Between 1918 and 1929 when 'business government' prevailed in America, the output per worker in manufacturing industry rose by 43 per cent—a greater advance than at any comparable period in history. However, 'the reward of labour for its contribution to each unit (i.e. labour cost per unit of goods produced, in dollars at constant purchasing power) was declining, whilst the rewards of "ownership and management" (i.e. overhead costs and profits in dollars of constant purchasing power) were increasing between 1922-9'.[38] Hence, while the total command over goods exercised by workers in manufacturing industry rose by 3·1 per cent a year, over the same period of time the rewards of ownership and management increased by 7·3 per cent a year. Because big business dominated government to an unhealthy extent, federal taxation policies were one-sided and served to increase rather than mitigate the mal-distribution of the national product. Under Mellon's Revenue Act of 1921 the Excess Profits Tax disappeared and the maximum surtax rate was lowered to 50 per cent (from 63 per cent in 1919). Between 1920 and 1928 the Treasury refunded some $3·5 billions of taxes, particularly to those in the higher income brackets.[39] By the time the effects of these taxation policies had worked themselves out, the 36,000 wealthiest families in America received as much income as the 12m. families—42 per cent of all those in America—who received under $1,500 a year.[40]

Some of the money that was passing into the hands of those with a high propensity to save was finding its way into the newer American industries. The output of capital goods, which had risen by 5 per cent a year between 1899 and 1914, rose by 6·4 per cent annually between 1923 and 1929. Investment was particularly heavy in industries making durable goods, which were increasing at the rate of 5·9 per cent a year. Although these figures indicate an unprecedented advance in material comfort for millions of Americans, the danger lay in the fact that much of the demand was of a once-for-all character. Furthermore, it was artificially stimulated by a rapidly growing volume of hire-purchase debt.

The increased overseas investment of the United States also had its unstable features. Some investment of a permanent value to British (and other European) industry took place between 1919 and 1929. Over seventy American-owned factories were built in Britain, including the huge Ford works at Dagenham in 1929.[41] But much of the early investment in Germany was for enterprises not strictly productive, such as municipal swimming baths and libraries, and American investment was of a less permanent kind than the pre-1914 British variety. It proved to be a precarious prop to European recovery, for when in 1928 investments made in the American stock markets promised better returns the dollars flowed back to America.

The influence of the Bank of England on American credit policy on the one important occasion when it was exercised was, on balance, harmful to American interests. Following Britain's return to the gold standard in April 1925, Montagu Norman, Governor of the Bank, had found difficulty in maintaining an adequate level of gold reserves in London because of the flight of 'hot money' seeking higher interest rates in New York. In company with the Governor of the Reichbank and the Governor of the Bank of France, therefore, he visited the United States in the spring of 1927 to plead with members of the Federal Reserve Board for a reduction in the rediscount rate of the Federal Reserve Bank. The Governor of the

Federal Reserve Bank of New York obliged by cutting the rate from
4 per cent to $3\frac{1}{2}$ per cent at a time when the Governor of the F.R.
Bank in Chicago and other American bankers were urging a 'tightening of the terms of credit to curb the wave of stock exchange speculation'. The decision to ease credit was subsequently described as 'one
of the most costly errors ever committed by the Federal Reserve
Bank'.[42]

The dilemma with which the larger commercial banks were confronted indirectly contributed to the 'overheating' of the stock exchanges before 1929. On the one hand they were under a continuing
obligation to pay interest on their customers' deposits; on the other,
opportunities for long-term investment in industry were declining
because of the increasing financial self-sufficiency of large industrial
concerns. The temporary (but dangerous) escape from this dilemma
was the creation of security affiliates which invested the surplus
deposits in stock exchange securities. The banks then added their
influence to the change in character of much post-war investment.
In the new conditions of the twenties there was a compulsive desire
for a quick and profitable turnover arising from appreciation of share
values, rather than from a steady long-term participation in the
profits of legitimate enterprise.

The 'blind relentless fear' which gripped the New York stock
exchange on 24 October 1929 marked the end of the buoyant era of
confidence of the 1920s. Some thirty years later, when events of the
first post-war decade could be viewed in clearer perspective, a leading
American historian pinpointed the main shortcomings of Government policy:

'The Federal Government . . . encouraged tax policies that contributed to over-saving; monetary policies that were expansive when
prices were rising and deflationary when prices began to fall, tariff
policies that left foreign loans as the only prop for export trade and
policies towards monopoly which fostered economic concentration,
introduced rigidity into the markets and anaesthetized the price
system. Representing the businessmen, the Federal Government had
ignored the dangerous imbalance between farm and business income, between increase in wages and increase in productivity. Representing the financiers it had ignored irresponsible practices in the
securities market. Representing the bankers it ignored weaknesses in
the banking system. Seeing all problems from the viewpoint of

business it had mistaken the class interest for the national interest. The result was both class and national disaster.'[43]

Notes

1 LEWIS, CLEONA, *America's stake in International Investment* (Washington, 1938), p. 349. *Historical Statistics of the United States* (U.S. Department of Commerce, Washington, 1960), p. 564.

2 FRANCIS, E. V., *Britain's Economic Strategy* (1939), p. 15.

3 SOULE, G., *Prosperity Decade* (New York, 1962), p. 9.

4 POLLARD, S., *The Development of the British Economy, 1914-1950*, (1962), p. 47.

5 *The Economist*, 5 December, 1918.

6 TAWNEY, R. H., 'The Abolition of Economic Controls, 1918-20', *Econ. Hist. Rev.*, XIII (1943), p. 15.

7 HURWITZ, S. J., *State Intervention in Great Britain* (New York, 1949), p. 290.

8 U.S. Department of Commerce: Bureau of Foreign and Domestic Commerce, *The U.S. in the World Economy, 1919-39* (Washington, 1943), p. 139 (reprinted by H.M.S.O., London, 1944).

9 BUXTON, NEIL K., 'Economic Progress in Britain in the 1920s', *Scottish Journal of Political Economy*, June 1967, p. 182. MILLS, FRED C., *Economic Tendencies in the U.S.* (National Bureau of Economic Research, Washington, 1932), p. 550. *Historical Statistics of the U.S.*, p. 139.

10 ASHWORTH, W., *An Economic History of England: 1870-1939* (1960), p. 301.

11 Committee on Currency and the Foreign Exchanges (Cunliffe Committee) *Interim Report*, 15 August 1918, P.P. 1918, VII, p. 853.

12 COMSTOCK, ALZALA, 'Reparation Payments in Perspective', *American Economic Review* (1930), p. 199.

13 See particularly SAYERS, R. S., 'The Return to Gold', in L. S. Pressnell (ed.), *Studies in the Industrial Revolution* (1960), p. 313, and WILLIAMS, D., 'Montague Norman and the Banking Policies of the 1920s', *Yorks. Bull. Econ. and Social Research* II (1959).

14 BOYLE, ANDREW, *Montague Norman* (1967), p. 209.

15 RICHARDSON, H. W., 'Over-Commitment in Britain before 1930', *Oxford Economic Papers* 17 (1965), p. 237.

16 COURT, W. H. B., 'Problems of the British Coal Industry between the Wars', *Econ. Hist. Rev.* XV (1945), p. 1.

17 YOUNGSON, A. J., *The British Economy, 1920-1957* (1958), p. 45.

18 ROEPKE, H. G., *Movements of the British Iron and Steel Industry, 1720-1951* (Urbana, Ill, 1956), cited in POLLARD, S., *The Development of the British Economy 1914-1950* (1962), p. 115.

19 League of Nations, *Economic Fluctuations in the U.S. and the U.K. 1918-1922* (Geneva, 1942), p. 65.

20 ALDCROFT, D. H., 'Economic Growth in Britain in the Inter-War Years: a Re-assessment', *Econ. Hist. Rev.*, 2nd ser. XX (1967), p. 311. MOWAT, C. L., *Britain between the Wars* (1955). p. 273.

21 Ministry of Reconstruction, *Reconstruction Problems: Electrica Developments* (H.M.S.O., 1919), p. 5.

22 Cited in SAYERS, R. S., 'The Springs of Technical Progress in Britain 1919-39', *Economic Journal* (1950), p. 275.

23 PIGOU, A. C., *The Theory of Unemployment* (1933), p. 252.

24 HAWTREY, R. G., cited in HANCOCK, K. J., 'Unemployment and the Economists in the 1920s', *Economica* n.s. XXVII (1960), p. 305.

25 BEVERIDGE, WILLIAM, *Causes and Cures of Unemployment* (1931), p. 56.

26 LEWIS, SINCLAIR, *Babbitt* (New York, 1922), p. 27.

27 PROTHRO, JAMES W., *The Dollar Decade: Business ideas in the 1920s* (Louisiana State University Press, 1954), p. 98 citing FAY, C. N., *Business in Politics*.

28 ALLEN, F. L., *Only Yesterday* (Penguin ed. 1938), I p. 237.

29 *Historical Statistics of the U.S.*, p. 383.

30 ALLEN, F. L., *Only Yesterday*, II, p. 388.

31 PAXSON, FRED L., 'The Highway Movement, 1916-35', *American Historical Review* (January, 1946), p. 236.

32 LEUCHTENBURG, W., *The Perils of Prosperity* (Chicago, 1958), p. 184.

33 *Historical Statistics of the U.S.* Series, P. 250-306, p. 420.

34 HAMILTON, W. H. and WRIGHT, H. R., *The Case of Bituminous Coal* (1925), p. 60.

35 HICKS, JOHN D., *Republican Ascendancy, 1921-1933* (1960), p. 70.

36 *Historical Statistics of the U.S.* Series K. 122-38, p. 283.

37 LEUCHTENBURG, W. L., *The Perils of Prosperity, 1914-1932* (Chicago, 1958), p. 245-6.

38 MILLS, FREDERIC C., *Economic Tendencies in the U.S.* (National Bureau of Economic Research, Washington, 1932), p. 550.

39 HICKS, *op. cit.*, p. 53.

40 LEUCHTENBURG, *op. cit.*, p. 193.

41 DUNNING, J. H., *American Investment in British Manufacturing Industry* (1958), ch. 1.

42 Cited in GALBRAITH, J. K., *The Great Crash 1929* (Pelican ed. 1961), p. 39.

43 SCHLESINGER, ARTHUR M., Jr., *The Age of Roosevelt I: The Crisis in the Old Order* (New York, 1957).

Suggestions for further reading

Texts

ASHWORTH, W., *An Economic History of England: 1870-1939* (1960).

FITE, GILBERT C. and REESE, JIM E., *An Economic History of the United States* (2nd ed. New York, 1965), part 4.

LEWIS, ARTHUR W., *Economic Survey 1919-39* (1949).

MOWAT, C. L., *Britain between the Wars* (1955).

PARKES, HENRY BAMFORD and CAROSSA, VINCENT P., *Recent America: a History* II (New York, 1963), ch. 1-3.

POLLARD, S., *The Development of the British Economy 1914-1950* (1962).

SOULE, G., *Prosperity Decade* (New York, 1962).

YOUNGSON, A. J., *The British Economy 1920-1966* (1967).

Specialized works

ALLEN, FREDERICK LEWIS, *Only Yesterday* (New York, Bantam Books ed. 1959).

GALBRAITH, J. K., *The Great Crash 1929* (Pelican ed. 1961).

HANCOCK, K. J., 'The Reduction of Unemployment as a Problem of Public Policy', 1920-1929', *Econ. Hist. Rev.* 2nd ser. XV (1962-3).

HICKS, JOHN D., *Republican Ascendancy, 1921-33* (1960).

LEUCHTENBURG, WILLIAM L., *The Perils of Prosperity* (Chicago, 1958).

LEWIS, SINCLAIR, *Babbitt* (1922).

SAYERS, R. S., 'The Return to Gold', in L. S. Pressnell (ed.), *Studies in the Industrial Revolution* (1960).

SCHLESINGER, ARTHUR M., Jr., *The Age of Roosevelt I: The Crisis in the Old Order* (New York, 1957).

1 The origins and characteristics of the economic crisis

In the two and a half years between the autumn of 1929 and the spring of 1932 the gains of the years of recovery in the 1920s were eroded in the most severe slump in world history. Between 1929 and 1932 the value of world trade declined by nearly two-thirds and its volume by one-third. The impact of the depression on the British and American economies is summarized in Table 30.

TABLE 30

Percentage change in some indicators of business activity in the United Kingdom and the United States, 1929-33[1]

	U.K.	U.S.A.
National income	−10·0	−51·6
Real national income	+ 6·4	−34·9
Industrial production	−18·3	−36·1
Mineral production (mainly coal in U.K.)	−13·2	−28·7
Electric power	+45·4	−12·3
Construction	+14·5	−78·6
Residential construction	+40·8	−87·4
Non-residential construction	−25·9	−73·9
Manufacturing	−24·8	−37·0
Consumer goods	−10·0	−24·5
Producers' goods	−29·9	−43·8
Employment	−10·6	−30·8
Wholesale prices	−26·1	−30·7

The American crisis, which was due mainly to weaknesses inherent in the domestic economy, arrived earlier, was more profound, of longer duration, and affected all aspects of economic and social life more severely, than did the crisis in the United Kingdom. The slump in Great Britain came mainly as a result of disturbances in the international economy which had their origin, in large measure, in the collapse of confidence within the United States.

The most spectacular feature of the American depression was the 'Great Crash' in the New York stockmarket in October 1929, when the index of security prices, which had rocketed upwards to 225·3 in September 1929 (1926 = 100), plunged downwards to 153·8 in December and continued to fall until 1934. But this collapse was the reflection of a more deep-seated imbalance in the economy rather than the originating cause of the decline. During the preceding decade investment in capital goods had outstripped the capacity of consumers to buy the goods produced. Entrepreneurs came to a realization of this fact before 'bearish' activity predominated on Wall Street. Constructional activity was falling for a year, and industrial production for three months, before the stock market debacle of October 1929. Once the boom in securities investment broke, the slump on Wall Street had its powerful repercussions on industrial production and employment. The financial collapse then aggravated the general collapse of the nation's economy.

The extent of economic decline in the United States may be gauged from the fact that national income in current prices fell from $87·8 billion in 1929 to $40·2 billion in 1933. Steel production declined from a peak of 56m. tons in 1929 to under 14m. tons in 1932. The number of jobless persons rose from 1½m. in 1929 to 13m. in 1933, when one in every four of the labour force was out of work. The nation's wages bill slumped from $50 billion in 1929 to $30 billion in 1932.

Partly because there had been no boom in the 1920s the recession in Great Britain was less severe and recovery began earlier than in America. The gross national product of the United Kingdom, at factor cost, declined from £4,632m. in 1929 to £4,024m. in 1933. After falling from a peak of 46·4 in 1929 to 41·4 in 1931 (1958 = 100), the index of manufacturing production already showed signs of recovery in 1932. The fall in production of crude steel was from over 9½m. tons in 1929 to 5·2m. tons in 1931. Unemployment rose sharply from a total of 1,263,000 in 1929 to 2,829,000 three years later but thereafter declined more rapidly in Britain than in America.

The longer duration of the American depression may be explained partly by the heavy involvement of the banking institutions with the speculative mania of the later 1920s. With the sharp fall in the value

of common stocks, the position of the security affiliates of the banks
that had gambled on the continuing appreciation of stock market
prices was seriously endangered. The collapse of the banks themselves quickly followed that of their affiliates. Bank suspensions were
not uncommon even in times of prosperity. No less than 491 had
occurred in 1928. But in 1929 the number rose to 642, and in 1930
failures were more than double those of the previous year. In the
following year, 1931, came a record number of 2,298 bank closures,
bringing in their train the insolvency and distress of millions of
depositors, both private customers and businesses. These cumulative
disasters dampened market expectations. Industrial production was
further curtailed, millions of wage earners were sacked, and the
wages of those lucky enough to keep their jobs were slashed. Because
of the weakness of the trade union movement and the absence of
government provision of old-age pensions or unemployment benefits,
there was little check on the downward plunge of consumer spending. At the same time, the fall in the index number of farm prices
(1926 = 100) from 104·9 in 1929 to 48·2 in 1932 gravely reduced
the ability of farmers to buy the products of industry.

In sharp contrast to the events on Wall Street, the rise of security
values in the London Stock Exchange had not been spectacular in the
1920s, and although the price index of industrial ordinary shares fell
by 36 per cent between 1929 and 1932 this was an orderly decline
compared with the 73 per cent fall in the same period in the Dow
Jones index of stock prices in the United States. British banks were
in no way seriously embarrassed by the depression of activity of the
London Stock Market, for they had not committed their resources
to any great extent into equity securities. Furthermore, the rapid
spread of branch banking over the two previous decades had obviated
the failures inherent in a unit banking system. Nor was the condition
of agriculture an important aggravating influence on economic depression in Britain. It had relatively a much smaller place in the
economy, and in the two years after June 1929 farm prices dropped
by some 15 per cent—considerably less than half the fall that took
place in America.

The short-lived financial crisis which occurred in Britain in the
summer of 1931 was principally the outcome of events in central
Europe and in America. In the later 1920s, especially after 1928,
when American loans to Austria and Germany were being recalled,

the London acceptance houses used funds deposited in London from Paris and Zürich to lend, at a higher rate, to German and Austrian banks. But in so doing they departed from the traditional ratio of capital to acceptances 1:4, which had been followed before the war. The post-war money market in London had become more of a *deposit* than an *acceptance* centre, and hence it was in a less secure position to counter a loss of 'hot money'. In the summer of 1931 the Bank of England, to forestall a general crisis of confidence, felt obliged to come to the assistance of the London acceptance houses whose position was endangered by the freezing of loans they had made to the German and Austrian banks. Simultaneously, the bank was called upon to subsidize the unemployment fund which had fallen heavily into debt as a result of the rapid increase in the numbers of the unemployed. Finally, the publication, on 31 July 1931, of the excessively gloomy report of the May Committee, appointed earlier that year to make recommendations for balancing the national accounts, aggravated the loss of confidence in the pound in international markets. Gold continued to flow from London until the recently formed National Government decided to abandon the gold standard on 20 September 1931. With this action the financial crisis was brought to an end.

The principal cause of the decline in industrial production in Great Britain between 1929 and 1933 was a sharp fall in export orders. Decisions taken by American investors and Members of Congress undoubtedly aggravated the difficulties of British exporters in these years. The drastic curtailment of American overseas lending from the fall of 1928, and the imposition of higher duties on imports under the Hawley–Smoot Tariff of 1930, together resulted in a reduction in the amount of dollars available to foreign countries from $6,500m. in 1929 to $1,500m. in 1932—a fall of 77 per cent in three years. Inevitably, foreign currencies were placed under great strain in relation to the dollar. Many countries, particularly the Latin American republics that depended on the export of a few primary products, experienced acute difficulties in balancing their payments. Their ability to buy British (and other countries') manufactures was seriously impaired. In the meantime, America's debtors endeavoured to pay in the only way left open to them—by exporting gold—and the proportion of the world's gold supplies stocked in the United States rose from 38 per cent in 1929 to 68 per cent in 1939.[2]

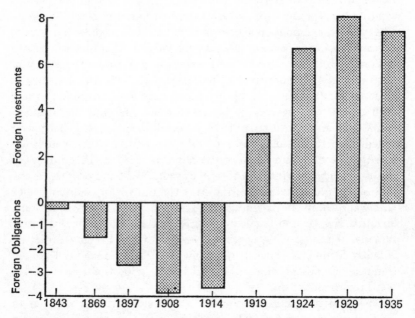

Figure 34. U.S.A.: net international financial position, 1843-1935,
(in billions of dollars)

2 Early policies for economic recovery

In both America and Great Britain the policy for economic recovery
advocated by those in charge of national finances during the early
years of the depression was to balance the national accounts by a
drastic curtailment of government expenditure. The British Government achieved a greater success in pursuing this objective than did
the American. The best that Hoover was able to achieve, in the face
of a severe decline of taxation revenues, was to keep the deficit within
bounds. His failure to balance the budget was not for want of trying.
In 1932 he made a personal plea to the Senate to make drastic
reduction in expenditure, and later that year in his annual message
to Congress he recommended a cut-back of government expenditure
of $830m. and an increase of revenue by means of a sales tax. Hoover

and his Cabinet believed the experience of past business depressions
had shown that recovery was soundest when it came of itself, un-
aided by Government interference. The collapse of prices and profits
would prune out the dead wood of the economy and lead to subsequent healthy growth. Their view is best summarized in the words
of a contemporary economist: 'Any revival which is merely due to
artificial stimulus leaves part of the work of depressions undone and
adds, to an undigested remnant of maladjustment, new maladjustments
of its own.'[3] The Republicans firmly resisted all proposals for major
artificial aids to recovery. In December 1931 a Committee appointed
by the President to consider the desirability of public works programmes to promote employment, reported that: 'borrowing of
large sums for public works emergency construction cannot be justified as a measure for aiding in the restoration of normal business
activity . . . the common-sense remedy is to stop borrowing except
to meet unavoidable deficits, balance the budget and live on our
income. . . . In the long run the real problem of unemployment
must be met by private business interests if it is to be permanent.
Problems of unemployment cannot be solved by any magic of appro-
priation from the public treasury.'[4]

On the other hand, it would be misleading to suggest that Hoover
had no policy for economic recovery. In January 1932 he established
the Reconstruction Finance Corporation, with funds loaned from the
U.S. Treasury, to aid the recovery of such industries, railways, and
financial institution as could not otherwise have secured credit. He
distinguished between what he called the 'the non-productive public
works' advocated by the Democrats, which would, he believed,
increase taxes, unbalance the budget, and provide only a small
amount of employment, and the 'income producing works', such as
the $55m. loan made by the R.F.C. to the Pennsylvania Railroad for
line electrification.

It would also be misleading to suggest that either during his
election campaign in 1932 or during his early weeks in office F. D.
Roosevelt advocated deficit spending as a remedy for unemployment.
Quite the contrary. In October 1932 he told a large audience in
Pittsburgh that he believed that a reduction in government expenditure was the most direct and effective contribution that could be
made to business recovery. By means of an increase in Federal taxation and severe restraint on Government expenditure, the size of

the budget deficit in the first five months of 1933 was reduced to only 60 per cent of the level in the corresponding period of the previous year. It was the tide of events, rather than the perceptiveness of the new President, which did most to bring about a new direction to Federal Government policy in the early summer of 1933.

Immediate reactions to the economic crisis were similar in Great Britain to those in America. The objectives sought were a curtailment of government expenditure and an increase in tax revenue. However, because the scope for economies was greater and taxation yields were more buoyant, the government in London succeeded in balancing the national budget by 1932, whereas the Government in Washington did not. For the fiscal year 1931-2 the British budget was balanced through a reduction in the pay of the armed forces, the police, the members of the civil service, the teachers, and the unemployed, and an increase in income tax, surtax, and taxes on beer, tobacco, and petrol. The greatest scope for economy was in the interest burden on the national debt. In 1932 some £1,970m. of 5 per cent War Loan was successfully converted to $3\frac{1}{2}$ per cent, bringing about a reduction of £80m. in Government expenditure, and a decline of debt redemption expenditures from a peak of $8\frac{1}{4}$ per cent of the national income early in 1932 to 4·65 per cent in 1935.

Of two major ways of restoring the profitability of business—the reduction of costs and the raising of prices—the experience of the early 1930s showed that British Government relied mainly on the first method to stimulate recovery, whilst American Governments depended principally on the second.

3 The new deal

One may well agree with Miss Frances Perkins, Secretary of Labour in the Roosevelt administration, that the New Deal 'was not a plan with form and content'. The new president had no clearer conception than had his predecessor of the measures needed for economic recovery. But he possessed greater energy, a greater determination to take positive action to relieve distress, and a greater willingness to experiment with new policies. Although his approach was a flexible one he demonstrated a sense of priorities. The pall of fear which oppressed the nation had to be lifted. Business confidence had to be restored. Relief and work had to be provided for the unemployed.

In March 1933 the immediate occasion for fear was the collapse of American banking. The president's inauguration coincided with an unprecedented wave of bank closures. The crisis was met by the proclamation of a national four-day bank holiday and the passage of the Emergency Banking Act, which passed through all its stages in one day, 9 March. The Act provided for the appointment of conservators to 'vet' the nation's banks, to separate off those whose insolvency, or threatened insolvency, was due to mismanagement, and those which were merely the victims of the general panic, and to sponsor measures of reform for the mismanaged banks. More Federal Reserve notes were issued to increase the banks' liquidity. When the banks were re-opened, the public, by returning their deposits rather than continuing to withdraw them, showed that fear was evaporating.

The keynote of the principal recovery measures of the first hundred days of the New Deal was reflation. This is true of the chief enactments for agriculture, for industry, and for the future exchange value of the dollar in international markets.

In the case of the Agricultural Adjustment Act passed on 12 May 1933, the government played a vital part in measures to raise farm

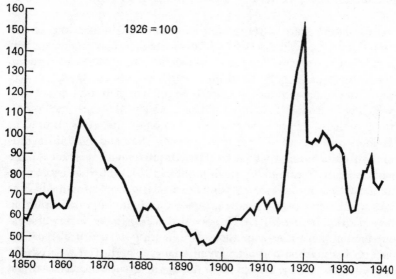

Figure 35. U.S.A.: wholesale prices 1850-1940

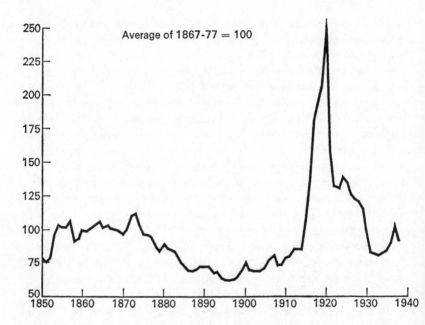

Figure 36. Great Britain: wholesale prices 1850-1940

prices. There were some six million farms in the country, and it
would have courted disaster to have invited farmers to devise their
own plan of reform. Therefore, farmers were induced to agree to
the restriction of production of wheat, rice, cotton, corn, tobacco,
pigs, and dairy produce by the offer of compensation payments,
which were financed from processing taxes levied on the first domestic processing of each commodity. Although the gross income of
farmers rose by over 70 per cent between 1932 and 1935, it is difficult to determine what part of the improvement was due to the
natural scarcity caused by the drought of 1934, and what part to the
artificial scarcity created by the efforts of the Department of Agriculture. In any case the adverse decision of the Supreme Court in
U.S. *v.* Butler *et al.* (the Hoosac Mills case) in 1936, invalidated
production control as a method of promoting agricultural recovery
before this method had been given a long enough trial to prove its
effectiveness. At least it can be said that the great disparity between
falling farm prices and relatively steady prices of manufactured

goods, which had been a persistent feature of the economy since 1920, and which it was one of the objects of the Act to correct, had been substantially lessened.

The central aim of the National Industrial Recovery Act of 16 June 1933 was to restore the profitability of industry by permitting the principal industrial groups to form 'codes of fair competition', which would raise prices and limit output while at the same time raising the rewards of labour and civilizing working conditions. In contrast to the situation in agriculture, it proved possible to entrust to the principal producing groups the main work of drafting the codes, the code administrator, General Hugh Johnson, acting mainly as arbiter. Although it was the most ambitious of all the New Deal measures, the Act was self-contradictory. The mistake made was

in assuming that whatever was mutually agreeable to the industrialists, the workers and (to a lesser extent) the consumers of separate industries would magically combine into a harmonious pattern for the whole industrial sector of the economy. . . . while individual industries, including their workers, may benefit from lessened production and increased prices, provided they are not followed by others, overall application of such a principle can clearly lead only to overall impoverishment.[5]

Nevertheless, the expenditure of some $3,300m. on relief works under Part II of the Act did contribute to the short-lived recovery of the summer of 1933, while the important section 7A strengthened the position of the trade unions in collective bargaining and helped to establish a national pattern of minimum wages and maximum hours. Roosevelt explained that the intention here was to encourage 'employers to hire more men to do the existing work by reducing the work hours of each man's week and at the same time paying a living wage for the shorter week'. But the aim could only be achieved if the employer in each trade adhered to the limitations imposed in the codes of fair competition. The Act was severely criticized by the anti-monopoly wing of the Democratic party on the grounds that small businesses were adversely affected and competition destroyed. The Supreme Court's invalidation of the Act in the Schechter case in May 1935, although wrecking this second important instrument of reflation, came as something of a relief to the administration, already in two minds about the future of this unpopular measure.

A more direct method of reflation was taken with America's abandonment of the gold standard. In an article in *The New York*

Herald Tribune of 15 April 1933 the famous newspaper columnist, Walter Lippmann, claimed that the country was faced with the alternatives of protecting the external value of the dollar or raising domestic prices. He believed that the second alternative was the right one. Roosevelt followed this advice. On 20 April 1933 he issued an executive order forbidding the export of gold except under licence. At the beginning of May that year he accepted the Thomas Inflation Amendment to the Agricultural Adjustment Act, increasing the government's power to inflate domestic credit. Before the month was out, Congress had approved the abrogation of the gold clause in government obligations so that debts might be paid in any form of legal tender. Under the Gold Reserve Act of 30 January 1934, gold coins were withdrawn from circulation; and on the day following the President's signature of the Act he announced that the gold content of the dollar was being reduced to 59·06 per cent of its former weight. Whilst these decisive steps were being taken in Washington, the International Economic Conference was meeting in London for the purpose of stabilizing international exchange rates. Although the American President's action in abandoning the gold standard and devaluing the dollar was widely condemned as having wrecked a serious attempt at international co-operation to restore world trade, Roosevelt answered these charges by asserting that 'the sound internal economic system of a nation is a greater factor in its well being than the price of its currency in changing terms of the currencies of other nations. . . . That objective means more to the good of other nations, than a fixed ratio for a month or two in terms of the pound or the franc.' The President certainly believed that if he tied his hands on the question of international exchange rates he would lack the freedom to promote recovery by raising farm and industrial prices.

The decision to opt for economic nationalism in the spring of 1933 adversely affected the chances of recovery of British export industries. The importance of the American market to British exporters declined still further after 1933, while the importance of the Commonwealth countries increased. America could more easily afford the luxury of economic nationalism, since foreign trade contributed only 5 per cent to the gross national product, compared with the 16 per cent contribution of overseas trade to the gross national product of Great Britain.

Throughout the period of the New Deal, Federal and state-sponsored work projects assumed a much greater importance than was ever the case with government employment projects in Great Britain. Apart from the $3,300m. already mentioned as being authorized under the National Industrial Recovery Act, the Emergency Relief Appropriation Act of 1935 provided for the expenditure of nearly five billion dollars on work relief—'the greatest single appropriation in the history of the United States or any other nation'.[6] As the letters of the alphabet were in danger of becoming exhausted with the proliferation of agencies providing work—W.P.A. (Works Progress Administration), C.W.A. (Civil Works Administration), C.C.C. (Civilian Conservation Corps), and N.Y.A. (National Youth Administration)—millions of persons, from youths just out of high school to middle-aged men long unemployed, were given useful spells of work which provided them with fresh hope and left the nation a legacy of fine new roads, libraries, schools, post offices, harbours, and forests.

But compared with the immense outlay of funds the contribution to recovery was disappointingly small. There were still 9m. persons unemployed in 1936. There are two outstanding reasons for the failure of the vast relief work expenditure to have a greater impact on the economic recovery of America. In the first place the administration was unduly sensitive of the need to avoid competing with private business. Works projects were selected for their labour-intensive characteristics and chosen only after there was a reasonable assurance that they would not be undertaken by business firms. Of every $100 spent under Harry Hopkins's Works Progress Administration, $86 went on wages, $3·50 on administration and only $10·50 on material. Compared with the expenditure of the same sum on building construction or automobiles, the secondary effects, in the shape of derived demand, were minimal. A far more important reason was that it was not until 1938 that the Federal Government accepted that deficit financing would be needed, not merely as a 'pump priming' stop-gap, but continuously for the forseeable future if unemployment was to be reduced to an acceptable level.

Looking at Federal Government expenditure figures alone for the years 1932-8, it is easy to be misled into false conclusions about the contribution made by increased government spending to economic recovery. Total expenditure rose from $4,659m. to $6,791m. during

these years. However, all forms of taxation were so much increased
that Federal Government receipts rose by nearly three times over the
same period. The revenue deficit was smaller in 1938 than it was in
1932; only in 1934 and 1936 was it substantially larger than during
Hoover's last year of office. Over the same seven years, state and
local government revenues increased—principally from higher taxes
—at a faster rate than expenditure. Collectively, between 1933 and
1939 total government revenue exceeded or roughly balanced expenditure in every year except 1936. Thus, at the same time as
Federal, state, and local governments were together paying out
billions of dollars to those employed in public works, ever larger sums
were being taken from the consumers in the form of increased income and outlay taxes, and the beneficial effects of vast employment
projects were to a large extent nullified. The first chart below shows
how Federal Work Relief schemes helped fill the breach caused by the
sharp decline in employment on private constructional works in the
late 1920s, while the second chart reveals the efforts made to match
increased government expenditures with increased revenues in the
years 1932-8. The third chart correlates the growth in the federal
deficit to the fall in the numbers unemployed.

In June 1934 the famous British economist J. M. Keynes talked to
President Roosevelt in the White House. This was a wonderful
opportunity for the visitor to explain, in simple terms, the necessity
of budgeting for a deficit as long as there was heavy unemployment.
Instead he treated the President as though he 'belonged to the higher
echelons of economic knowledge' and left 'a whole rigmarole of
figures' with his host, who commented that Keynes 'was more like a
mathematician than a political economist'. (Keynes' comments about
Roosevelt were no more flattering: he had expected the President
to be 'more literate, economically speaking'.[7]) The consequences of
the Englishman's failure to effect a conversion were that Roosevelt
was still at times prepared to be influenced by the conservatives
among the Democrats. Early in 1938 he yielded to their demands
and made a determined attempt to balance the Federal budget by
cutting recovery and relief expenditures by one-third. The result
was disastrous. The numbers out of work, well below eight million in
1937, suddenly shot up to over ten million. This shattering experience taught the President a lesson. In the second half of 1938 relief
expenditures were sharply increased and the number of the un-

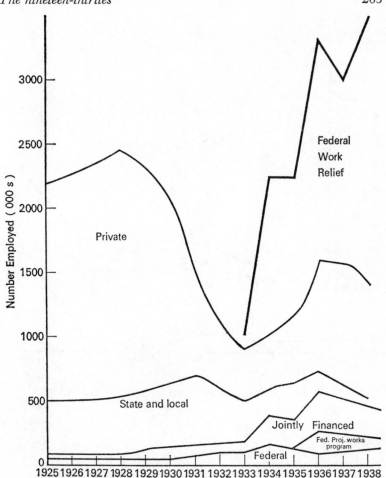

Figure 37. Estimated on-site employment on new construction U.S.A., by sources of funds 1925-38. *Source Galbraith J.K. The Economic Effects of the Federal Public Works Expenditure 1933-8, Washington (1940)*

employed immediately began to fall. From this time onwards the administration was more fully committed to Keynesian policies. But the level of deficit expenditure which was required virtually to eliminate unemployment was only revealed after America was at war. Only when the budget was unbalanced to the tune of over $45 billion

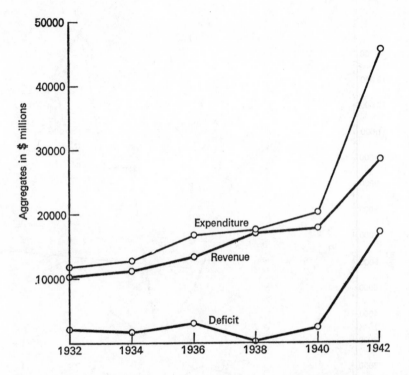

Figure 38. Federal, state and local government revenue and expenditure, 1932-42. *Source, Galbraith J.K. The Economic Effects of the Federal Public Works Expenditure 1933-8 Washington* (*1940*)

in the course of 1944 was the number of unemployed reduced to well below the million mark.

At the same time as the measures for relief and recovery were being applied throughout the nation, plans for the reform of commercial institutions were pushed ahead. Although most of the new measures were enacted by the end of 1936, in many cases their beneficial effects were not experienced until the 1940s and 1950s.

Apart from the Emergency Banking Act of 9 March 1933, two other important measures, the Banking Acts of 16 June 1933 and of 23 August 1935 were designed to ensure that the kind of financial disaster which confronted Roosevelt at the time of his inauguration

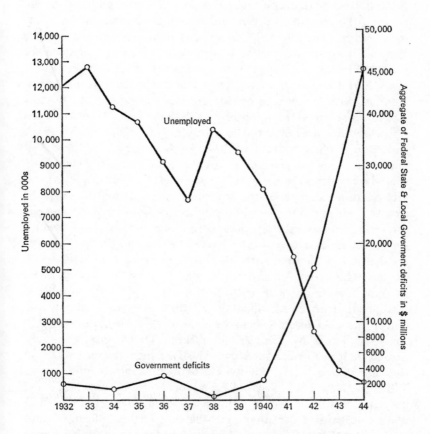

Figure 39. Federal state, and local government deficits and unemployment, 1932-44

did not recur. The earlier Act effected the separation of the security affiliates from the commercial banks, established a Federal Deposit Insurance Corporation to insure the deposits of the banks' customers, prohibited the payment of interest on demand deposits, encouraged National Banks to open branches, and in other ways increased the security of commercial banks. The Act of 1935 laid stress on enhancing the powers of the Federal Reserve system by providing powerful inducements to state non-member banks to affiliate to the

Federal Reserve Bank of their district. This was achieved by increasing the reserve requirements of member banks, and by many
other means. The effect of this legislation, which must be counted
among the most constructive of the New Deal, was to reduce the
number of bank suspensions from an average of 2,877 a year in the
years 1931-3 inclusive to fifty-five a year in the three years 1934-6.

Allied with the reform of banking was the reform of the stock
markets and the elimination of speculative abuses. Here the most
important measures were the Securities Act of 27 May 1933, and the
Securities Exchange Act of 6 June 1934. The first of these Acts
embodied two of the principles of the British Companies Act of 1844,
that the investing public should be provided with adequate background knowledge about the securities being offered for sale, and
that the seller was to be held legally responsible for providing the
correct information the law demanded. (The maxim *caveat venditor*
replaced that of *caveat emptor*.) A Securities and Exchange Commission was established with the task of ensuring compliance with
the law. The second Act gave the Federal Reserve Board power to fix
margins of profit on securities traded, and it listed a large number of
manipulative practices which the Commission was to stamp out.
Under the able leadership of its first three chairmen: Joseph P.
Kennedy; James M. Landis, and William O. Douglas, the Commission helped to raise the standards of business practice whilst at
the same time it helped the investor to obtain accurate information.
When the New Dealers looked for a model for securities legislation
they turned to the British example of some ninety years earlier;
when the British Government considered a further reform of company law in 1966 the methods of work of the Securities and Exchange
Commission in Washington were taken by many as an exemplar.[8]

By two important laws, passed in 1935, two 'built-in stabilizers'
were provided for the American economy, although their influence
was not much felt until towards the end of the decade. The National
Labour Relations Act (Wagner Act) which guaranteed the right of
wage earners to bargain collectively through unions of their own
choosing, was signed by the President on 5 July 1935, but its provisions were defiantly challenged by powerful employers until the
Supreme Court upheld its constitutionality in April 1937. Thereafter the unions, whose membership rose rapidly from 3,728,000 in
1935 to 8,980,000 in 1939, stood as one safeguard against the kind

of decline in earnings that had occurred in the depths of the depression. The Social Security Act passed on 14 August 1935 eventually helped to reduce the fall in consumer spending caused by unemployment or retirement, but in 1937-8 it had the opposite tendency. Millions of dollars were collected from the public in payroll taxes (the insurance contributions), but 'payments out' were not to be started until 1942. The deadening effects on employment of the deflationary payroll taxes eventually persuaded the government to advance the date of the first benefit payments to 1 January 1940.

One of the worst features of American farming had been the destructive effects on the soil of the practice of continuous cash cropping, especially where the crop was a straw one. In the hot May of 1934 the top soil of a large part of the nation's land was blown away, an experience immortalized by John Steinbeck in his novel *The Grapes of Wrath*. One of the worst-hit areas was the Tennessee Valley, where out of $8\frac{1}{2}$m. acres of cultivated land in 1933 some 7m. were damaged by erosion. The Tennessee Valley Act of 18 May 1933 was based on a project begun in 1918, but stifled during the Republican era, to build a dam at Muscle Shoals on the Tennessee River in order to generate cheap electricity and provide irrigation. But it went much further and envisaged the comprehensive planning of the entire river basin under the direction of the Tennessee Valley Authority. The scheme was remarkably successful in reviving the agricultural, industrial, and social life of important parts of the region. Designed to serve much the same ends of soil protection was the Soil Conservation and Domestic Allotment Act of 1936, which made available to farmers who terraced their land and planted soil-conserving grasses the sum of $500m. It was measures such as these that led the well-known radio commentator, Alistair Cooke, to observe that the New Dealers' concept of the 'common man' was 'one who could take up contour ploughing late in life'. The value of these 'rescue' operations to the country's well-being may best be summed up in the words of a contemporary journalist: 'It is conceivable that when the history of our generation comes to be written in the perspective of a hundred years the saving of broken lands will stand out as the great and most enduring achievement of our time.'[9]

How successful was the New Deal in redirecting America towards economic growth? If the more measurable features of the economy above are considered, the inevitable conclusion that emerges is one of very incomplete recovery. The index of manufacturing production had still not quite recovered its 1929 level ten years later. At the outbreak of the Second World War gross private domestic investment was only two-thirds of the amount of the late 1920s, and the number of unemployed was in excess of nine million. On the other hand some of the imbalances in the economy which had been a prominent cause of the depression, notably the impoverishment of large sections of the farming community, and the failure of wage rates to rise as fast as productivity, had been substantially reduced by 1939. Through the provisions of the two Agricultural Adjustment Acts of 1933 and 1938 the average of farm prices in the years 1935-9 was raised above the 1909-14 level, and by means of the National Labour Relations Act of 1935 and the Fair Labour Standards Act of 1938 labour was able to secure a reward more closely matched to its contribution to increased productivity. The reforms in the banking structure and in the stock markets resulting from the legislation of 1933-5 made it less likely that any future business recession would be aggravated as a result of major weaknesses in banking and the stock exchanges.

The full significance of what was achieved in the New Deal era can be better understood when the difficulties encountered by the administration are recalled. The achievements were all the more impressive in the light of some underlying trends of the American economy in the 1930s. The reduction of the volume of unemployment was made more difficult because of the continuing growth of the population and consequent increase in the size of the labour force from 47m. in 1930 to 53m. in 1940. A rise of productivity per man-hour by more than one-fifth during the same period strengthened the tendency towards technological unemployment.

The work of reform was undertaken in the face of bitter opposition from vested interests. Richard Whitney, the President of the New York Stock Exchange, claimed in 1933 that legislation to curb the kind of practices which had contributed to the collapse in 1929 was 'a great mistake' since the stock exchange was 'a perfect institution'. When proposals for reform were drafted, there was mobilized 'the most powerful lobby ever organized against any bill which ever came up in Congress'. In more homely language, Will Rogers observed at the time that: 'those old Wall Street boys are putting up an awful fight to keep the government from putting a cop on their corner'.[10] The opposition of the bankers to the Glass—Steagall Banking

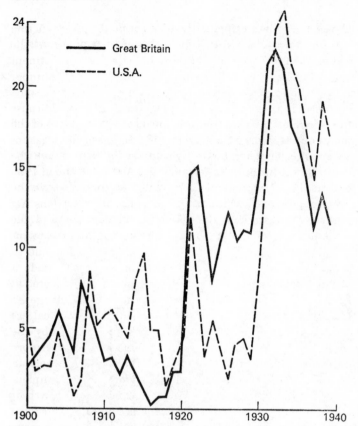

Figure 40. Great Britain and U.S.A.: unemployment 1900-40
Expressed as a percentage of civilian workforce.

Bill of 1933 was equally determined. The president of the American
Banking Association fought 'to the last ditch' proposals for a federal
deposit insurance scheme which he regarded as 'unsound, un-
scientific, unjust, and dangerous'. As if this was not enough, the
administration had to contend with the conservatism of a majority
of the Supreme Court judges who, at least until the latter part of
1936, declared unconstitutional some of the most important Acts of
the New Deal era, including both the Agricultural Adjustment Act
(1933) and the National Industrial Recovery Act (1933). Only after
1936 when the membership of the Court was changed were the
judgements of its members more sympathetic to Roosevelt's policies.

Politics played a big part in tipping the scales of public policy. Roosevelt's campaign for re-election in 1936 was a great popular crusade for the endorsement of his reforms.

4 The British economy in the nineteen-thirties

During the New Deal era the American Government made repeated and strenuous efforts to drag the economy out of depression and promote a revival of economic growth. By contrast the British Government, if we except its immediate reactions to the crisis in the balance of payments in 1931-2, was more of a spectator of economic recovery than its active promoter. Without much conscious effort on the government's part, Britain in the 1930s experienced some of the features of expanding domestic demand for housing and consumer

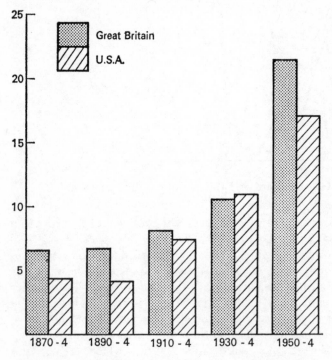

Figure 41. Great Britain and U.S.A.: government expenditure as a percentage of gross national product 1870-4–1950-4

durables that had been characteristic of the American economy in the previous decade. A number of reasons have been advanced for the expansion of domestic demand in Britain after 1932: the abandonment of the gold standard; the cheap money policy of the years 1932-9; the improvement in the terms of trade; the housing boom and its repercussions; the Import Duties Act of 1932; and the switch from overseas to domestic investment have all been suggested as important contributors to recovery. It is necessary to examine the influence of each in turn.

Once Britain had left the gold standard on 20 September 1931, the old argument for maintaining the bank rate at a relatively high level no longer applied since there was no longer a necessity to keep a fixed exchange rate with other currencies. But there was fear that with an inconvertible paper currency the danger of inflation would increase. The value of the pound fluctuated embarrassingly between September 1931 and April 1932, a circumstance detrimental to the restoration of business confidence. The Bank of England wanted to stabilize the external value of the pound but at first lacked the power to do so. The market price of gold in London rose rapidly to 113*s*. per standard ounce, but under the terms of the Gold Standard (Amendment) Act of 1931 the Bank was under obligation to pay not more than 77*s*. 9*d*. per standard ounce. Hence it was impossible for it to act in the market as buyer. Under the Finance Act of 1932 an Exchange Equalization Account was established in the Bank of England to enable the Treasury, in co-operation with the Bank, to bypass the limitations imposed by the Act of 1931 and smooth out fluctuations in the external value of the pound caused by seasonal changes in demand and the operations of speculators. At first the account was limited to £150m., but through subsequent increases it eventually reached a total of £567m. in 1937.[11] By this device Britain was able to free herself from the strait-jacket of dear money without involving herself in the twin perils of inflation and violently fluctuating exchange rates. The establishment of the Exchange Equalization Account must therefore be seen as an essential precondition for a cheap money policy.

From 30 June 1932 until 24 August 1939 bank rate stayed at 2 per cent, the longest period of stable discount rates in the long history of the London money market. How important was cheap money, available continuously for over seven years, in the revival of economic activity? In so far as speculative builders were able to borrow money at less cost than they had been in the 1920s, cheap money was a contributory factor in the building boom. Nearly three million houses were built in Great Britain in the 1930s, compared with less than a million and a half in the previous decade. But cheap money alone would not have been sufficient to create a building boom: a rising demand for houses was also essential. However, the new financial conditions of the early 1930s were favourable to the borrower who wished to buy his house through a mortgage. One outcome of the financial crisis of September 1931 was a government ban on foreign investments, except where they directly aided British industry through purchase of British capital goods or where they helped countries in the sterling area increase their London balances.[12] Hence the volume of funds available for domestic investment increased. In the years 1927-30 inclusive, new domestic issues had formed only 60 per cent of all new capital issues; in the years 1933-5 the proportion had grown to at least 80 per cent.[13] The decline in yields of gilt-edged investments encouraged the investor to lend more to building societies whose funds became more abundant and whose rates to borrowers fell by a quarter between 1932 and 1937. However, cheap money in itself is insufficient to explain the housing boom. It made the boom possible but was certainly not its sole cause. It is difficult to maintain that the lower interest rates after 1932 had any great influence on the volume of industrial investment for many of the larger investment decisions were not greatly influenced by the cost of borrowing. This certainly applied to the $33·8m. raised by the Central Electricity Generating Board in 1932-3 for financing the construction of the grid. A great proportion of the investment of large firms was made out of ploughed-back profits, while the increased investment which took place in smaller firms in these years reflected expectations of economic recovery. The conclusion of a recent writer on this subject that 'recovery began under its own momentum; cheap money merely helped it to run smoothly'[14] seems inescapable.

Between 1930 and 1933 the terms of trade of Great Britain (i.e. the average value of exports divided by the average value of imports) moved strongly in her favour. The cost of her imports of food and raw materials was falling in relation to the prices of exports of manufactured goods. Although the terms of trade moved against

Britain between 1934 and 1937, only part of the advantage gained up to 1934 was lost in the following years. One consequence of this overall improvement was that for the years 1929-33 the real incomes of those in work rose by 2 per cent, whereas had the terms of trade remained unchanged they would have fallen by 3 per cent.[15] Money saved on food could be spent on radios, electric irons, or mortgage interest payments. The fact that the terms of trade were more favourable in the 1930s than they had been before 1929 imparted a degree of buoyancy to domestic demand which was important for economic recovery. In the U.S.A., over the same four years 1929-33, average weekly earnings fell by a third whilst the consumer price index fell by only a quarter. Even those lucky enough to keep their jobs were substantially worse off in 1933 than they had been four years earlier. It is scarcely surprising that recovery was more elusive in that country.

In contrast with the situation in the 1920s when most building was government-subsidized for local authority letting, the outstanding feature of the building boom of the mid 1930s was the private construction of houses for sale. Powerful influences increasing the demand for houses were rising standards of domestic comfort and the spread of publicity about these new standards; the increasing availability of cheap electricity; and the more liberal policies of the building societies, which were prepared to advance money for longer periods, to lend a larger proportion of the purchase price, and to lend to more families in the lower income groups. At the height of the boom, between 1933 and 1937, investment in housing accounted for between one-third and two-fifths of the total of domestic fixed capital formation.[16] For this reason it played a major part, though not the sole part, in bringing about economic recovery. In Britain, as in America in the 1920s, the housing boom was associated with rising sales of consumer durables such as furniture, radios, and motor-cars; but in the British case the boom did not assume such large dimensions and, therefore, did not have so significant an impact on employment. The extension of hire-purchase arrangements for the sale of consumer durables associated with housing improvements was not so rapid in the Britain of the thirties as it had been in America in the preceding decade. One reason for this slower growth was the lower level of earnings of the British worker, who was not in a position to set aside more than a shilling or two a week for hire-purchase payments.[17]

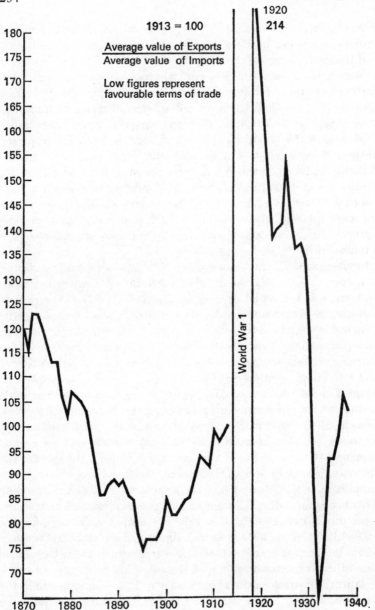

Figure 42. Great Britain: movements in the terms of trade
1851-5–1950

Recovery in Great Britain followed hard on the heels of the Import Duties Act of 1932, and it is therefore tempting to suggest that the introduction of the protective tariff played an important part in stimulating industrial revival. In the case of one important industry, iron and steel, there is some truth in the assumption. The depression in this industry before 1932 was severe. British iron and steel exports fell from 4,379,000 tons in 1929 to 1,979,000 tons in 1931, whilst retained imports rose from an average of 1,035,000 tons in the years 1919-22 to an average of 3,480,000 in 1926-9. In 1931 British pig-iron production was only half what it had been in 1929. Whilst a part of this sharp decline may be explained by the heavy fall in demand for capital goods characteristic of a slump, it was also the case that Britain had become a dumping ground for other European iron and steel producers. The Import Duties Act of 1932 established an Import Duties Advisory Committee with power to raise duties above the general level of 10 per cent stipulated in the Act, and these powers were quickly used to raise duties on imported iron and steel to 33⅓ per cent *ad valorem*. Faced with this new obstacle, the members of the continental steel cartel promptly switched their competition to markets where British exports were important. After negotiations with the cartel to establish an assured share of export markets for British producers had broken down, the I.D.A.C. imposed a temporary duty of 50 per cent on imports into Great Britain. Agreement was then reached with the Cartel for Britain to have a larger share of the export markets. In 1937 an ironical situation developed when domestic demand for iron and steel increased to such an extent that it could not be met from home supplies and British iron and steel firms urged the Committee to remove the duty entirely as a temporary measure until the necessary supplies were obtained from the continent.[18] This was done in March of that year. Through the years of tariff protection British steel production rose from 5,261,000 tons in 1932 to a peak of 12,984,000 tons in 1937, before falling again to 10,398,000 tons in 1938. It is certainly arguable that, but for the tariff, a greater proportion of this demand would have been met from imports.

Apart from this particular case, however, it would be difficult to maintain that the new tariff made any substantial contribution to industrial recovery. Among the awkward facts that belie any claim that the new tariff had an appreciable impact on the revival of business are the smaller fall between 1930 and 1935 of imports of newly protected industries than the imports of other industries; there was also the fall in employment in newly protected industries between 1930 and 1934 and the rapid rise in employment in industries not subject to protection. The most important influence of the tariff was to make possible a partial redirection of British overseas trade. After its imposition the British Government was in a stronger bargaining position with the countries of the Commonwealth to secure a larger share in their markets in return for accepting a greater volume of their exports. As a result of the Ottawa Agreement in 1932 the proportion of British imports coming from the Commonwealth rose from 28·6 per cent in 1931 to 39·1 per cent in 1937, while the proportion of British exports going to the Commonwealth rose much less impressively from 43·5 per cent in 1931 to 48·0 per cent in 1937.

Although less spectacular as an explanation of recovery, the buoyancy of total consumers' demand in Great Britain was more important in stimulating new investment and the expansion of employment than was the tariff. Between 1929 and 1937 average real wages rose by 9 per cent at the same time as the numbers in employment rose by 11 per cent. In consequence of more comprehensive social security benefits, even the unemployed, the widows, and the aged poor were prevented from falling into that degree of destitution which many Americans experienced in the early years of the decade. With food, clothing, and coal costing substantially less in the 1930s than they did in the 1920s, the British consumer had some money available for the purchase of the products of the newer industries.

The kind of impression that an outside observer would have gained of the degree of prosperity enjoyed by British industry in the 1930s would have varied enormously both between geographical regions and between industries. In the 'Special' or 'Depressed Areas' of Wales, the North-east, the North-west, and Scotland, where throughout the years 1929-36 over 22 per cent of the insured population were unemployed, the impression would have been one of practically unrelieved decay and gloom. In the London area, the South Midlands, the South-east, and South-west, the percentage of unemployment was less than half that in Wales and the North. The impression in these areas would have been one of new factories and employment opportunities with, in many parts, an air of modest prosperity. This contrast arose from the heavy geographical concentration of the declining industries coal mining, shipbuilding, cotton textiles, and ironfounding on the coalfields of Wales, the North of England, and the Lowlands of Scotland, and the confinement of the newer, expanding industries to the Midlands and the South.

Apart from their own defects in industrial organization and technology, the industries of the depressed areas were all adversely affected by the developments in international trade and payments in the early 1930s. Exporting had been their life-blood before 1914, and twenty years later the growth of economic nationalism and the collapse of the international payments system damaged their prosperity more seriously than it did the newer industries in which production for domestic demand assumed a greater importance.

One consequence of the financial crash in America in the autumn of 1929 was a sudden decline in the demand for raw materials. Merchants preferred to draw on existing stocks until future economic prospects proved reassuring. This reduced demand aggravated the existing tendency towards over-production of primary products and led to a slump in world commodity prices. The balance of payments of all countries which depended mainly on the export of foodstuffs and raw materials—particularly those of Latin America—became heavily adverse. A severe reduction in demand for manufactured goods was the inevitable result of the impoverishment of these economically underdeveloped regions. British exports of ships, coal, iron and steel, and textiles slumped. Along with a decline in the value of world trade went the collapse of the international payments system. By April 1932 the gold standard had been abandoned by twenty-four countries and was inoperative, though not legally abandoned, in seventeen others. By June of the same year restrictions on the use of international exchange were in force in no less than thirty-one countries.[19] The restrictive effects of higher tariffs were being buttressed by import quotas which placed strict physical limits on the quantity of goods imported, irrespective of price. The cumulative effects of all these measures were to aggravate the plight of the older basic industries of Great Britain.

In the 1930s the central government showed a greater willingness to intervene in order to help the re-organization of the older basic industries than was the case in the previous decade. A common characteristic of most of the measures taken was an attempt to blunt the damaging effects on profits of unrestrained competition and the existence of surplus productive capacity. In the case of the coal industry the Coal Mines Act of 1930 established, in the Coal Mines Re-organization Commission, the necessary machinery for regulating production, supply, and sale. But during the next nine years it was discovered that the control of output, even within the main producing districts, was no guarantee of stable and remunerative prices. Nor did it pave the way for rapid re-organization and modernization of the pits. It is true that by 1938 some 59 per cent of the coal was cut by machinery as compared with only 22 per cent in 1926, but the regrouping of the mines under more efficient leadership came painfully slowly. An official historian summing up the effects of the Act just over a decade after it had been passed, wrote: 'Instead of being translated, as some had hoped, into a scheme of control over prices and sales aimed at restoring the profitability of the industry so that long term re-equipment could be financed, the law became a device by which the available business was spread among weak concerns and strong, efficient and inefficient; all enjoyed the benefits of fixed prices and restricted output while the expensive and systematic technical re-equipment of which the industry was beginning to stand badly in need after the lean 1920s was postponed indefinitely.'[20]

The fall in employment in the industry from 1,226,000 in 1920 to 702,000 in 1938 was as much due to the failure to retain export markets or to develop with sufficient energy new domestic uses for coal, as to the displacement of labour by machinery.

A similar kind of task was performed by the government on behalf of the cotton industry. The work of destroying spindle capacity surplus to requirements in the light of the reduced post-war demand, which had been started by the Lancashire Cotton Corporation in 1929, was continued on a more substantial scale by the Spindles Board set up under the Cotton Industry Re-organization Act of 1936. An Act of the same name, three years later, set up a Cotton Industry Board to fix compulsory minimum prices. Neither Act made any positive contribution to the improvement of productive efficiency in the industry.

The breakdown of the international payments system and the shrinking volume of World trade in the early 1930s caused the depression in British shipbuilding to be particularly severe. The shipyards of Great Britain had a capacity for building over three million tons of shipping a year, but annual launchings fluctuated between 1,400,000 tons in 1930 and only 133,000 tons in the worst year, 1933. The task of eliminating surplus capacity in this industry was undertaken by a company, National Shipbuilders Security, formed in 1930 for the express purpose of buying up redundant shipyards and putting them out of action for at least forty years. The plan had government approval since some of the capital for the operation was provided by the Bankers' Industrial Development Corporation, an offshoot of the Bank of England. In the first four years of its existence the company bought up yards with a launching capacity of over a million tons a year. The revival in the industry after 1935 was partly due to direct Government subsidies and partly due to re-armament. Under the Shipping (Assistance) Act of 1935 subsidies were given for the construction of new tramp steamers and motor vessels, while the North Atlantic Shipping Act of 1935 subsidized to the tune of £9½m. transatlantic liners, including the renowned *Queen Mary*. Despite these blood transfusions, at the peak of revival in 1937 the industry was still working well below capacity, and the proportion of the labour force unemployed was still as high as 24·4 per cent.

The Import Duties Advisory Committee made the re-organization of the iron and steel industry a precondition for making permanent the higher duties on imports imposed in 1933. This re-organization was carried out under the direction of the British Iron and Steel Federation, formed in April 1934 to fix prices and organize production quotas in the industry. The Bank of England also helped much more in the 1930s than it had done in the 1920s to salvage large firms threatened with bankruptcy, such as William Beardmore, and to contribute large loans to aid modernization, as in the case of Richard Thomas Limited in South Wales in 1937.

In the case of all these older industries there was a greater emphasis on the elimination of surplus capacity and the avoidance of damaging competition than there was on technological and managerial modernization. Despite all efforts of both individual industries and Government departments much surplus capacity remained in the late 1930s, and the level of unemployment continued depressingly high.

In respect of employment and the level of industrial production the newer industries, such as the manufacture of electrical appliances, artificial fibres, chemicals, and motor cars, improved upon the promising start that they had made in the 1920s. In the case of the automobile industry the annual output of motor vehicles rose from 238,000 in 1929 to 511,000 in 1937, whilst the number employed in the industry rose from 295,000 in 1930 to 380,000 in 1939. Employment in the manufacture of electrical equipment rose from 230,900 in 1930 to 367,000, in 1937, and the number of units of electrical power produced more than doubled over the same period. The big weakness in the newer industries was the failure to give sufficient attention to exports. Most manufacturers took the easy road of exploiting the new opportunities in the home market without bothering unduly about the harder task of increasing exports. The proportion of British cars exported never rose above one-seventh of the annual production, and the value of electrical goods exported in 1937 at the height of the 'boom' was actually less than it was in 1929 (£18,240,000 compared with £19,444,000). A contemporary authority on this industry commented as follows in 1938: 'It is a somewhat unsatisfactory condition that few of the new firms are making any serious effort to develop export business and that the principal export activity of the country still remains with firms which have always specialized in it. To that extent therefore the industry on the export side is probably more vulnerable now than it was some years ago . . . It has not made it its business to develop outlets in export markets for the new and specialized products which are now being turned out in such immense quantities.'[21]

Another reason why it is impossible to take a very optimistic view of the achievements of British industry in the 1930s is the failure of both private business and government to use the vast idle resources of capital equipment and manpower in the distressed areas. The halting efforts of the government in Westminster to reactivate economic life in regions of heavy unemployment stand in marked contrast to the magnitude of the works projects of the American New Deal. In 1934, under the Special Areas (Development and Improvement) Act, commissioners were appointed 'to initiate, organize, prosecute, and assist measures such as the establishment of trading estates' in South Wales, Durham and Tyneside, West Cumberland, and Scotland. They were given enhanced powers and more money under the Special Areas Reconstruction (Agreement) Act of 1936, and the Special Areas Amendment Act of 1937. By the end of September 1938, expenditure of some £17m. had been authorized for grants

towards the establishment of trading estates, land settlement, and
sewerage construction, and some 15,000 workers had been found
jobs. A future Prime Minister, Mr. Neville Chamberlain, in introducing the second Bill in May 1936 conceded that it would not 'set
the Thames on fire or provide any great revolution in the affairs of
the depressed areas'. Another future Prime Minister, Mr. Harold
Macmillan, said that in comparison with the size of the problem, the
Act of 1934 was 'a mouse—a nice mouse, a good little mouse, but a
ridiculous, microscopic, Lilliputian mouse'.[22] There is no doubt that
re-armament expenditure after 1935 created more jobs than the
number that had been made available under the special areas legislation. It is as true of Great Britain as of the United States that the
principles of Keynesian economics were only beginning to be understood at the end of the 1930s, and that it was only through extraordinary wartime demands that idle capacity in manpower and
resources found full employment.

Notes

1 RICHARDSON, H. W., *Economic Recovery in Britain, 1932-9* (1967),
p. 16.

2 MORTON, WALTER A., *British Finance, 1930-1940* (Madison, University of Wisconsin Press, 1943), p. 34. LARY, HAL. B., *The United States
in the World Economy* (U.S. Department of Commerce Economic Series
No. 23, Washington, 1943), p. 174.

3 SCHUMPTER, JOSEPH A., cited in J. K. Galbraith, *The Affluent Society*
(Penguin ed., 1962), p. 46.

4 MYERS, W. A. and NEWTON, W. H., *The Hoover Administration: a
Documented Narrative* (New York, 1936), p. 156.

5 FAINSOD, M., GORDON, L., and PALAMOUNTAIN, J. C. Jr., *Government
and the American Economy* (New York, 1960), p. 542-3.

6 LEUCHTENBURG, WILLIAM E., *Franklin D. Roosevelt and the New
Deal* (New York, 1963), p. 125.

7 PERKINS, FRANCES, *The Roosevelt I Knew* (New York, 1946), p. 225-6.

8 See the article 'Into the S.E.C. Searchlight' by Anthony Vice, *The
Sunday Times*, 5 June 1966.

9 'The Grasslands', *Fortune*, XI. November 1935.

10 SCHLESINGER, ARTHUR M., Jr., *The Roosevelt Revolution* II (New
York, 1959), p. 429.

11 WAIGHT, L., *The History and Mechanism of the Exchange Equalisation Account* (Cambridge, 1939), pp. 8-9.

12 STEWART, ROBERT B., 'Great Britain's Foreign Loan Policy', *Economica* N.S. V (1938), p. 54.

13 GRANT, A. T. K., *A Study of the Capital Market in Post War Britain* (1962), p. 134.

14 RICHARDSON, *op. cit.*, p. 206.

15 JONES, J. H., Introduction to *Britain in Recovery* (British Association, 1938), p. 2.

16 BRAAE, G. P., 'Investment in Housing in the U.K., 1924-38' *Manchester School* Vol. XXXII No. 1 (January 1964), p. 15.

17 P.E.P. Report on the Market for Household Appliances, quoted in Richardson, *op. cit.*, p. 89.

18 MACROSTY, H. W., 'The Effect of Tariffs', in *The Times: Iron and Steel Number*, 14 June 1938.

19 ASHWORTH, W., *A Short History of the International Economy* (1962), pp. 236-40.

20 COURT, W. H. B., *Coal* (History of the Second World War U.K. Civil Series, H.M.S.O., 1951). p. 22.

21 JONES, J. H., 'The Electrical Industry' in *Britain in Recovery* (British Association, 1938), p. 271. For an assessment of the growth of British output and the dangers of too rigid distinction between 'old' and 'new' industries see J. A. Dowte 'Growth in the Inter-war Period: Some more Arithmetic'. *Econ. Hist. Rev.*, 2nd ser. XXI, 1968, p. 93.

22 DENNISON, S. R., 'Effect of Recovery on the Various Regions', in J. H. Jones (ed.), *Britain in Recovery*, Hansard, 5th ser. vol. 295 col. 1256, and vol. 312 col. 55; *The Times*, Special Areas Supplement, 27 June 1939.

Suggestions for further reading

Texts

ASHWORTH, W., *An Economic History of England: 1870-1939* (1960).

FITE, GILBERT C. and REESE, JIM E., *An Economic History of the United States* (2nd ed., New York, 1965), part 4.

LEWIS, W. ARTHUR, *Economic Survey 1919-39* (1949).

MITCHELL, BROADUS, *Depression Decade* (New York, 1962).

MOWAT, C. L., *Britain between the Wars* (1955).

PARKES, HENRY BAMFORD and CAROSSA, VINCENT P., *Recent America: a History* II (New York, 1963). ch. 1-2.

POLLARD, S., *The Development of the British Economy 1914-1950*, 2nd edn. (1962).

WILLIAMSON, HAROLD F. (ed.), *The Growth of the American Economy* 2nd ed. Englewood Cliffs, N. J., 1951). part 5.

YOUNGSON, A. J., *The British Economy 1920-1966* (1967).

Specialized works

ALLEN, FREDERICK LEWIS, *Since Yesterday 1929-1939* (New York, Bantam Books ed., 1961).

BLYTH, RONALD, *The Age of Illusion: England in the Twenties and Thirties 1919-40* (Pelican ed. 1964).

GREENWOOD, WALTER, *Love on the Dole* (1933).

LEIGHTON, ISOBEL (ed.), *The Aspirin Age 1919-41* (Pelican ed., 1964).

LEUCHTENBURG, WILLIAM L., *Franklin D. Roosevelt and the New Deal* (Harper Torchbook ed., New York, 1963).

LILIENTHAL, DAVID E., *T.V.A.: Democracy on the March* (New York, 1944).

ORWELL, GEORGE, *The Road to Wigan Pier* (1937).

RICHARDSON, H. W., *Economic Recovery in Britain, 1932-9* (1967).

SCHLESINGER, ARTHUR M., Jr., *The Roosevelt Revolution* (3 vols., 1957-61).

SHANNON, DAVID A., *The Great Depression* (Englewood Cliffs. N. J., 1960).

Supplementary bibliography

Some recent work on the economies of Britain and America 1850–1939

Since the appearance of the first edition of *Britain and America*, a number of new introductory texts dealing with one or other of the two countries have been published. These include: P. Mathias, *The First Industrial Nation* (1983) and E.J. Hobsbawm, *Industry and Empire* (1968) (both of thes go back a century or more before 1850); and on the United States, J.M. Peterson and Ralph Gray, *Economic Development of the United States* (1969) and J. Potter, *The American Economy between the World Wars* (1974). Readers wishing to supplement the necessarily concise account given here will do well to make a choice of further reading among these texts.

There are also a number of recent advanced texts which students, especially those specializing in economic history, might wish to study. These books are examples of the new qualitative trend in the study and writing of economic history which has been gathering influence (more especially in the United States) over the past twenty years. In this 'new economic history' attempts are made to estimate in precise terms the effects of certain major influences or developments, as for example in Robert W. Fogel's estimation of the contribution to the national income of the United States made by the American railroads (in his *Railroads and American Economic Growth* (1964)). A useful introduction to this modern approach will be found in Peter Temin (ed.), *New Economic History* (Penguin Modern Economics Readings, 1973), while an overview of it, and some systematic criticism, are provided by the following: Albert Fishlow and Robert W. Fogel, 'Quantitative Economic History', *Journal of Economic History*, 31 (1971); Fritz Redlich, 'New and Traditional Approaches to Economic History and their Interdependence', *Journal of Economic History*, 25 (1965); and Harry N. Scheiber, 'On the New Economic History – and its Limitations', *Agricultural History*, 41 (1967).

Of the texts which are of general usefulness in adopting this new approach the following are important: *Britain*: Phyllis Deane and W.A. Cole, *British Economic Growth 1688–1959* (2nd edition, 1967);

R.C.O. Matthews, C.H. Feinstein and J.C. Odling-Smee, *British Economic Growth 1856-1973* (1982); and Roderick Floud and Donald N. McCloskey (eds), *The Economic History of Britain since 1700* (1981). *USA*: S.P. Lee and P. Passell, *A New Economic View of American History* (1979); and Sidney Ratner, James H. Soltow and Richard Sylla, *The Evolution of the American Economy* (1980).

In addition to the above some recent specialized works of a less quantitative character are referred to below in the order in which their subjects appear in the chapters of *Britain and America*.

Internal transport

D.H. Aldcroft's *Studies in British Transport History, 1870–1914* (1974) and British Transport since 1914: An Economic History* (1975) provide thoughtful coverage of most of the period studied in this book. P.S. Bagwell's *The Transport Revolution from 1770* (1974) has the merit of giving fuller consideration to the coastal trade and inland navigation than do other transport histories. E. Haites, J. Mak and G. Walton, *Western River Transportation: the Era of early Internal Development, 1810–60* (1975) fills some similar gaps in American transport history. For British railway history an outstanding work of scholarship is J. Simmons, *The Railway in England and Wales, 1830–1914*, volume I (1978). In the USA the main area of controversy has been over the application of the 'new economic history' to the sphere of inland transport. The chief participants have been R.W. Fogel, *Railroads and American Economic Growth* (1964), and H. Fishlow, *American Railroads and the Transformation of the Ante-Bellum Economy* (1965). A 'good tour guide' to the controversy has been provided by P. O'Brien, *The New Economic History of the Railways* (1977). Fogel's methods were applied to British railways by G.R. Hawke, *Railways and Economic Growth in England and Wales, 1840–70* (1970).

Agriculture

Two major works to appear on English agriculture in this period are G.E. Mingay (ed.), *The Victorian Countryside* (1981), and Volume VIII of *The Agrarian History of England and Wales: 1914–1939* (1978) by E.H. Whetham. The first contains a large number of essays by leading specialists which cover a wide variety of aspects of the English countryside, including landownership, farmers and farming methods, the agricultural labour force, and social conditions. Edith Whetham's volume, by contrast, concentrates mainly on the technical changes and trends in farming.

On American agriculture two important words are G.C. Fite, *The Farmer's Frontier 1860–1897* (1966), and Clarence H. Danhof, *Change in Agriculture: the Northern United States 1820–1870* (1969). Fite's book supplements, if it does not replace, the important older work by Fred Shannon, *The Farmer's Last Frontier* (reprinted 1973), and is particularly valuable for its new material and for modifying some of Shannon's views. Danhof's book is more strictly concerned with changes in farming itself, and although confined to the North is a useful addition to the older texts.

International trade and the movement of factors

Among the more recent work published on the topics discussed in this chapter should be mentioned one of the pamphlets in the Studies in Economic History series (Papermac): P.L. Cottrell, *British Overseas Investment in the Nineteenth Century* (1975). Two important articles which appeared in the *Economic History Review* should also be consulted: H.W. Richardson has a new discussion of 'British Emigration and Overseas Investment 1870–1914' (Vol. XXV, 1972), and G.R. Hawke analyses the effectiveness of the protective tariff in 'The U.S. Tariff and Industrial Protection in the late Nineteenth Century' (Vol. XXVIII, 1975).

The money and capital markets

Important newer writings on the development of the British banking system include D.K. Sheppard, *The Growth and Role of UK Financial Institutions, 1880–1967* (1971), and B.L. Anderson and P.L. Cottrell, *Money and Banking in England: the Development of the Banking System, 1694–1914* (1974). S. Howson's *Domestic Monetary Management in Britain, 1919–38* (1975) is an outstanding book on an important subject. For America, two useful additions to the literature include: B.J. Klebaner,

Commercial Banking in the United States: a History (1974), and J.A. James, *Money and Capital Markets in Post-Bellum America* (1978).

Industrial developments 1850–1914

Another valuable pamphlet in the Studies in Economic History series relevant here is S.B. Saul, *The Myth of the Great Depression 1873–96* (1969), an acute analysis of the controversy surrounding the performance of the British economy in this period, Covering a much longer period and broader field is Francois Crouzet's *The Victorian Economy* (1982) which provides an up-to-date and balanced assessment of Britain's economic development over most of the nineteenth century. On America, an important article concerning the growth of big business is A.D. Chandler and L. Galambos, 'The Development of Large-Scale Economic Organization in Modern America', *Journal of Economic History*, Vol. XXX (1970). A valuable comparative study with useful source material is S.B. Saul, *Technological Change: the United States and Britain in the 19th Century* (1970).

Trade unions

For a well informed, critical survey of developments in the American labour movement, particularly for the post 1914 period, D. Brody's *Workers in Industrial America* (1980) is invaluable. For Britain, A.E. Musson's *British Trade Unions, 1800–75* (1972), and J. Lovell's *British Trade Unions, 1875–1933* (1977) are useful study guides. C. Wrigley (ed.), *A History of British Industrial Relations 1875–1914* (1982) includes contributions from leading authorities on British labour history. The hitherto largely neglected area of women's employment and organisation has been tackled by A. Kessler-Harris, *A History of Wage-Earning Women in the United States* (1982); and by S. Lewenhak, *An Outline History of Women in the British Trade Union Movement* (1977), and N.C. Soldon, *Women in British Trade Unions, 1874–1976* (1978). The widening of interest to include sociological influences on labour history is reflected in H.G. Gutman, *Work, Culture and Society in Industrialising America* (1976), C.R. Littler, *The Development of the Labour*

Process in Capitalist Societies (1982), and in the stimulating essays of E.J. Hobsbawm in *Labouring Men* (1964) and *Worlds of Labour* (1984).

Social progress

A number of specialized works have appeared in this field on the British side, notably John Burnett, *A Social History of Housing 1815–1970* (1978), M.E. Rose, *The Relief of Poverty 1834–1914* (1972), and D. Fraser, *The Evolution of the British Welfare State* (1973). Of broad general interest is the long-term perspective offered by François Béderida, *A Social History of England 1851–1975* (1979), while over a shorter period J. Stevenson, *British Society 1914–45* (Pelican Social History of Britain, 1984) is important. For America valuable contributions include: D. Brody, 'The Rise and Decline of Welfare Capitalism' in his *Workers of Industrial America* (1980); P.K. Conkin, *F.D.R. and the Origins of the Welfare State* (1967); and E.E. Witte, *Development of the Social Security Act* (1962).

The Atlantic economy, 1914–29

For the international background A.G. Kenwood and A.E. Lougheed's *The Growth of the International Economy, 1820–1960* (Part II, 1971) is essential reading. For the restoration of the Gold Standard in Britain an authoritative account is to be found in D.E. Moggridge, *The Return to Gold, 1925: the Formulation of Economic Policy and its Critics* (1969) or in the same author's shorter *British Monetary Policy, 1924–31: the Norman Conquest of $4.86* (1972). For both the 1920s and the 1930s, D. Winch, *Economics and Policy* (1972) and M. Stewart, *Keynes and After* (1971) provide valuable insights on the impact of fiscal and financial policies on the development of the British economy. For America, J. Potter, *The American Economy Between the World Wars* (1974) has a lucid summary of some major trends. For the crisis at the end of the decade J.K. Galbraith, *The Great Crash, 1929* (1972) is essential reading. Still very userful is W.P. Leuchtenberg, *The Perils of Prosperity, 1914–32* (1958).

The nineteen-thirties

Writing about the economic and social history of the decade has tended to concentrate on the themes of the great depression (1929–32) and subsequent recovery. For Britain useful starting points are P. Fearon, *The Origins and Nature of the Great Slump, 1929–32* (1979) and B.W. Alford, *Depression and Recovery? British Economic Growth, 1918–39* (1972). H.W. Richardson's *Economic Recovery in Britain 1932–39* (1967) is valuable for the author's analysis of the housing boom. For the decade as a whole, N. Branson and M. Heinemann, *Britain in the Nineteen Thirties* (1973) provide a very readable account. For America, a good introduction is D.R. McCoy, *Coming of Age* (Volume 6 of the Pelican History of the USA, 1973). Studies in greater depth include A.L. Hamby, *The New Deal: Analysis and Interpretation* (2nd ed. 1981); D.L. May, *From New Deal to New Economics: the American Liberal Response to the Depression of 1937* (1981), and J.J. Wallis, 'The Birth of the Old Federalism: Financing the New Deal, 1932–40', *Journal of Economic History*, March 1984.

Index